4/89

Dear Mother,

Happy Birthday!

Happy Fall!

Love,

Krystal & Tom

Dreaming Myself, Dreaming A Town

Susan M. Watkins

also by Susan M. Watkins

Conversations with Seth: The Story of Jane Roberts's ESP Class, vols. 1 & 2

Dreaming Myself, Dreaming A Town

(Field Notes from the Land of Dreams)

Susan M. Watkins

Illustrations by George Rhoads

Kendall Enterprises Inc. ◆ New York

Published by Kendall Enterprises Inc.
P.O. Box 5258
Rockefeller Center
New York, New York 10185

Book design and typography:
Brad Allan Walrod/High Text Graphics
Cover design:
Denise Vannucci
Cover illustration:
Kat Reviaska

Printed in the United States of America

Library of Congress Cataloging-in-Publication Data

Watkins, Susan M., 1945–
Dreaming myself, dreaming a town (field notes from the land of dreams)/Susan M. Watkins; illustrations by George Rhoads.—1st ed.

p. cm.
Includes index.
ISBN 0-945512-01-5: $21.95 (est.)
1. Dreams. 2. Watkins, Susan M., 1945– . 3. Dundee (N.Y.)—Miscellanea. I. Title.
BF1091.W43 1989
135'.3—dc19 88-37068
CIP

1 2 3 4 5 6 7 8 9 10

First Edition

This book is dedicated to the memory of
Jane Roberts Butts,
and to her vision of a world of psychic naturalists,
collecting species of private dreams and peculiar notions
in a universe of meaning and fulfillment.

With Special Thanks to
the Dreamers of Dundee, N.Y.

—and especially to Susan Benedict,
"Snoop Sister" and friend.

CONTENTS

"The answer . . . [is] to stack unofficial experience against official experience, to acquire our own body of evidence by paying direct attention to what actually happens *in our lives, as opposed to interpreting those events as we've been taught. The answer [is] to begin trusting ourselves and our impulses now—and starting out with some sense of adventure, not looking over our shoulders at the official world."*

—Jane Roberts
The God of Jane: A Psychic Manifesto

PREFACE

It's taken me more than seven years to put this book together, and now that I look back across that time, it's clear to me that in working on the manuscript in fits and starts as I did, I was following impulses of which I was not even consciously aware, waiting for the passing of a certain "block" of experiences to finish this work. There were connections to be made between my stance in that time and the material I'd collected on dreams, impulses, precognition, and coincidence—and recognitions of what I could comfortably reveal about my private odysseys and what meanings such revelations might have in public terms.

In that regard, this book represents two sides of a story; two halves of a whole—the inside and the outside of a span of time as I experienced it. On the one hand is the little dream-collection experiment that I carried out in the village of Dundee, New York. On the other is the inescapable element of my private life and its own dreams and challenges and the story of how these two elements merged, as they inevitably must.

I left my second marriage in late 1981, and for a while my son and I occupied a two-room efficiency apartment in a hillside complex overlooking Dundee. In many ways, it was the pleasantest place I'd lived in up to then, filled as it was with sunlight and the smells of new spring mud and flowers from the nearby woods and vineyards. A tentative title for my book and the outline of it, chapter by chapter, fell into my mental lap one afternoon as I sat at my desk, idly watching my cats zoom around the place in great gymnastic carefree cat-ness. I had all the material from my Dundee dream-project; it needed only the right form to put it in. Again, I assured myself—just as I had with the inception of *Conversations with Seth*—that I could report on the dreams of a town and keep my personal travails out of it. I worked up a prospectus and sent it off to an editor at Prentice-Hall. It seemed like the natural follow-up to my first book. The Prentice editor agreed, and in a couple of weeks, I had a book contract in my hands.

Nothing happened. Trying to write the book was like pushing wood through stone. Eventually I gave up and cancelled the contract, feeling ashamed and stupid with terminal writer's block. Moreover, despair haunted all the corners of my private world. I was in the process of mourning a marriage whose inevitable end I'd foreseen, almost stubbornly, when I'd entered it. Beyond that, by

March of 1982, my friend Jane Roberts was suffering such severe complications of rheumatoid arthritis that she was forced to go to an Elmira hospital for a long and painful stay. At the same time, my father's health was rapidly deteriorating as scar tissue left from an old chest injury* began to constrict his breathing like a slowly-closing fist. On top of this, my mother was experiencing serious difficulties with lupus erythematosus, the same disease that had caused her own mother's death in 1956. Within three years, all three would be dead: my father of sudden cardiac arrest in December of 1983; Jane passing away in September of 1984; my mother dying in October of 1985 after a year's slow destruction from cancer of the liver and stomach. Other emotional issues weighed heavily upon me during all of this; and following my mother's death there was the added burden of trying to decide whether to keep or sell my childhood home now left to me in my parents' estates.

Throughout, I took notes, compiled and collected dreams, and even wrote a chapter here and there for my unfinished dream book, crammed as it was in a box on my desk. It wasn't until late May of 1985, when I *impulsively* took the box of stuff with me to read while staying with my mother, that I finally saw the unity hidden in all those notes and scrawls. It was a bright spring afternoon, my mother's favorite season, and she lay on the sofa, dozing, listening to the birds in the feeders outside the big picture windows. I didn't hear a single squawk. I read through that thick batch of material with increasing astonishment at what I had there: at the journeys I'd been heir to in the village of Dundee, and at the way my private life dovetailed and . . . filled in, as it were, with public events; two sides of a coin, the dreams of a town and mine. Precognition . . . public and private, weaving in and out fast as light. Coincidence, like witty clues scattered along the path. Impulses, terrifying and exhilarating, leading always into unexpected adventure. Well, even a lousy adventure is still adventurous, I mused.

My mother stirred. "What are you reading, dear?"

"I'm not sure," I said, "but I think it's finally my next book."

---

*He was stabbed in a bar fight in Topeka, Kansas, in 1940; an incident he always recalled with great humor, in spite of the fact that he lost a lung as a result. I still have a clipping from the Topeka newspaper that reported it, complete with his typically cryptic non-remarks about what "really" happened. Ironically, by the time my father died of those wounds forty-three years later, the brawl itself had achieved immortality as a Mullin family legend.

"Oh, that's good," she said. "Is it finished yet?"

"Christ, I don't think the damn thing will ever be finished," I answered. "The more I put it off, the more it goes on and on."

"Lucky book," my mother said, dozing. Never once did she consciously believe that she, too, might, in some form or another, go on and on. I'd like to think that if nothing else, this book will serve as a catalyst to the contrary; as a springboard into the realms of natural knowing that all of us share here, and elsewhere, as part of our true heritage.

Susan M. Watkins
Dundee, New York

Proposal

(for Roy, August, 1979)

I
You knocked
on my door
with a hammer.

Holes appeared
in my space.
I let you in.

You said,
"What is it that you
want?"

I said,
"To be a great
writer. To
be up there
in the ranks."

You said, "Sure,
and I want
to sing in
Nashville."

You said,
"What are
the percentages of
writers who get
up there?"

You said,
"I would try
in every way I could
with my hard-
working hands,
to make you
happy."

II
O my dear,
how do I say it?
You don't believe.
You don't believe
in beliefs.

You believe in
values.
These are different
things.

Like the two
of us.

You see facts
as practical
laws to be
obeyed, or
at least
not denied
respect.

I see facts
as the best-selling
works of
fiction:
Most of them are
trash.

I want to play
with them.
I want to
re-write the
best-seller list.

How practical is that?
O my dear,
it's the only way
we got here to
begin with.

III
But most of all
I want you to
believe that *I*
believe.

Not what—
just *that*.

You say you want
to make me
happy.
I think the
accent
is on the
make.

IV

But part of me
wants your
definitions;
part of me
wants to be
crammed
inside those
walls—

I knew
a man who
wrote books in
prison.

His rent
was always
paid.
He never
went hungry.

He had endless
time.
He also died
while on
parole.

He killed himself,
in fact.

I want a
safe universe
to write in.
And to make
my own,
I have to

re-write
the biggest
Best-Seller
of all time.

All *you*
have to do
is face
the facts
and go on
living—

In, of course,
the same old
place.

V

I think
we are talking
about
Divine Conceit.

I have it
to the hilt.
But then, so
did the gods,
and they,
after all,
invented you
and me.

They filled
the Earth
with secrets.

They seeded
a crop of
Divine Conceit.

It grows
like weeds among
the facts.

But metaphors
aside,
I am conceited enough
to think

that your universe
will not protect me.
That, frightened as
I am sometimes,
I know
your definitions are
too small
for me.

That I would
die while
on parole.

VI

You went home.
You left
your hammer
on my table.

O my dear,
I love you when
I'm frightened—
that best-seller
list is
so goddamn
huge.

—SMW

ONE

Of Dubious Disciples, Gobbledygook, and Ghosts

I'm going to write about someone who might become famous.

To know somebody who might become famous by writing literature is great. And Sue Watkins won't change the way she is if she becomes famous.

It is just the same actually, as if she were to make me a cake and all I can say is she always has a sense of humor and I don't think she'll become a Sniff and not make jokes about everything.

She could also spend a lot of money and show off if she gets famous, not using it wisely you know.

Not writing for the [*Observer*] as much is sad for the paper, but good for her. I always thought she was a good writer but I never expected she would write a book.

All I can say is I hope she has a great seller in a book!

—"*Lynn's Lines*" by Lynn Renée Backer (age 10)
(weekly Dundee *Observer* column)
January 18, 1979

"I quit," I said. "I'm never going to write another goddamned thing again."

Spilling out of the publisher's envelope were a dozen reviews of my first book, *Conversations with Seth: The Story of Jane Roberts's ESP Class*.[1] Ten of those reviews were great—not only did they say nice things about the author's talents, they actually seemed to appreciate the subject. But I hardly noticed. The 11th and 12th reviews lashed out like a public slap in the face.

"Gushy and indulgent," one remarked, adding, "Susan Watkins was one of the disciples [of Jane Roberts] . . . who hung on every word uttered by Roberts in the guise of 'Seth' . . ."

My knees went weak, my mouth dry as dust.

". . . and if Seth says an old fellow on the street is an aspect of Watkins's dead grandfather,[2] then, by gum, that clinches the matter for everyone," the review went on. "Nonsense about reincarnation, telepathic powers, and such—lent dubious authority by a ghost."

Humiliation wrapped around me like a suffocating weight. None of the other, quite positive reviews existed—only these. Never mind that both negative reviews gave an inaccurate description of the book's events and missed its point altogether; they carried the punch of disapproval from the literary establishment, and I was temporarily devastated. *Was* I guilty of the one thing that I held to be different about the Seth material and Jane's ESP class? Had ghostly guru-ism indeed crept into those Tuesday nights; had I given Jane/Seth power over my self-awareness; *did* we all sit there lapping up any old metaphysical metaphor just because it was presented in a clever, articulate manner? Had I been spared all the God-myths in my childhood only to put Seth on that throne as an adult?

At the time that I wrote *Conversations*, I didn't want to be burdened with such questions. For one thing, I was writing a chronology, and clacking on about what the hell we all thought we were doing there didn't seem appropriate. Still, the fact was that Seth had for me blossomed as a larger, symbolic event—symbolic of what I saw as the rise of a new personhood in myself and the world at large—though it was terrifying for me to declare, publicly as it were, that I believed the Sethian ideas, and by association Seth's origins, to be not only valid but true. I had grown up an only child in a family that heaped savagely witty ridicule upon anything smacking even remotely of religion or mysticism—despite (or perhaps precisely because of) the mystical realizations and sense of the mysterious that my parents experienced (and often spoke of) throughout their lives. Those reviews, then, carried a double punch. Though my parents were surprisingly reticent about my friendship with a woman who *pretended to be sombody else* half the time and then *wrote books about it,* they obviously believed that their daughter had fallen for some sort of religious baloney—the worst kind. Yet whenever the subject came up, my father always asked, "Just find out what the hell happened to Zeus, will you?" Only much later did I understand how direct that question really was.

"It's the search for God, or for new gods," Jane said to me one day as we talked about my ideas for this book. "Even five years ago, I couldn't have said that—it would have been too terrible to say. But it's natural to start looking around for new gods when the old ones wear out. Maybe it's time to stand up for our human characteristics again," she added.

So in a way, I couldn't blame the so-called literary establishment for being at least suspicious of my book. In the realm of ESP, precognition, dreams, and related matters, there are few guideposts and little common sense applied. Most of the books written in the so-called "occult" or "spiritual" fields were worthless nonsense in my opinion—as were treatises that debunked all subjective experience as "unscientific." It was certainly a dilemma, and reviewers aren't supposed to solve it—they take what comes to them and judge it according to their feelings, as I was doing. The real question for me, then, was how to learn to trust my ideas as a valuable commodity in the world, and not worry about the reactions of those who were, after all, only trying to find answers for themselves. It was obvious to me now that I could not rely on the literary hierarchy for approval—or on any other hierarchy, for that matter. I'd have to take my own stand and find my own source of approval, if that's what I wanted; my own network of feedback and value. But where?

In 1973—one year after the Hurricane Agnes-fed floods ravaged the Chemung-Susquehanna river valleys—I moved from my Elmira, N.Y., apartment to the village of Dundee, 40 miles north and several hundred feet *uphill* from the city where I'd grown up. A year later I started work as co-editor of the weekly Dundee *Observer* with its owner (and only other staff member), Dundee native Susan Benedict. The two of us spent the next six years covering local news (mostly municipal business), writing it up, typing it up, pasting it down, driving it to the printer in nearby Canandaigua, addressing and mailing 2,000 copies, and even, occasionally, selling advertising for the thing. In the process, we managed to achieve rather a flamboyant image in Dundee, winning a New York Press Association prize or two in the process and inspiring grassroots-municipal news coverage in several other area newspapers.

Early in the summer of 1978, the Dundee radio station announced that a nationally-known psychic, whom I'll call Faith Godwin, would appear for a week on the noon talk show to give readings and advice to callers. This really struck me as odd; for one thing, the station manager himself thought that anything relating to psychic phenomena was so much hormonal mumbo-jumbo ("Men are logical, women are emotional—so of course you're interested in that stuff," he told me several times). For another, I just couldn't imagine—I couldn't imagine *then*—who in little old Dundee would call up and ask for such information on the air. Even though nobody had to give names, if this Faith Godwin were any good at all, she might come up with enough revealing details right there on all 5,000 watts to let everybody in five counties guess who you were. But the disgusting part of it all was that despite myself, I was also feeling that old siren song: Maybe, an irritating little voice whispered from somewhere behind my good sense, maybe she could tell me the answers to those eternal questions . . . maybe, just maybe, if I could speak with her, maybe *she* would take up where Seth left off (leaving me on my own, in his annoying fashion) and tell me . . .

Of course, it didn't matter what the question was—the answer had to come from the Self or it wasn't an answer at all, right? I *knew* that. Or thought I knew that. What else had Jane's class and the body of her work been *about* but that? And here I was succumbing easily enough to the temptations of . . . well, the age-old lure, wasn't it? Yet, I asked myself, what difference did it all make, really—a little touch of the Twilight Zone on small-town radio never hurt anybody; things haven't changed since the days of the Elixir salesmen in their horse-drawn wagons. Maybe it would even open up some doors for people, I told myself. After all, I was about to sign a contract for *Conversations with Seth*, a venture designed for commercial success—right? The world is roomy enough for all.

Despite such attempts at logical reasoning, however, I dogged myself with contradictions and questions about it all until Susan finally suggested (partly to shut me up and get back to municipal earth) that we interview Faith and let *her* say what she thought about these issues. Plus, it seemed like a good tie-in with her talk show.

We made an appointment to talk with Faith at the radio station before her first program and then spent a half-hour or so compiling some questions. When did you start doing psychic impressions on the air? Do you travel all around the country doing this? Do you ever follow up on what you've told people—whether or not it's helped, or come true? And so on, turning readings into story-routine, making my relentless crabbing seem overblown—until the moment we walked through the station's parking lot. There by the studio door was a showroom-new Cadillac, completely unscathed by dust or road dirt—with license plates to match. The letters spelled out PSYCHIC in gaudy blue and gold, in perfect complement to the car's mirror-finish baby-blue and gold paint job.

"Weird," Susan remarked—but I felt the hair stand up on the back of my neck. Forget weird—this was a personal insult. No *wonder* books in this field were passed off so often as the delusions of dopes! Look at what my contemporaries were doing! I stood there for a minute staring and sputtering, but Susan had already gone inside the studio, apparently unconcerned. And why shouldn't she be, I told myself—what difference did it make what anybody put on their license plates, for crying out loud?

I followed Susan inside, trying to sort out this emotional miasma and be a good, objective reporter. Faith, a pleasant-looking woman of about 40, was standing in the station's back room next to a movie-star handsome man dressed in that carefully-styled and coiffed fashion of born-again television ministers. He was speaking earnestly to Jack, the station manager, about arranging for some sort of follow-up deal on Faith's air time: People, he said, would pay at least $25 for a personal reading once they heard Faith's show, and the radio station could have a percentage if it would advertise her consultations for free. His voice was smooth, liquid. His eyes never left Jack's, even when Susan and I walked into the room. He was none other than Faith's husband-manager, and Roland Godwin was certainly doing the managing.

And Faith, I noticed with wicked glee, was standing quietly, hands folded, like a serene Madonna—except that she was sporting the meanest-looking black eye you ever saw in your life.

She smiled up at us. "You must be the girls from the newspaper," she said in a syrup-sweet voice.

At this, Roland whipped his attention away from Jack and riveted onto us.

"The newspaper?" he said. He literally rubbed his hands together. You could see advertising possibilities roll through his eyes like the dials on a slot-machine. I didn't have the heart to tell him that "the newspaper" was an eight-page weekly typed up in the hallway of an apartment building by exactly two of us.

"Yes indeedy," I said brightly. "We have an appointment to interview Faith."

"That'll be fine," Roland said, "but before you get into that, maybe you'd like to hear about the idea Jack and I are cooking up here." He gestured toward Jack, who looked hypnotized. "See, Faith can't give a complete reading on the air; there's just not enough time to go into all the impressions that she picks up, so we've got this package deal that would probably benefit you girls too. The thing is, Faith writes this weekly column on psychic stuff, you know, and you would publish . . ."

"Hold it," I said, interrupting. Silence filled the room.

"Yes, what?" Roland prodded, impatient. I glanced at Susan. She raised her eyebrows and sighed, an established signal.

"Well, we haven't even gotten to the interview yet," I went on, smiling.

"Oh, I'm sure *that* will go just fine," Roland said, smiling, smiling, smiling. "Of course you do realize, don't you, that Faith usually gets a retainer for interviews? That she charges a basic fee for them?"

Jack giggled nervously. The air in the room was turning thick as wool. A retainer to interview a psychic who wants to *help* people?? A $25 tease on the airwaves for a package deal rammed down all our throats?

"You know," Roland suddenly interjected, apropos of nothing, "my wife made one woman wet her pants."

"She what?" Susan blurted.

"She made one woman wet her pants," Roland purred, leaning toward me. "She was giving this woman a reading and the woman didn't believe in what Faith was saying, so my wife just made a dresser drawer move out and then move back in and the woman saw that and just wet her pants."

More silence. "Terrific," I said, lamely. I wanted to get the hell out of there and go home, but at that moment, Faith finally spoke up. "Oh, that's all right, Roland dear, this will only take a minute," she chirped. "You can talk with the ladies about other things later on."

I pulled my notebook out of my purse with ice-cold fingers, all eyes in the room upon me. (Jack took that moment to dash out of the room and disappear down the hallway.) "Well," I said, "I guess my first question is, uh, how did you get started doing impressions on the . . ."

Faith took a sudden gulp of air and touched her forehead. "Just a minute," she whispered, "I'm getting an impression."

And the worst of that moment was that the back of my neck

tingled in anticipation. An impression, I thought, holy cow, here it comes! The answer that will whisk back the curtain, tell me everything I ever wanted to know, reveal the identity of my own true love, inform me of impending fame and fortune, tell me something miraculous and true . . .

Oh, stop it, my nice, faithful, common-sense self yelped: This is pure horseshit, and don't you forget it.

"I am seeing someone," Faith murmured. "I am seeing an older woman, possibly a grandmother. She has blue eyes and a rosy complexion and white curly hair. She is standing beside you, and she wants you to know that she loves you."

Faith looked up.

"That's it," she said.

I laughed. I honestly thought that she was putting me on. "Oh, wow," I said. "That's funny."

"What's funny??" Roland snarled. He was hovering over Faith, glaring at me with real fury.

"Uh, well," I stammered, "I mean, well, take a look at me and tell me how hard it is to deduce that my grandmother had blue eyes, curly hair, and a rosy complexion."

They just stared at me.

"Uh—it's the Irish in us and all," I said, making it worse.

"I think we'd better get on with the interview," Susan cut in, stepping up next to me and removing the pen and reporter's notebook from my hands. "So tell me—when *did* all of this start for you? How old were you at the time?"

Faith stared briefly at me. "You're also psychic—I can always tell by the eyes," she said, and then turned to Susan for the interview. Roland stuck a cigarette in his teeth, never taking his eyes off me, conspicuously ready to strangle me with his bare hands. As it turned out, none of us made him too happy, as neither Jack nor Susan and I took him up on his package deal. But I could see that Roland was betrayed to the fighting point by my skepticism. His message was clear: Don't screw with the psychic gameplan, sister—people want to hear this and they'll buy it at any price, so bug out. And the thing was that for a second, just a second, really, they'd nearly sold *me* the package by going for the psychic gut—the vulnerability in us all: the desire to *know,* to understand, to find an answer to the cries of the human soul.

And actually, as I listened during the week to her talk show, I realized that despite the blatant show-biz payola context, Faith did have some genuine abilities. It turned out that she'd helped the police department in her home town solve numerous crimes, including a murder and a kidnapping—and all for free (she said).

And the talk show had so many callers that Jack extended the program for an extra half-hour every day. So maybe she'd earned that awful license plate, but why turn it all into such a carnival, complete with barker and shill?

Of course, I had to remember that Jack was selling advertisements for Faith's week-long show and I was sure that the *Observer* would sell a few extra issues that week, too. So there was a commercial value there for us all. What seemed cheap, though, was the exploitation of desperate yearnings—except that from the way calls stacked up in the phone lines, people apparently didn't mind the possibility of exploitation . . . or didn't connect it with the possibility of being given something they thought they couldn't otherwise get. In terms of this small village, they were willing to risk exposure on the air in their search for new answers where the old ones no longer worked. I'd never expected that, of all things—I'd assumed that everyday people would pass Faith's information off as bunk, as I thought they must therefore pass me and my book off as bunk—unless they were completely without healthy skepticism; in which case, I believed, they would of course accept not only Faith, but any old whack-o gobbledygook psychic glop and, yea, verily, me—all in the same category.

It was then that I began to realize that in my way, I'd already lumped myself in with the crazies and the bunksters by default; that even I did not know how to define the so-called "real" stuff that I wanted my book to express. No wonder I was hesitant about putting myself out there in psychic book-land! It was all so formless, clumsy, burdened with worn-out words and concepts that didn't fit or were just plain stupid. Maybe the problem was that we were all groping across unknown continents together, nobody knowing how to behave on the trail: I'd been panned for being too credible and for being too hard-nosed—sometimes by the same people. And I later ran head-on into those feelings of vacuous clumsiness whenever I was asked to discuss my book or Jane Roberts' works; but it took a long time before I understood that it was not because of my inability to articulate, but precisely because I refused to resort to the smooth, polished catch-phrases that would have made me a better lecturer but a lesser explorer.

One of the first promotional assignments for *Conversations* that I received from Prentice-Hall was (ironically) a series of radio talk show interviews on stations all across the country. Almost without fail, the questions directed to me, from both program hosts and callers, came from two diverse and warring factions: either people wanted to prove that ESP-related matters were nonsense by definition, or they wanted "psychic" answers for everything. A man claiming to be a scientist informed me that *nothing* existed except what was provable in a laboratory; the very next caller wanted to know if Seth would tell her what her "karma" was this time around. Still another person wanted Seth to stop Russian telepaths from finding our MX missile sites. One program moderator said that Jane must be faking it all because the Seth material was "too good"; in the next breath he accused Jane and me of consorting with demons because Seth (and the rest of us) used four-letter words . . .

All of this was confusing enough to try to keep in perspective; but worse, whenever I was asked the inevitable question of who this Seth character actually *was*, my mouth, and my brain for that matter, filled instantly with lead. The "energy essence personality no longer focused in physical reality" explanation just didn't do it—did that mean that Jane Roberts was speaking for a ghost? Well, no; the idea of "ghost" and "dead" is just too limited, and . . . Then did that mean that Jane was holding seances like Madame Blavatsky? Gawd, no; Jane was primarily a *writer*, producing an excellent work of *art* and unlike the majority of quote, psychics, unquote, who never questioned . . . Then Jane wasn't speaking in trance for a dead person? Well, yes and no, sort of, except that, um, well, if you think of Seth as maybe a future Jane, uh . . . Then just what kind of claims was this Seth making, anyway? Well, uh, understand that I don't speak for Seth *or* Jane and we're supposedly talking about *my* book here, but nobody was making any *claims*, see, the Seth material is a philosophical approach to . . . Really? Wasn't Jane claiming to speak for the spirit of a dead . . .

It was endlessly frustrating. But I found myself enjoying the give-and-take, despite my difficulties. At least people were asking eccentric questions; at least there was some sort of dialogue going on here that couldn't happen just anywhere—it was a cinch that you couldn't raise your hand in school and ask about the mechanics of speaking for a dead anything, let alone wonder aloud about focusing (or not) in physical reality. Perhaps I was asking too much of people. Where, after all, in the midst of this noisy psychological drama, could the everyday person—ordinary human beings living daily lives—find practical, sensible answers to extraordinary questions? And how does anyone learn to evaluate whatever information is available? How does anyone find new frameworks of reference in the midst of chaos and ready-made definitions?

And that was it. By god, I thought, why do any of us think we have to go anywhere else at all? Why not just throw Faith Godwin right out the window and trust that each of us possesses that *knowing* we seek so fervently? I'd kept track of my own dreams for years, for instance—and I was finally understanding that I could trust their insights implicitly, simply because if nothing else, my dreams were an expression of my being, of my Self. So what if "authorities" didn't agree? So what if standardized dream analysis didn't apply?

All right, I thought, then there must be some way to show people once and for all that the *knowing* they'd always ascribed to others was theirs for the asking; that it came naturally from within; and that if necessary, it could be documented, recorded, verified—whatever; that *knowing* was as natural as breathing, and that we've spent too many centuries giving that knowledge to outside authorities: to gods of all descriptions; to oracles and psychics; to science and politics and medicine; to parents, friends, therapists, mystics, madmen—whomever; to Jane and Seth and even me (well, probably not me, but you never know). And I was fed up. I'd had it. I was tired of dunderheadedness, my own included. I was going to cut through the crap once and for all and uncover the "natural knowing" I really believe is inside everyone; the *knowing* that forms our individual, intimate lives and that we can turn to always (and do, even when we exteriorize its source). A knowing of the future, the past, and the miraculous mix of the present. Always. Inviolate.

And to my surprise, I ended up peering into the dreams of Dundee to find it.

NOTES

1 *Conversations with Seth: The Story of Jane Robert's ESP Class,* Vol. 1, 1980; Vol. 2, 1981, Prentice-Hall, Inc., Englewood Cliffs, NJ 07632.

A brief explanation of Jane Roberts and Seth: As described by Roberts herself in her many books, Seth, "an energy-essence personality no longer focused in physical reality," appeared in the lives of artist-writer husband and wife Robert F. Butts and Jane Roberts Butts late in 1963, as Jane and Rob were experimenting with a Ouija board as part of a book project (later published as *How to Develop Your ESP Power,* 1966/1974, Frederick Fell, Inc.; reissued by Pocket Books in 1976 as *The Coming of Seth*).

"The pointer paused," Roberts wrote in *The Seth Material (*1970, Prentice-Hall, Inc.) of her initial perception of the Seth personality. "I felt as if I were standing, shivering, on the top of a high diving board, trying to make myself jump while all kinds of people were waiting impatiently behind me. Actually it was the words that pushed at me—they seemed to rush through my mind. In some crazy fashion I felt as if they'd back up, piles of nouns and verbs in my head until they closed everything else off if I didn't speak them. And without really knowing how or why, I opened up my mouth and let them out . . ."

Once "let out," those words and Jane's development of the Seth material would in the next twenty years create among other works such books as *The Nature of Personal Reality; The Individual and the Nature of Mass Events; Dreams, "Evolution," and Value Fulfillment; Seth Speaks;* and a vast range of material as yet unpublished, delivered by Jane in trance as Rob wrote it all down by hand. In the Seth material and in her own books (such as *Psychic Politics* and *The God of Jane: A Psychic Manifesto*) that include novels, non-fiction, and poetry (*Dialogues of the Soul and Mortal Self in Time* and *If We Live Again,* for example) Roberts displays an astonishing progression of original thought, reflecting the great intellectual adroitness—on many levels—that she possessed. My book, *Conversations with Seth,* chronicles in two volumes the discussion group (somewhat mislabeled as a "class" in "ESP") that met in the Butts home from 1967 until December of 1978. Roberts died in September of 1984.

2 As more thoroughly explained in my first book, this "old man" was a character I used to notice standing around behind the spectator seats in local bowling alleys during my high school's Saturday morning games. I can still see him clearly in my mind's eye, watching me with a sweet, simple gladness on his ancient face, holding his brown hat in his hands and wearing a ratty-looking ankle-length brown coat. Whenever I spotted him,

he would bend forward slightly, nodding, with an eager smile; once, I remember, he made a little hello-wave gesture with his right hand and I waved back; he obviously *liked* me, and I felt drawn to him, too.

Probably I caught sight of him a couple of dozen times altogether in the space of two or three years—always in Elmira bowling alleys (located miles apart throughout the city), and always wearing the same heavy-looking brown coat, summer or winter. I recall pointing him out to my girlfriends, but I don't remember if they acknowledged seeing him or not. I never walked back to speak to the old fellow (and what would have happened if I *had,* I've asked myself a million times since), though it would have been perfectly safe to do so, since the alleys were always crowded and noisy with people milling about. The thing is that I instinctively *knew* there was something extraordinary about this old fellow's presence, though I could never quite put it into words.

Part of Seth's explanation of that old man, quoted here from *Conversations with Seth,* Vol. 1, pp. 128-129, was in response to a question I asked in a 1970 class: "[The old man] was a probable self of your grandfather's . . . He was a portion of your grandfather [Baker] that your grandfather as you knew him could not be, and in many ways he was much freer than your grandfather. He did not know . . . your name or who you were. He lived in Germany in his reality. He was born in his reality in 1831 and died in 1897. But you were able to see him. In out-of-body states, he projected into your reality . . . and you were able to see him because of your own abilities."

My grandfather Baker, as I knew him in usual terms, died in 1963 at the age of 71, when I was 18.

TWO

Tales Told to the Shaman

A Nightmare in Harlem and Secrets Revealed

. . . the idea [is] that solitude in nature may mean a temporary replentishment of selfhood, but to remain solitary is to risk impoverishment . . . to risk vanishing like a cloud dispersed, or sink . . . into the woods.

—John Gardner
Mickelsson's Ghosts

What does it signify when I dream of you every night?
—Distant Cousin Mary

(Postcard from vacationing Dundee native & cousin Mary L., mailed April 23, 1979, from Charlotte Amalie, Virgin Islands)

In the fragrant night air of spring, when the wind whispers of lilac and mock orange and flowering trees, and the new maple leaves play hand-shadow with the streetlights—in the mystery of a May night, when the gods seem capriciously ready to reveal all of their secrets, and the far-off sounds of car motors and barking dogs and fuzzy radios blend into the language of those gods—it is then that the soul of a small town emerges from its mortal disguise and you understand why it is that people live here, stay here, come back here, belong here, and are buried here in the churchyards and forested cemeteries guarded by corn flowers and the silence of a rural moon.

Dundee, New York, has often revealed its soul to me, as it has across time to most of its residents. It is a village of 1,600 or so, settled in a dish of land between Keuka and Seneca, two of the Finger Lakes of upstate New York. First explored by scouts from Jemima Wilkinson's Rhode Island Society of Universal Friends, the area was formally purchased after the Revolutionary War by one Issac Stark, who sold parcels off to later-arriving settlers, some of whom were my mother's ancestors, the Harpendings. (Stark apparently offered the entire tract to someone for a pair of grey workhorses, but the horse owner wouldn't trade.) For a time, the settlement was known as Stark's Mills, then Harpending Corners; finally, it was named Dundee in 1834 by a local contest-winner who picked the Scottish reference out of his favorite hymnal.

Like many rural communities, Dundee's industrial heyday has long passed by, although during the 1800s and early 1900s it was a milling center and was known as The Berry Capital of the World. A sulphur spring in nearby Crystal Valley made Dundee a popular health spa in the late 1800s, with a succession of huge hotels built to accommodate the thousands who flocked to the promised elixirs and cures. And actually, Dundee was more accessible 100 years ago than it is today: All passenger trains, and most local rail freight service, have disappeared; the main state highways are far to the north and south; major airports are at least an hour's drive away. The nearest communities of any size are Penn Yan, the Yates County seat, some twelve miles north; and Watkins Glen, site of the old Grand Prix races, ten miles south in Schuyler County.

And so Dundee remains an insular village in the heart of New York's wine country, surrounded by vineyards, dairy farms, and woods still deep enough for an occasional lynx or fox, growing populations of great blue heron, beavers, turkeys, and the ever-burgeoning deer. Except for changing store names, paved streets, utility lines, cars, and the inevitable trailer park, Dundee looks virtually untouched from photographs of Main Street taken in 1885, its gracious old homes and ancient maples like guardians of innocent small-town America. Yet there is a subtle vitality here beneath the provincial quiet: At least a dozen working writers and artists live in or near the village; new businesses have started up in town (including a revival of the Crystal Valley springs),[1] and numerous people in communications, education, business, and the arts have moved here in recent years. Perhaps they, and those whose lives have focused here for generations, respond, as I do, to the extended family of a small village, with all the joys and exasperations of family life. And it is safe. A safe universe. I haven't taken the keys out of my car in fifteen years.

I became an official part of Dundee on a March evening in 1977 during the Rotary Club's annual fund-raiser. At the time, this event was patterned after television's "Hee-Haw" show, with everyone taking harmless potshots at each other—Mark at the hardware store, Frank at the post office, Allan at the supermarket —all pleasantly corny, all for a good cause. And then Bob, the town clerk, stepped out front stage in his country-hick costume and made me his adopted daughter.

"Hey—you know what I heard about Sue Watkins??" he bellowed at the audience.

"No—what?" the stage company yelled back, from behind him.

"I heard she was walkin' along the beach down there in Florida—you know, in her *bikini??*" Bob shouted. "In her *bikini,* right??? Well! She was walkin' along on that beach and she had this *canary* in her hand, right?"

The audience roared. "And the first fella that comes along, ole Sue sez, Hey! If you can tell me how much this canary weighs, I'll let you make love to me! And so the guy sez . . . Well, lemme see . . . I guess it must weigh about a *ton!!!* And Sue sez . . . Hey! *THAT'S CLOSE ENOUGH!!!"*

Waves of laughter and applause washed over my head. I sat still, riveted to the seat, stunned. In that instant, I was born into the psychic structure of Dundee, child of my ancestors, part of a community and its network of people for the first time in my life.

It was an initiation that until that moment I'd never thought possible. My seven-year old son Sean and I lived then in a second-floor apartment overlooking a wooded lot on the edge of the village; and sometimes, sitting at my desk above the trees, I'd imagine that I was piloting a flying saucer rushing soundlessly across the face of the Earth. And in fact, I often felt as though I must be from another planet entirely. The years I spent as co-editor of the *Observer* seemed a disguise on what I imagined to be my true character. I believed that it was desirable—superior, even—to be eccentric, but that unofficial philosophies were ultimately dangerous and would only serve to isolate me from my contemporaries, from love and approval, and from myself (particularly the female self).

And the one thing that I didn't expect—the one reaction that I would never have predicted then—was embodied in that silly Rotary joke: acceptance. Acceptance of my character as it is. Not always *liked,* but accepted—and accepted not only as a fact, but as a necessary *function.* In its own way, Dundee had already made me its tribal shaman—a dream-shaman of sorts—long before I came up with the idea to gather up, and give recognition to, the dreams of a town.

It was while I was working on the class dream chapters in *Conversations* that the idea of collecting Dundee's dreams occurred to me. Those chapters were frustrating and difficult, mainly because of the lack of decent dream records. And from an ESP class, yet![2] I recalled that during class I'd noticed people reading their dreams from things like checkbook stubs and pieces of scrap paper, but for some reason we never took the step to establish guidelines for dream record-keeping. Which was really sad, because by the time I started my book project, there were few complete dream records left. I'd kept my own notes on correlating dreams, but damnit! I wanted all of those old records intact; a written history that would back up my book's declaration that we had lucid group-dream recall. I managed to put those chapters together, but they seemed like ghosts of what really went on. *Damn* the precariousness of ten-year-old notes, I thought. *Damn* trying to dig up the past with precision. Damn, damn, damn.

I considered starting my own dream class and doing it right this time; making sure that everyone (at gunpoint, maybe) kept *excellent* records—and turned them all over to me. But I really didn't want to hold a class in my apartment, even though the idea had merit. And then in one of those coincidences that isn't, another, concurrent project dovetailed into my dream-musings and took off on a direction of its own.

In one of our last *Observer* efforts together, Susan Benedict and I started a series of histories on the big old village homes. The newspaper printed one history per week, complete with photos and as many fascinating little gems as we could glean from local folks who remembered human-interest tidbits about each house. It was a popular series, even though we couldn't use half the items we uncovered, such as the fond moment recalled by the sweet elderly lady whose three young sons had gathered around the upstairs floor register and peed down through it onto a card table below, where an earnest game of bridge was in progress.

I was sitting at my desk one afternoon, taking a break from that impossible dream chapter by reading over the latest house history installment in the *Observer*. It made me think of the notions of official vrs. unofficial history: the difference between formally-recorded facts ("The house was built by So-and-So, who later became a State Senator . . .") and that lady's delightful memories of home life with three waggish sons; memories considered at least by the post office as unsuitable (weirdly enough) for a *family* newspaper. One's true, interior life, for the most part, had to be cleaned up to be acceptable. And I understood that, because I tended to operate under the precept myself.

Idly—on impulse—I went to the bookcase and took down the little self-published book[3] that my great-grandfather, Dr. Asbury Harpending Baker, had written about his childhood in Dundee. Born in 1860, Asbury put the book together for his grandchildren three years before his death in 1933. According to his preface, it was a family history, meant to be continued by each succeeding generation. I leafed through its yellowing pages and soon found myself absorbed in his descriptions of Dundee events that were now, for me, as distant as the stars. In 1859, the first of several major fires ripped through Dundee's downtown section, as well as part of the nearby residential area, reducing the whole block to a cinder. The following year, the entire west side of downtown burned to the ground. And then, according to Asbury, came the "Great Fire" of 1861, when great-grandfather was just a year old. Starting in a nearby barn and fanned by high winds, the fire gutted Dundee's main four corners, consuming 40 buildings in all—including the house where my great-great grandparents and baby Asbury lived.

"Our lot was deep and extended through from Seneca to Hollister Street," Asbury recounts. "And when it became evident that the house was going to burn my mother and grandmother carried me in my crib back through the lot to Hollister Street . . .[4] The blankets in the crib caught fire many times, making it necessary for them to brush out the sparks with their hands and slap out the fire." The next day, so history says, there was not a building left on Dundee's four corners—just a heap of smoking rubble.

A heap of smoking rubble. Hmmm. Like a war, I thought; the old photos I'd seen of that day-after certainly looked like the rubble of war. But one of the reasons I liked living in Dundee was because it seemed disaster-proof. No major floods, no hurricanes, only occasional "lake effect" tornados, no earthquakes, no avalanches, no forest fires or mud slides or toxic waste hazards or . . .[5]

Now why, I wondered, would the people of Dundee participate in a disaster in which their entire downtown burned not once, but several times? What was going on in the Dundee of 1861—going on beneath the surface, that is? Of course, that was the beginning of the Civil War, a conflagration all its own, literally and figuratively. But . . . my thoughts persisted, prodding at the funny feeling I was getting about it all. What were those fires really all about? A community event of another kind. A localized reflection of larger issues, maybe. Naturally, all of this presupposed (as I do) that such events are a creation of the village residents, individually and en masse . . .

Too damn bad, I thought, that you couldn't have everybody's *dreams* from back then—the dream history, the *truly* underground activities; the psychological fabric of the physical act. Oh, yes, my mind clattered, how wonderful, if everyone wrote their dreams down and preserved them and compared them. What if, just imagine, what if everyone in Dundee held a community meeting on, oh let's say, New Year's Day in 1861, to compare their dreams; and what if it were like ESP-class days and lots of people remembered—ye gods, what if they'd discovered that half the town remembered dreams about this great big *fire* burning down the whole damn dream block; and then what if Dundee's newspaper had *printed* all of those dreams and then everybody decided to go searching through the buildings and they'd discovered this smouldering hay or whatever in the barn on the four corners and . . .

"Ho-lee SHIT!!" I yelled, leaping to my feet, scattering papers, sending my cat scrambling under the couch. "Of course! Of *course!* Whoo-*EE!*" I literally hopped around the room, bursting with this sudden, crazy idea. Why not? Why not do it? Why bother with a little dream class in my apartment, two or three people dutifully turning in half a dozen dreams a week, WHEN THE WHOLE DAMN VILLAGE WAS RIGHT OUT THERE, dreaming away every night as naturally as rain?

What if Dundee—what if any town—had dream records that were checkable before and after objective events? What would the dreams of a community be like in the time surrounding a major fire, or accident, or whatever? I didn't think such a thing had ever been done before—and I knew that if anyone could collect people's dreams, I could. As a newspaper reporter, I'd been asking oddball questions for years—surely people would trust me with this. And the paper! Of course! The perfect outlet! Why not come right out in the *Observer* and ask for dreams . . . and then report on what I discovered?

It made instant sense. It seemed such an audacious thing to do . . . but so correct. And I knew that people would respond. The idea tingled through me like an electric shock. What a project—what a *book*.

And respond they did. But not precisely in the way I expected.

That week, I wrote up and published the following letter for the March 28, 1979, edition of the *Observer*:

Does Dundee Dream About Dundee?

I am interested in studying the correlations between the waking and dreaming activities of people who live in the village of Dundee. To do so, I need your participation and trust.

Dreaming is a necessary, biological function. Scientific experiments have proven that people who are allowed to sleep but kept from falling into the RM dream state quickly develop severe neurological disorders. Dreams and their haunting, symbolic nature have also been a source of mystery and speculation for centuries. Many books have been written on dreams and their interpretations, but never has there been a study done of the correlations between the dreams and waking life of a community.

Is there, for example, such a thing as a precognitive dream? And if there is, then is it possible for an entire group of people who have roots in common ground—such as the residents of Dundee—to have similar dreams about the same event?

If you are interested in being part of my experiment, all you have to do is tell yourself that you will remember your dreams every Friday night. That's all—just one night a week. Then, when you wake up on a Saturday morning, write down as many dreams as you can recall and include as much detail as you can, plus the date of the dream and, if possible, the time.

It won't matter if your dreams aren't about Dundee—write them down anyway. If some details, or some of the people in the dream, need explanation, include that also. And if anything happens to you during the week that happened in your Friday dreams, please make a note of this for me. Or, if you have an interesting dream on a night other than Friday, you can record that, too. You don't have to include anything that's too personal, of course; and you may have weeks in which you don't remember any at all.

In any case, after you've written down your dreams, you

can mail them to me at [my address]. Please understand that your identity will remain strictly anonymous, and that any published study that I may do on this experiment will preserve your anonymity without exception.

You may insist that you never remember your dreams, or that you don't remember enough of them to write down. However, if this whole idea interests you, you may find that the interest alone sparks dream recall. The act of recording dreams also tends to help you remember more of them.

So—if you would like to participate in a dream study of Dundee, please fill out the form below and mail it to me, or hand it to me on the street. I will contact you and answer any questions you might have. Thank you!

Sincerely,

____

I didn't know what to expect from the publication of this letter—except that I had the wonderful feeling that I was about to start recording a kind of history that up until that moment had never been recorded ("To boldly go . . ."). I did feel that all impulsively, I'd taken a big risk, exposing myself at last to my friends and neighbors—declaring my eccentric ideas to this extended family of mine. Now, I thought, people will see the self that I "really" am—not just the news-reporter-person from "outside"—and I realized that I wanted affirmation in that way; that I sought it; that I wanted my musings about dreams and the underside of reality to pass the test of practical daily life and mean something to people; to be more than a neat philosophical treatise.

A week went by. Nothing—but these things take time, I told myself, and ran the letter again in the next edition of the *Observer*. Several days passed—still nothing. I began to feel a little embarrassed; what if nobody responded at all? Maybe I really *was* the only one who cared about such things.

Then one afternoon two or three weeks into April, I walked down to the local post office and ran into Thaddeus, a big, burly farmer dressed that day in coveralls and muddy work boots. He was standing at the counter thumbing through a clump of bills and he looked as though he'd had a trying day at the office, to say the least.

"Hullo," he grunted when I came in the door. "I see yer puttin' together a book on dreams and stuff like that."

"Right," I said, surprised. Thad and I had managed to achieve a friendship based on mutual disagreement about almost everything, with his picking on my liberal views and my needling his more conservative ideas—never really arguing, just fencing. "Got any dreams for me?" I teased, assuming that he'd laugh and make some arch comment, as usual.

To my complete shock, he responded with, "Yeah, I got lotsa dreams—I remember 'em all the time." And then, to fill in the stunned silence, Thad added, "You know what I think? I think that it'd be a good thing if everybody in town—in this town, hell! Everybody!—wrote their dreams down every mornin' and then talked about 'em!"

"Urrrk!" I garbled, unable to make my mouth work.

"Sure," Thad continued, "mebbe that'd be a good way to find out what's *really* goin' on! You know, like mebbe you could tell if somebody was mad enough to wanna shoot somebody or somethin' like that or mebbe . . ." He looked at my frozen expression and laughed—*blushing*. "Aw, hell, who'd do that kinda thing anyway? It's just a dumb idea. Nobody's gonna send you no dreams, either. Naw—that's just dumb."

"Uh—No! No, it isn't!" I squawked. "No, no, it'll work, of course it'll work—that's my idea, sort of! Why won't it work?!"

Thaddeus laughed. "Sure, why not?" He was backing off now—kidding me again, back to normal—but he'd spoken his true thoughts the first time. Why was he acting as though he'd said something he shouldn't?

"So, you say you remember your dreams?" I persisted.

He sighed, shrugged. "Yep, all the time. Two and three a night, sometimes—sometimes more. Sometimes none."

I held my breath. "Do any of them ever come true?"

He laughed again, looked away. Then he stared straight at me—seriously, about to tell me a great secret. "Yeah, once in a while," he said. "Why—you lookin' for dreams that come true?"

"Sure," I said. "But I just want dreams—any dreams."

Thad stuck his hands in his coverall pockets and backed toward the door. "Well, I think that's a good thing," he said, making his escape. "Round 'em all up and read 'em on the radio every morning! *That* would sure be interestin'! Better'n gossip!"

He fled. I watched him go, ecstatic. Thad, a man in his sixties immersed from childhood in the crushing religion of the work ethic, was exactly the sort of person least likely in *my* mind to care about such things as dream experiments. And yet he had responded with a beautiful childlike playfulness, an approach that nearly everyone in Jane's ESP class had been obliged to *learn.* And I wondered: Does everyone, in secret moments, have this native understanding of the inner self? Is there an underground naturalism out there that no one has ever discovered because we're all so adept at keeping it to ourselves?

As it turned out, Thad's revelations were the beginning of a flood. A day or two later, I went to the local hardware store to buy a paint brush. I'd spent several minutes mulling through the mysteries of bristle types before I noticed that Sid, the clerk, was cracking his knuckles and clearing his throat in a frenzy of nervous impatience. Hastily, I took several brushes up to the counter and spread them out between us. "Sid," I said, "which is the right brush to put latex paint on over old woodwork with oil . . ."

"I hear you're writin' a book about dreams," Sid interrupted.

"Oh—well, maybe, but not before I paint the woodwork," I said cheerfully.

"Are you collectin' recurring dreams?" he asked casually, as though someone else wanted to know.

"Sure, I guess so," I said.

"What does it mean when you have the same dream—I don't mean all the time, but maybe, oh, on the average of, say, once or twice a year or so ever since you can remember?"

"Well," I said, "it's hard to say—it all depends on . . ."

"And *what,*" Sid went on, "if that dream is a *nightmare?!!*" His eyes widened.

"Well, a nightmare . . ."

"The scariest nightmare you can *imagine!!*" he hissed, his voice echoing up into the ceiling above us. The store, overwhelmed as it was by towering, jam-packed shelves dim in the dusty, old-fashioned lighting, suddenly seemed filled with the mutterings of bad dreams.

"Uh—well, nightmares," I said, lowering my voice, "can be anything, but maybe if you've got an unresolved problem or fear . . ."

"*THIS* nightmare," Sid growled, "is one I've been havin' since I was a kid—and it always scared the heck right out of me!"

Oh, wow, I thought, this one's going to be a beaut. I turned on my reporter's ears. "Tell me about it," I said eagerly.

"Well, now," Sid began, "I don't know if you'll want to use this in your book or anything, but—" he wiped his lips with the back of his hand. "In this dream, now, I'm drivin' a car in New York City and it's night—it's right in the middle of the night!"

"Yes?" I urged.

" . . . And it's in the pitch black of *night,* and I'm drivin' a car, and all of a sudden I realize that I'm lost and I don't know where I am at all . . ." He made a sweeping gesture with his hands.

"And all of a *sudden,* I realize that I've gotten myself *into the middle of Harlem!!!* And then you know what happens??!!"

"What?" I breathed, neck hairs dancing in anticipation.

"The car conks out," Sid said. He looked at me.

"Uh—" I waited. "That's it?"

Sid nodded vigorously. "Well, yeah!"

"That's all of it? That's your nightmare?"

He glared at me, offended. "Well, Jeeze, woman, isn't that *enough???"*

* * * *

I approached the dream study, of course, with numerous prejudices. For one thing, I already believed that precognition existed as a natural function of life (and who knows, maybe of what seems to be non-life: Do chairs dream of who will sit upon them?). I anticipated the existence of dream connections (and so resolved to make sure that I didn't read connections where none existed). I was most of all predisposed to think of dreams as meaningful, intimate symposiums in the creation of private and public life. And I hoped that all of this would be borne out in a written record of village dreams and days.

To begin with, about twenty people started sending me their Friday night dreams—not anywhere near what I'd hoped, but enough to make it interesting—and it soon became evident that as they kept going, their dreams got "better" in a certain way. This observation prompted me to look over my own dream records, which I've maintained since the early 1960s; and I discovered that the same was true of my dreams, too. As I became accustomed to keeping dream records, the dreams themselves got "better," with more direct information and precognitive "hits." It wasn't exactly that my dream recall improved; most of my earliest dreams were great long tangled masses of stuff, sometimes ten to fifteen pages long, with a lengthy Star Trek scenario every few days (some not bad story lines, actually). The problem wasn't memory; my memory was almost *too* good back then. Maybe it was that after a while, your dreams got used to being paid attention to and your daily recall knew what was important and what was not . . . or maybe the chore of writing all those dreams down caused automatic dream-editing.

And my Dundee dreamers plunged ahead, definitely improving within each dream style. And I'll get to those dream records later. Because the *other* fascinating thing that started to happen was that the whole project split into "official" and "unofficial" records. The written dreams were my official records, and they were interesting, sometimes astonishing—but they couldn't begin to compare with the stuff that I collected from people who wouldn't write anything down; who sometimes refused to acknowledge that the experiences were even worth talking about. These I scribbled down in a notebook I carried in my purse—usually after the person was out of sight. And the funny thing was that those who scoffed openly at my dream idea were most often the ones who later sought me out on the sly to "confess," as it were, their dreams or psychic experiences.

"You probably won't believe this," one person told me as he checked to make sure no one could hear, "but I'll tell you anyway and you can forget it if you want. My mother died when I was a kid, but afterwards she used to walk in my room to tell me that she would always watch over me." The man looked at his feet, glumly, waiting for me to laugh or pass him off or make a joke. "I suppose it was a dream, but I swear to you I was just as wide-awake as I am right now," he went on. "I've never told that to anyone—but I always felt that it *was* my mother, not a hallucination or whatever." "I wouldn't tell this to just anybody," another person said, "but I saw something in the sky a couple years ago that must have been one of those UFO things. It was bright silver and moved back and forth and it wasn't any airplane—but anyone else would think I was crazy."

A local businessman called me up one afternoon to reveal that he "knew" he'd lived before, during the Civil War, and how could he go about finding out more? When I suggested that he try asking for more information in his dreams, this businessman then "confessed" that he'd recently dreamed of meeting a local retired real estate broker in the Dundee bank—and that the two had shaken hands and said good-bye to one another—the night before this broker died.

"Funny thing is," my businessman friend said, "I didn't even *like* the old buzzard—but there he was, plain as day! I guess that means dreams really do 'work'!" He concluded the phone call by saying that he'd see what he could get about the Civil War in his dreams, or maybe he'd try hypnosis—he'd let me know (though he never did).

Another businessman told me, "in confidence," over a cup of coffee in the local restaurant, that he and his cat shared a special communication. "I get an image in my mind of the cat sitting outdoors, and I look out the window and there she is, in the back yard, looking back toward the same window," the man said. "I've always had the feeling that this is okay, you know, a natural thing; but what I wonder about is, does the cat *know* that she can get ahold of me this way? Does it work the other way around, too?" I told him that at least in my opinion, it certainly did work "the other way around."

"Oh, I see," my friend said, "then you mean that dreams and real life work back and forth the same way?"

Sure they do, I told him, though I wouldn't call one side of life less "real" than the other—"differently organized," maybe. So we discussed how dreams "come true," a conversation that later reflected back to me when several of Sean's friends told me that they'd had dreams that "came true"—usually dreams concerning incidents in school, or events in the news. At about this same time period, Sean's own dreams, always vivid, seemed to splash out into his waking days; one afternoon he told me he'd happened to glance inside the school windows as he walked along the sidewalk toward the elementary section's doors—and sitting in the otherwise empty classroom was C., a schoolmate who'd died in a house fire some months before. Sean said that he stopped abruptly and stared in at the girl's apparition, or presence, sitting there—staring back. "She looked like she knew exactly what effect she was having," Sean said. "Wisenheimer, you know—like ha, ha, I can scare you! I looked at her for a while and then it was as though she hadn't been there at all. She just disappeared."

Then there was the afternoon that I met Mrs. Densig on the steps of the local dress shop. She and her husband managed a large farm in the northern part of the county, and though I'd met her once or twice while gathering farm news, I didn't know her well enough to remember her first name. Plus, she lived way outside of the *Observer*'s circulation area, so I was a bit surprised when she greeted me that afternoon and with no preamble launched into a story about a series of recent deaths in her family.

"I knew about them all," Mrs. Densig stated, staring sadly into my eyes. "I dreamed about every one of them dying, every time, just before it happened. Then, after my father-in-law died, I dreamed that I was talking to him." Her lips trembled. "I know this must sound crazy, but if I hadn't had those dreams, I would have *gone* crazy. I dreamed that I saw my father-in-law sleeping in the barn, right by the milkhouse. When he—when they found him, that's where he was, by the milkhouse." She struggled with tears. "I don't know why I'm bothering you with this," she said.

I cleared my throat, feeling badly for her on one hand, and trying not to skewer her with questions on the other. "Ah—well," I said. "Your dreams certainly don't sound crazy to me—they sound perfectly natural. Do you remember the conversation in the dream with your father-in-law?"

Tears spilled down her cheeks. "Yes, I do," she said. "And the reason I remember it is because I—well, I had the same kind of dream after each one of my relatives died. They all told me that they were okay now, that they were all right, they knew they were dead and it was okay, I shouldn't worry." She took a deep breath. "That's all," she said. "I didn't dare tell my husband about it because he'd think I was—what do you think it means?"

"Oh, boy," I thought. Once again, the old words and definitions seemed idiotic in the face of this woman's questions. What could I say? What if I offended her in some way? "Well," I said, hesitantly, "I think that you were involved in some kind of genuine communication with your relatives."

Mrs. Densig nodded, her eyes never leaving my face.

"I, uh, also think," I went on, "that you picked up on their deaths exactly to the extent that you wanted to know about them." I said this off the top of my head, but it made instant sense. "Probably there were other signals of their upcoming deaths—you may have known unconsciously that they were about to die and the only acceptable way you had to acknowledge the information was in your dreams." I smiled. "You could just pass it all off as a dream, right? But you remembered them. Not everybody remembers dreams, you know."

"And they all came true," she said, intensely.

"Uh—well, yes," I said. "But the point is, you were prepared to some extent—the deaths weren't a total shock to your psyche, right?"

"No," she agreed, "they weren't—I *knew.* But why?"

I shrugged. "Maybe we always know and repress the information out of habit, or whatever."

"Yes," she said. "In the one dream, my father-in-law was *sleeping,* not dead. Maybe . . ." she blinked back more tears. "Maybe that's all I wanted to see, is that what you're saying?"

"Well," I said, "I guess so, yes. But whatever, the dreams helped you through a time of great difficulty. And afterwards, I would say that you communicated at least with your *idea* of your relatives, and . . ."

She glared, almost angry. "What do you mean, my 'idea' of my relatives?"

Delicate territory. "I mean that I don't think after death, we stay the same people—I mean, we don't even stay the same people throughout life, right? We change all the time, grow, learn new things?" She nodded again. "I just think that maybe the process goes on after death—maybe on a scale we can't imagine . . ."

Abruptly, Mrs. Densig burst into sobs.

"Oh, you're right!" she cried, swiftly pulling a kleenex out of her pocketbook. "I don't know why I worried that there was something wrong with it all! I knew those dreams were good and came to me for a reason!" She blew her nose, mopped her face. "Oh, you're so good and kind! Thank you! Where did you learn all of this? You know so much about these things!"

"Ah, well, no, not really," I stammered. "I'm, ah, just writing a book about Dundee peoples' dreams, and . . ." She'd stopped listening. "It's just the kind of thing I like to think about."

"Well, it's a *good* way to think," Mrs. Densig said, squeezing my hand. "There's my ride, now, so I have to go. Good luck on your book." She walked down the sidewalk and got into a waiting car. And I have no idea what made her tell me about her dreams, because as I thought about it, I realized that she didn't know about my dream project, apparently—she'd brought up the subject out of the blue.

I was still thinking about Mrs. Densig's dreams a few days later—wondering where in god's name people get the idea that such innocent things as dreams might be "wrong"—when I ran into an old friend from a nearby town. We hadn't seen one another in a while, although I knew that her father had died several months before. She said she was visiting relatives in Dundee but she'd been meaning to talk to me because she'd heard that I was collecting dreams and . . .

She burst into tears. Oh *shit* why me, I thought; emotional displays embarrassed me and now this damned dream thing was pulling me into such scenes every time I turned around . . .

"I dreamed about my father's death before it happened," my friend said. She went on to explain that for at least six months she'd had little dreams two or three times a week in which her father would carefully explain to her that he was dead, but that he would look out for her always. "The dreams were sort of fleeting and, like, really kind of inconsequential," she said. "I barely remembered them, even—it was more like a feeling that I remembered—reassurance, or some kind of mystical, I don't know, *rightness* about to occur. Do you know what I mean?

"If I hadn't had those dreams," she said in a rush, "I think I would have fallen apart when Dad died. I think they helped me get through what happened, maybe even get *ready* for it, even though they didn't tell me, you know, *right out loud* that he was going to die and I really didn't remember anything. And even though his death was a complete shock, I wasn't surprised. I realized that I'd *known.* Am I making sense?"

"Perfect sense," I said, struck by the fact that, like Mrs.

Densig's dreams, my friend's experience had given her exactly the right emotional support at precisely the right time and with the right amount of information—enough to prepare, not enough to overwhelm: a subtle balance.

"The only thing is," my friend went on, "I keep thinking, maybe I could have done something to prevent his death. I mean, maybe if I'd remembered the dreams better I could have made him get a checkup . . . I don't know. But I really didn't have a *warning,* damnit! It was more like—like a dim memory of something *before* it happens, you know? But—then I think, why have any dreams like this at all if you don't remember enough to be able to act on them?"

"Why couldn't you have been a better daughter, right? Couldn't save your father's life, right?" We smiled ruefully at one another. Guilt I understood; and inducing guilt is not the purpose of dreams, that much I knew. But in each case of foreknowledge, the information suited the needs and psychological framework of the perceiver—and who knew, maybe of the object of the dream . . .

A fascinating idea began to play around the edges of these unofficial records: Precognition as a facet of daily life, of natural ability—like the natural ability to learn one's own language from babyhood. Precognition as a portent of the *dreamer's* role in the event, as well as the role of the *dreamed.* Like the Great Fire of 1861 in Asbury's book—what migrations of public and private purposes must have crossed in that terrifying disaster? And if people *do* know of future events, then what processes of acquiescence and intent combine to keep such knowledge hidden (or at least cloistered) until after the fact? What role is played by the will of the participants?

It was an interesting riddle, to muse on how these "unofficial" dreams were precognitive to some degree, but not direct, exact descriptions of the actual physical events; Mrs. Densig had seen her father-in-law *sleeping* on the barn floor, with no aura of pending death. She'd simply prepared herself, or so it seemed, to find the man lying there, without giving herself any worry-hint of his physical end. And while my friend's dreams with her father were definitely about death, these reassured her without "mentioning," as it were, the actual event, which was abrupt and terrifying (the man died in a local store while buying cigarettes, his family waiting for him out in the car). So maybe by searching for exact correlations between dreams and events and discounting whatever didn't seem to fit in that regard, we'd been overlooking what was *really* going on in "precognition" by applying what was probably an extremely limited form of expectation in the first place . . .

though again, I cautioned myself, I had to be careful not to read in all sorts of interpretations and connections that weren't there . . .

And then I was presented with a glimpse of dreams coming "true" in a way that I'd only vaguely imagined.

NOTES

1 Crystal Spring water has recently been revived as a business; a local company is now in the process of bottling and distributing through state retail stores. According to tests made by state health officials, this water has exactly the same mineral content that it did 120 years ago—and is so pure that it's being bottled without additives or filtration.

2 See Chapters 13 and 14 in Volume 2 of *Conversations with Seth.*

3 *Memories* by Asbury Harpending Baker, 1930, The Commercial Press, Elmira, NY.

A note on Asbury himself: My great-grandfather Baker grew up in Dundee and in 1878, at the age of eighteen, went to work for the *Observer*, which had been founded that year by Dundee native Eugene Vreeland. Asbury set type (a profession I spent many classes learning in the Syracuse University Newhouse School of Journalism in the years just before "hot type" was replaced by offset) and ran a job press for $1.50 a week, a salary raised the following year to $3.00. At that point Asbury purchased a power press and other "modern" printing equipment for the paper with money borrowed from his mother. He was then made a full partner in the business, though he left it in 1882 to enter Buffalo Medical College. Besides all of his subsequent medical records and lectures, Asbury left behind a batch of short stories and the original handwritten manuscript for his *Memories*; and it is with rather a breathtaking sense of serendipity that I contemplate how 100 years later I came to be co-editor of the same newspaper with owner Susan Benedict; purchased our "modern" IBM composer-typewriter with money borrowed from my mother; and later left the *Observer* to go my own way, too—with the writing of *Conversations with Seth*, the gathering-up of Dundee dreams, and other projects.

Meanwhile, on my father's side of the family tree, my paternal great-grandfather, Ernest Lorain Disbro, was publisher and editor of newspapers in Oberlin and Elyria, Ohio, at the turn of the century . . . which would seem to make a case for genetic printer's-ink-in-the-blood.

4 And this is the same lot where the Hollister Street house I bought in 1984 was built, in 1869.

5 Though maybe I shouldn't have mentioned it! In late August of 1988, a devastating storm later classified as a tornado ripped a path through Yates and Schuyler Counties, destroying 80% of the 1,000 acres of vineyards affected with a combination of 125 mph winds, torrents of rain, and hail literally the size of golf balls. It was all over in less than ten minutes, leaving one person dead and a lot of ruined property behind. Some of the vineyards along Seneca Lake looked as though they'd been run through a food processor. Though the hail beat holes in my son's car and dented up the siding on my house, the tornado itself missed me by a couple of miles. Just a few hours before the storm, I'd been sitting at my dining room table proofreading this book's galleys—specifically, *this chapter*, in which I mention the area's "occasional 'lake effect' tornados!"

I should have been on the alert for this sort of coincidental tie-in between my book and exterior events, since it's happened before, as I explain in this book . . . and as happened just a week before this tornado! In my first of several read-throughs of these galleys, I'd started going over Chapter 12, in which I mention an incident involving two Jehovah's Witnesses coming to the door of my Florida condo. *That* incident had occurred in 1980 just as I was typing up the final chapters for my book, *Conversations with Seth*, and so connects with ideas presented in *Dreaming Myself* on coincidence and impulses.

Reading over this incident in 1988, the thought came to me that I hadn't seen any Jehovah's Witnesses at my door in quite some time. There's a large congregation of Witnesses in the Dundee area, and for a while it seemed they were showing up two or three times a month. Sitting there with my book's galleys before me, I thought to myself that this probably meant that I was going to get a visit from them that day! And sure enough, no more than an hour later, a battered old blue station wagon pulled up my driveway. In it was a young couple and their small, very skinny son. Much to my surprise, the man looked so much like a friend from Jane's ESP class that I was momentarily taken aback. Equally astonishing, the woman was bristling with ill-concealed hostility and even made a couple of rude remarks. But the funny thing was that I was intrigued enough by the man's resemblance to my ESP class friend that I found myself with the impulse to ask them in for a chat (where we'd have ended up sitting at the table with my book's galleys strewn all over in plain sight). Had the woman not displayed this hostility, I might have acted on the impulse and possibly discovered other connections offering themselves to me here.

Later I wondered about the woman's immediate reaction to me and its consequences in terms of *my* impulse, which, after all, "fit" their own purposes. Her husband, on the other, hand, was more than polite—he was actually sympathizing aloud about invading my privacy, a stance that to me felt contrived and *cunning*. At least the woman's anger was honest. But altogether, the two of them were charged up with stuff I decided I'd rather not have in my house, so I turned them away. Watching them rumble their car back down my driveway, their stick-thin, runny-nosed son staring wide-eyed out the back window, I saw them as an inside-out version of (Chapter 13's) Annie and Harold, seeking salvation in a shabbier sort of Spiritual Home on Wheels.

All of this tied in so nicely with my book—with both of my books, and the connections between them—that I decided to include these incidents here.

THREE

Unofficial History, Underground Events

The Man Who Died and the Puzzle of Dreams

I've known before that earth and mind are one,
and heaven's wasteful dark is the mind's same dark.

John Gardner
"Desire on Sunday Morning"
Poems

I hadn't slept well that night, and the one dream I recorded in the morning was as dark and gloomy as I felt.

"I am looking at an article in a magazine that seems to be about a startling discovery recently made by deep-sea explorers," I wrote. "In a slick, glossy article with strange, golden photographs, I read that x-rays taken from a bathysphere down through layers of coral and rock, miles below the surface, have revealed a sunken city. Not Atlantis—another, lost, city. This is in a canyon in the Atlantic. I see this little round diving bell drifting down through the water, wending its way through the reef, which here has layers of caves and cobwebbed coral, arranged in shelves that jut out and threaten to catch the bathysphere. The city is far below, in an almost bottomless place, in cold, cold water: A city suspended in timeless cold somewhere beneath the sea."

My dream notes add that in that morning's mail (which I picked up after writing down this dream) was the week's edition of *The New Yorker* magazine. In it was a John McPhee piece entitled "Annals of the Former World, Part I," an article about the coastal plates of the U.S. Eastern Seaboard.

A quirky little precognitive peek, I thought, but who cares? So what if I pick up on some article written in a national magazine? I put the dream away and forgot about it. Until the next day.

That next morning, a Sunday, I went down to the local restaurant for breakfast, as many people do. Immediately, I could tell that something was wrong. Folks were sitting in small, quiet groups, unlike the usual Sunday morning cacophony of breakfast chatter. I soon found out what had happened: a young man I'll call Donald S., a lifelong resident of Dundee, had drowned early that morning in Seneca Lake. His body hadn't been recovered, and most were of the opinion that it never would be.

According to information later gleaned from those who'd been at the scene, Donald had been with friends on a sailboat just offshore at about 2 a.m. when the accident happened. It was a dark night, with fog rolling across the water, and Donald, who couldn't swim and wasn't wearing a life jacket, slipped on the fog-slick deck and fell overboard. Apparently, the waters had closed over his head with barely a splash; and Donald never cried out or surfaced again. One of the women on board leaped into the lake after him, but it was too dark and foggy, and all efforts to rescue him proved futile. (Local fire departments conducted a three-day search, but to this date in 1988, Donald's body has never been found.)

As I listened to this sad news, I thought immediately of my

dream. Seneca is the deepest and coldest of the Finger Lakes, reaching known depths of nearly 700 feet. In addition, the lake is filled with unpredictable currents and narrow, jagged canyons and caves, and is considered dangerous for divers and swimmers alike. (I know from experience that swimming in Seneca on the hottest summer days can be a numbing shock.) And Donald was hardly the first to disappear forever beneath Seneca's waters: people have drowned there frequently enough, and their bodies are often never recovered. I thought of the diving bell in my dream, drifting down past those jagged reefs toward a cold, silent timelessness—and knew, with a shudder, that it was indeed connected with Donald's death.

And I sat there, puzzling over the nature of my dream, getting more and more annoyed with the whole business of precognition. I felt as though I'd reached out and captured at least the *cast* of Donald's tragic end. But it wasn't a precognitive dream in what you might call conventional terms. *And why the hell not,* I demanded. Why such an eerie, filtered picture—why not the whole thing, or nothing? Why in *hell,* if I were going to have any premonition of this at all, couldn't I have had one clear enough to use as a warning? Donald was a friend, as he was to most everyone in town. But who in Dundee had more faith in dreams than I did? Why hadn't I seen the picture as it was going to happen, if at all—I'd connected it with a magazine article, for chrissakes.

Or . . . I sighed, watching people whisper to one another in a small town's acknowledgment of a native son's passing. Or maybe Donald's decision was made and sealed in some way, in his reality, and cut off from change on whatever level these things occur. I knew, for instance, that several years before, Donald had nearly been drowned during a fistfight with another local man while the two of them were standing on a Seneca lakeshore dock. Had Donald been "considering" death then, and backed away from it, only to confront it now? Whatever the answer, why had the event punched through into *my* dream world so oddly—and yet so powerfully?

I was soon to find out that my questions didn't even begin to take in the whole picture. The following morning, I walked into the post office and ran into a fellow who'd gone to high school with Donald. "I want to tell you something," he said. His face was troubled and grim, not at all like his usual self. "I had a dream about Donald the night before he died," my friend said. "At least I *think* it was about Donald, but it wasn't actually *about* Donald—it just feels like it was about Donald." He shook his head. "I'll just tell you about it and you can make what you want out of it."

"Go ahead," I said.

We walked back out onto the sidewalk. "What I dreamed was this," my friend said. "I saw this big, dark rowboat in the garage next to my father's house. It was at night, and it was absolutely quiet. There was no sound at all in this dream. And then the rowboat—which was empty, see, nobody in it—the rowboat started tipping up on one side, and then it tipped on up and up, and then it fell over—still without any sound, just all dark and quiet. It fell over and hit somebody's arm and broke it. I don't know whose arm it was, but the whole thing was weird."

I agreed—it *was* weird, like a little side-addition to my own dream. "Gee, that's not what happened, but it sort of sounds like what happened," I said, lamely.

"I know," my friend replied, obviously very unhappy about it. I quickly described my own dream. "So maybe we both picked up on what was going to happen, sort of," I said. "Your dream sure reflected the atmosphere on the lake's surface—the darkness, no sound, you know . . ."

My friend looked a bit pained. "Are you saying that we helped make that happen to Donald?" he asked.

"No, no, of course not," I answered. "But I think maybe we both perceived the death, don't you?"

"I don't know," my friend said. "I wonder if anyone else dreamed about it?"

"I wish I knew," I said. Briefly, I thought about asking this question in the newspaper, but that seemed in bad taste, considering the circumstances.

As it turned out, I didn't have to ask. The network of "unofficial" dreams swung smoothly into operation. Within a day or two, three more people stopped me on the street to tell me about their "strange little dreams" that they said "felt" attached to Donald's death. One person dreamed of sinking, fully-dressed, down through the water of a swimming pool, looking all the while back up at the fast-retreating sunlight, feeling a vast sadness for leaving the things of the earth behind. Another said she'd dreamed just one tiny thing: of standing in the fog on the shore of Seneca Lake, waiting for friends to return from a boat ride. The third person's dream was a fleeting image: a feeling of doom and disaster.

All the dreams had occurred before that Sunday morning; none of them had been written down.

Listening to the dreams, I was struck again by the jigsaw-puzzle sense of connection. None of these dreams by themselves showed what would happen to Donald, and none had named Donald as the victim or alluded to him in any way. Yet when pieced together, the dreams all formed major portions of that event, like a painting coming together in a chorus of brush strokes—with the results whispering through each touch on canvas. Would the dreams of all 1,632 Dundee residents have filled in the complete picture?

Of course, you could come to the conclusion that people were making the dreams up—after all, I'd made my interest public and Donald's death was a well-known fact of news and discussion by the time people started telling these dreams to me. And I considered that possibility. But if anyone were going to play such a hoax—and really, Donald's passing was too great a community tragedy (his wife, son, and parents living on among us) to be a subject for practical jokes. And the obvious trick would have been to tell me dreams of the event exactly as it had happened. The cooperation necessary to *contrive* this puzzle-picture, not to mention coming up with the idea in the first place, would have required a heartless cunning that just doesn't exist among ordinary people.

The dream connections with Donald's death didn't stop with these few people, either. During the next couple of weeks, at least a dozen others described dreams to me that fell into one of two categories: those that occurred before Donald's drowning and nightmares that followed soon afterward. One person dreamed that his own son had drowned; another dreamed that his pet dog fell off his fishing boat and swam away into darkness.

Remarkably, and somehow more chilling than this, was a kind of mass-repercussion nightmare that people started reporting to me, in which they'd dreamed that Donald was still alive under Seneca's waters and was trying to crawl out of the lake through the rock strata or gas springs (which are common around these lakes). Many of the details in these dreams were identical (again, unofficially, because no one wrote these down for me); in most, Donald was trapped and needed help; in others, he had reappeared and was walking the village streets; or he had been caught by authorities who couldn't figure out who he was; or he had changed his identity and was living under a pseudonym in another town.

And I wondered: If you could see the dreams of any town, or neighborhood, or family, or any group of people, would all waking events appear there in bits and pieces? Do all living creatures dream of the world this way? Were my dreams my own, and yet a five-and-a-half-billionth of the world's giant puzzle of a dream?

I made up a chart of the "before" and "after" dreams as reported to me and stared at it for a long time, making criss-cross lines between the dreamers, and marking how they connected in village life with Donald. Some of the people whose names I put down had rarely, if ever, spoken with me before about *anything*. There were funny little tendrils of association, too, here and there . . . one man, who'd been particularly upset by a "before" dream, couldn't swim either (like Donald) . . . reminding me of my phobic airplane-crash dreams that seemed eerily predictive sometimes. A woman whose "after" dream saw Donald rising up out of the lake, alive, had recently joined an area religious sect . . . so *that* fit with her ideas about death—or maybe *all* of these "after" dreams were based on the dreamers' ideas about death. Or ideas about "new life": the fellow who'd dreamed that Donald was living in another town with a new identity was himself in the midst of changing jobs and wasn't really happy with either one. Perhaps his dream reflected a yearning to become someone else altogether, with Donald's death as metaphor (they were about the same age).

And it was funny, it really was—looking at this bunch of dreams made me almost think that there was something "precognitive" about the dreams that happened *afterward*, too. What was it? It was all provocative as hell.

I had nothing conclusive, of course—just a small collection of dreams from people mourning a friend; certainly nothing that any scientist would take as a statement of any sort of fact. Yet there was a "truth" here that was most exciting. If only we were as civilized as the Indian nations that once gathered daily in the longhouse to tell their dreams . . . perhaps then we could have discovered that one of our tribe was headed for disaster on the dark waters of the lake, and perhaps . . .

It was then that I started looking more closely at the relationship between the details of my dreams and my daily life; between dream "bits" and the odd little waking coincidences of happenstance. And a very engrossing pattern began to emerge from this sideways contemplation, one that should have been obvious to me from the beginning of my dream notebook-keeping days so many years before.

FOUR

K. and Me and the Pits Make Three . . .

(from the *Observer*)

The world's parts come spontaneously together, with an order that basically defies the smaller laws of cause and effect, or before and afterward. In that regard, again, your dreaming state presents you with many clues about the source of your own lives and that of your world.

—Jane Roberts
Dreams, "Evolution," and Value Fulfillment

(May 10, 1979)[1]

Ever since I started asking for dreams from Dundee residents, people have not only been sending them to me faithfully, but at least a dozen folks have come to me to relate dreams or ask questions about my dream study. One of the more persistent questions I've been asked in one form or another is of what "good" such a study will do. People send me their dreams. Maybe there are some correlations; maybe some precognitive ones. So what?

Much of our knowledge of dreams and the dream state has been gleaned under "scientific" conditions in which the dreamer is wired to a type of electroencephalograph (brain wave scanner) while sleeping. As the subject's brain waves begin to indicate dream activity, he is awakened and asked to describe what he or she was dreaming about. From this, scientists have discovered a great deal about how the brain functions during sleep, and the psychological effects of various kinds of dream states. But very little has been recorded on the relationship between dreams and the constructions of daily life beyond the consideration of dreams as a symbolic reflection of life—which, of course, they are.

I want to look into the notion that we literally make the days and world we know within the magic elasticity of our dreams. That sort of creation would naturally have to include precognitive abilities—as well as a power of synthesis beyond our wildest—

Uh, well, dreams. And I already have an example—just a small one; a hint, a clue—from my Dundee dream collection.

On the night of February 12/13, 1979, I had a long and rather involved dream that ended up with my father and me in a car, driving down a peaceful country road. In the dream we stopped at a large white house by the side of the road. We soon discovered that the house was perched on the edge of a steep, bottomless pit, the banks of which were stony and crumbling, descending sharply down into darkness. Water was leaking into this pit from all around the sides, making it slick and dangerous. But I got out of the car and walked around the house until I found a way to get down the hill to the bottom of the pit from outside it.

There I found an opening to a cave leading into the side of the pit—and entering, I discovered that the cave was filled with valuable antiques. Guarding these antiques were two men—my great-uncle Templer, and Jack C., owner of Dundee's radio station. I made my way inside the pit itself and finally came across a set of doors leading up into the outside world from below. The pit wasn't so dangerous after all—there was a way out! I noticed that the doors had a system of locks that worked like puzzle rings—where each piece fits together in a tricky way. Then I woke up.

The next day, I was in the *Observer* office when I received a phone call from K., a village resident I've known for five or six years but whom I've talked to only a few times—and never about personal matters or dreams. However, mutual friends had told me that her husband was struggling with cancer of the bowel and had gone through some frightening surgery.

"What were you doing in my dream last night?" K. immediately demanded, in an excited tone of voice. She then proceeded to tell me the following, prefaced by the assertion that she *never* remembered her dreams—but that this one was a "shocker."

In K.'s dream of the night before, February 12/13, she and I were riding in a car down a country lane when we came to a huge pit in an otherwise peaceful field. Men were working in the bottom of the pit. We stopped the car and I got out to see what the men were doing. As I walked back to the car, it lurched forward suddenly and nearly fell into the pit. I spoke again to the men and they helped K. out of the car, after which it fell to the bottom.

Although K. hadn't been in my own dream of the night before, the correlations involved were obvious to me—more than they could be to K., since some of the linking details included facts that she couldn't have known. First off, obviously, both of us had dreamed vividly of a huge pit in the ground—both of these dangerous, and both with men working at the bottom (in mine, the men were guarding antiques; in hers, they were performing the physical labor of excavation). Secondly, and K. did not know this, my father (who was in *my* dream) had gone through emergency surgery a few years before when several intestinal diverticulae had burst through the wall of his bowel. Both of those sets of physical difficulties involved "pits" in the intestines, and physical "excavations" in the form of similar surgical techniques.

"But why would *you* appear in my dream?" K. asked me again, almost indignantly.

Well, for one reason, I had announced in the January 18, 1979, edition of the *Observer* that I was quitting my editorial position there to write a book on dreams and ESP. K. said that she'd read that announcement at the time. "So that might have influenced your dreams," I said.

"Well, probably, but why *this* dream?" K. persisted. From the way she spoke, I could see that it mattered very much to her to know why she had dreamed about me. Of course, my immediate interpretation of the dreams' possible symbols might not mean the same to her at all, and I didn't want to drag out any painful subjects—the fact was that her husband had nearly died and at that time was not entirely out of the woods. (My father's condition had been touch-and-go for a couple of days, too.) I like K. a great deal, and I have a kind of awed respect for her territory, so I was hesitant to tread more than lightly. But still, K. had called *me*, and it was a good question. Assuming that dreams have their own reasons for things—crafty replicas of ourselves as I believe they are—why had I appeared in K.'s dream? I could surmise what people in my dreams might symbolize to me. What would I mean to K.?

"You might try asking yourself what thoughts you have about me as a person living here in the village," I suggested. "Or think about how you feel about the dream study I proposed in the paper."

"Hmmm, well maybe," K. responded. I had the feeling that we were both dancing around the same unspoken area of her husband's illness: K. wanting to ask and my wanting to suggest and neither one of us wanting to go very far. "The thing is, I might represent 'new' questions that you might be asking about, uh, areas where you're feeling powerless," I said. "I mean, not that I have any answers, but that my book announcement and the rest of it suggested other directions if the standard ones haven't satisfied your needs. Maybe—well, maybe you can ask for help in your dreams. I always have."

"Oh, really?" K. said. "That sounds pretty good."

Then I told her my own dream, and pointed out how wild it was, that in my dream, I'd found doors leading to the outside—to safety—from the bottom of the pit, and in *her* dream, I'd talked the men into helping her get to safety. "See, in both dreams, I made the pit area safe—benign," I said. "I could be symbolizing your hopes. Maybe in my dream, I'm showing myself that I can venture where I don't dare to, I don't know. I also think it's really funny that my dream's locks were actually puzzles! Maybe that's an observation about all of this 'fitting together'!"

When I hung up, Susan, who had heard my side of the conversation, expressed genuine surprise that K. would remember a dream at all, let alone call me up about one. "That's really unusual," she said. She's known K. for more than ten years (and as of this date in 1988, K. hasn't spoken about her dreams to me again; she and her husband seem to be doing just fine, too).

Some of the "good" of this dream study of mine, then, if there must be a "good" (as opposed to "no good?") occurred to me as I thought about K.'s dream and mine. What fascinating psychological impetus and revelation are embodied not only in the people we meet in our dreams, but in the people we meet and relate to as we go about our usual business? How is it that we utilize, in realms so subtle and innocent that they escape our worldly eye, the presence of everyday friends for our own individual "good?"

Area newspapers have reported University of Rochester [N.Y.] research studies showing that dreams by their nature exert healing influences on the physical body—moreover, the researchers were speculating that dreams can warn of incipient, and even *probable*, illnesses by using objects such as buildings and people to symbolize cells or organs. (I was quite surprised to read this account, which as far as I know wasn't mentioned again in area dailies.) Had K. also read about this and consciously forgotten the possibilities implied—or had this item, plus my *Observer* articles and an unknown host of other associations, together with the force of her love for her husband, triggered my appearance in a dream that was vivid enough to get her to call me up and ask questions that might in turn lead to some help and comfort?

In other words, what do my own ideas mean to K. and what do K.'s beliefs and ideas mean to me? For apart from whatever analytical interpretation can be applied to them, those two dreams are inescapably connected. K. and I exchanged some sort of communication. And what if such communication goes on all the time between relatives, friends, members of the same community—members of the whole human race? It could open up our eyes to avenues in the human psyche that could even surprise our "enemies." And on a small scale, that's one of the things I'm trying to find out in my dream study of Dundee.

NOTES

1 I wrote the original versions of this chapter and Chapter Seven ("What IS This Thing Called ESP . . . ??") for the *Observer* editions as dated. They appear here in somewhat altered form.

FIVE

Patterns of the Future

How Dreams Came True by Bits

Because it can happen . . . that the symbols you put next to one another will modify themselves without your choosing it, and that when next you call them forth, they may say something new and revelationary to you, something you didn't know you knew. Out of the proper arrangement of what you *do* know, what you *don't* know may arise spontaneously.

John Crowley
Little, Big

Actually, the dreams surrounding Donald's death in Seneca Lake that fall were not the first examples that I'd noted of what I'd come to think of as precognition in "bits"—although those particular Dundee dreams were the first examples I'd come across of what appeared to be group premonition. In my own dream records, I'd discovered that precognition tends to run in cycles, or in groups of dream events; and that at the end of such a cycle, a formed (though not at all finished) unit of experience has often jelled in a loose, psychologically astute framework that seems to add *up* to the waking event. Dreams, I realized, come "true" as our days come "true"—not, usually, in the huge slam-bam literally-as-you-dreamed-it "hit" commonly associated with the idea of precognition. I think that dreams give us the inside of probable upcoming events, and that the events themselves accumulate in bits and pieces, according to our individual purposes, moving back and forth across the screen of our psyches between the awake and the dreaming self.

I suspect, then, that dreams and days both come "true" by bits. A bit here in the dream state—a chunk there in waking life. Even your feelings can be precognitive: you can literally experience the emotions of a future event, like sensate radar. Furthermore, I've discovered by reading through my old dream notebooks that precognition can reach across years of time, and, for me at least, tends to be seasonal. A dream in the fall of one year, for example, might relate to something that happens the *following* fall, or even several years later in that time of year. (Perhaps some physical experiences take longer to "accumulate" than others.) And so I believe that dreams act in concert with waking perceptions and actions to create the structure of our lives—always with our individual selves as creator.

Very Sethian, of course. Yet precognition is far too commonplace a phenomenon to label with any one philosophy. I'm going to elaborate here with examples of what I mean by dreams coming true in "bits." All are from my own notebooks. Some of the details and the names have been changed for reasons of privacy, but the progression of events is essentially as it occurred.

I always thought of Emily Dennis as my "first fan." She'd picked my name out of Jane Roberts' books, and through some kind of operator fluke managed to get ahold of my unlisted phone number. Emily called me from her Alabama home one night in 1978 to talk with me about the ideas in Jane's books. Usually, when my phone number is given out without my okay, I tell the caller off and hang up. But somehow I couldn't resist Emily's sincere and lighthearted enthusiasm. She didn't want anything more than someone to talk with about philosophical possibilities, and so we struck up a long-distance friendship. She'd call me once or twice a month and tell me about her life in the rural south; and even though we often had such a hard time understanding each other's accents that we'd have to spell out words, our conversations were a lot of fun. We exchanged letters now and then, and I began to understand that Emily, in the extremely conservative context of her environment, was a true scholar. She was intellectually restless, curious to bursting about the nature of things, unwilling to accept anyone else's answers unless she tried them out for herself, and quite willing to risk reprisals of one sort or another to ask new questions. Plus, she'd kept a dream journal for years before coming across Jane's books. I developed a good deal of respect for Emily, and I guess she did for me.

On October 4, 1979, Emily called to talk about how worried she was about her son. Tommy was in his early twenties and severely retarded, unable to talk or take more than minimal care of himself. He lived at home with his parents, and Emily never complained about the caretaking that Tommy must have required. The problem now was that Tommy's right hand had swollen up grotesquely the day before, and since he couldn't explain the source of his pain, Emily couldn't figure out what had happened. Tommy had a slow-acting allergy to bees, and Emily was trying to decide whether to take him to the hospital, which was located in a city several hours' drive from her country home and was always a traumatic ordeal for her son. Could I, Emily asked, try to "pick up" something on Tommy's condition?

The request wasn't demanding in any way, but I was uncomfortable with it. Besides a host of other cautions, I just didn't want the responsibility of trying this out on Tommy, who was more or less at the mercy of guesses about his physical problems, and I certainly didn't want to offer anything under the gossamer authority of a "psychic" impression. What if I guessed wrong, and Emily took my word for it, didn't go to the hospital, and Tommy died? I finally decided that despite her worries, Emily was capable of making decisions on Tommy's behalf without me. If I picked up anything, it would have to be in my nice, safe dream state—and offered as that: a nice, safe dream.

On Tuesday, October 9, I went to the regular meeting of the Dundee village board, part of my regular reporter's routine. Village business was pretty routine too—until minutes after the meeting adjourned. And then for reasons that I could never recall afterwards, I suddenly—*impulsively*—started quizzing board member Al S. about why his sports association wasn't politically involved in the questions surrounding nuclear power and its waste disposal problems. (Although the issue had been of local interest three years before when the Energy Department made preliminary studies of area salt veins for waste storage possibilities, it hadn't been mentioned during the board meeting and wasn't on my *conscious* mind at all.) To my surprise, Al's reaction was vehemently and vigorously pro-nuclear power, with no doubts or reservations whatsoever. Normally, I hate arguments about anything, so why I started this is a mystery—because the whole thing blew up into a savage, emotionally brutal shouting match. In fact, I became so upset about it all—and about Al's sharp, belligerent attacks on my ideas—that I left the room and burst into tears.

"I felt reduced to a cinder," I later noted in my journal. "I felt that in that moment, I was the only defender of ecology; the only one in the world who cared, in fact; and that I had to 'win' that argument there, on the spot, single-handedly, or lose it for the entire world and all of its wild creatures—that all of nature was depending on me. And I'd failed.

"I went home feeling totally useless; more, I was convinced in those moments that the universe is without options in the face of human greed and stupidity; that nature is too fragile to hold out against the power of human evil and destruction; and that I—my personality, my being, my life purposes—was completely out of sync with all other members of my own vile, ugly species—that I was alone in the world and always would be."

Of course I knew that this was an exaggerated reaction—that I'd blown the whole incident all out of proportion and that we'd both put more into the stupid argument than it merited. I fell into a restless sleep that night, and the next morning (October 10) recorded the following dream:

"Adrienne S. [*the board member's wife*], Emily Dennis, and I are responsible for giving away a litter of puppies. The pups are about three months old, bright-eyed and healthy, little fluffy black and white cutie-pies. I think that we must be very careful who gets these puppies, because they are, after all, just helpless puppies. The three of us go inside a dark barn with one of the pups. But we don't like it in there and decide not to leave him. Then through a forgotten series of dream-events, I see that the puppies will be okay—just by the protective nature of their puppy-hood. Nature, I know, will keep them safe no matter what, just because all things have their own natural protection."[1]

When I contemplated this dream, I somehow couldn't shuck the feeling that this was some kind of answer to Emily's worries about Tommy. On the surface, that conclusion seemed pretty farfetched—there wasn't anything in the dream about Tommy; more likely, it was a reaction to my fight with Al the night before. A nice way of reminding me that nature didn't need my defense! But the feeling of connection with Tommy didn't leave me, and so for the heck of it—and because, even stubbornly sometimes, I'd learned to trust these feelings about my dreams—I typed up a copy of the dream and sent it out two days later (on October 12) to Emily. I added a note that the puppies might have represented Tommy, who was in many ways puppy-like. "The universe, as well as Tommy—and for that matter all of us—does have its own protections and natural healing abilities," I wrote. (*Oh, yeah?* my mind chattered, *then how come you don't have more faith in the ability of nature to heal itself, huh? Who are you trying to kid?*)

Hmmm. Another irritating question.

Then on Saturday, October 13, Emily called me again, this time to tell me that Tommy's hand was much better and she'd decided not to take him to the hospital. She hadn't received my letter of October 12th, though; so I described my Oct. 9/10 dream about the puppies.

I'd barely gotten the dream information out of my mouth when Emily interrupted me in a rush of words. She said that during the recent summer months—unknown to me—a stray beagle had "adopted" the Dennis family and in August presented them with a litter of fluffy black and white mongrel puppies. Emily said that she'd managed to give away all but one of those pups, but that on Saturday, October 6—two days after we'd last talked on the phone—a telephone company truck had run over it.

"I didn't think he would live," Emily said, "but I had a real deep desire to help him, so I brought the puppy inside and gave him some medicine, barbiturates and stuff."

Aack, I thought, she gave barbiturates to a puppy? But Emily said that by the 10th, the pup had apparently recovered and was running around as usual. Emily added that Tommy's hand had returned to normal by the evening of the 7th.

What a weird connection, I thought after hanging up the phone; what a strange combination of picking up something on an unknown (to me) puppy and picking up some insight on creaturehood taking care of itself—an insight that Emily needed at that moment and that I, apparently, had yet to get through my head at all. My curiosity piqued, I called Jane Roberts and told her about the whole thing—including a brief summary of the argument I'd had with Al.

"*That's* interesting as hell," Jane said. "Just this morning Rob and I were talking about that argument you had last April 13th, remember, with Bill Gallagher? The fight about whether or not the world is going to hell in a hand basket? And you tried to defend the world, and ended up in tears?"

I remembered that incident clearly, though I hadn't connected it with Al S.; but now it seemed obvious, another little piece of a puzzle whose picture wouldn't quite focus. "Peg and Bill were at our house last night, too," Jane continued, laughing. "Bill was in the same sort of mood—he was even mad at the paperboy! Too bad you weren't here!"

Now when I hung up the phone, I looked through my dream records again. On August 31, 1979, I'd had a dream in which Emily and Al S. were both in my apartment, reading aloud from my ESP class sessions (which were all over my desk in messy stacks, both in the dream and in actuality). About a month after this, I'd asked for a dream "to help me get on the right track" in the writing of *Conversations with Seth.* Part of the long dream that followed that request of September 21, 1979, involved Al S.: In it, I was telling him that he should go back to school and become a conservation officer so he could *help police* the area lakes.

Dimly, I recalled that one of my first comments to Al that night of October 9th was to ask him—in an angry, condescending fashion, I had to admit—why the local conservation clubs didn't take a more active role in *policing* the lakes and other parts of the environment. I looked again at my "help" dream of September 21: Toward its conclusion, Al S. appeared again, this time driving Mike B., a boy from my childhood, to a special "environmental school" (the dream's words). Mike—like Emily's son—is mentally handicapped. And at the end of the dream, Emily was sitting in the back seat of the car as we all approached this "school."

By now, I was really intrigued. How far could you take layers of interconnections, anyway? I spent the rest of the day reading through my 1979 dream notebook—and starting with dreams a few nights before my April 13th argument with Bill, the correlations went on and on—back and forth, across waking and dreaming; an infinite network of events accumulating in a strange progression completely unlike—and yet in concert with—the usual "logical" means of assessing cause and effect.

I came to the dream I'd recorded for the night of April 13/14, 1979—after my argument with Bill. In it, Carl K., an old teenage flame of mine, appeared as some sort of political bigwig with Al S., the two of them discussing Dundee municipal business. And later that week, I'd received some of my "Dundee dreams" from Jeanette R., who is also what you might call a local political "bigwig." *Her* dream, dated April 13/14, included a brief scene with me—waiting for "an old boyfriend" to show up.

"But there is something not good about this with Sue," Jeanette's dream adds. "Something hurtful."

Interesting, I mused, that today Carl K. is a *policeman* in a nearby city . . .

I made some notes, trying to comprehend what was behind all of these *apparent* connections; trying not to create something out of . . . nothing? My dreaming unconscious, at least, was weaving a tapestry of connections between Bill and Al; between the hassle with Bill and the blow-up at the board meeting six months later . . . with Emily and Tommy drifting through this progression, apparently embodying the underlying notion (or lesson) that the creatures of the universe have their own natural defense, no matter how it looks . . . or do they, I wondered, still unconvinced. There were literally dozens more interconnections, crisscrossing in and around dreams and daily life, the people involved and their relationships with me, my underlying beliefs, and some pretty blatant precognitive information.

In fact, there were so many of these correlations that an entire book could be written on the time span between the "Bill argument" and the "Al spat," as it were. Elements "built up" in my dream and waking states, springing from the first incident and winding down through the second—riding on the waves of my private beliefs about the world, and pushing some pointed psychological lessons up into my conscious mind. In other words, not only did I bring the arguments upon myself, but the combination of my dream and waking awareness pulled together a deeper synthesis than that available to what I usually *thought* of as my "normal" analytical appreciation. And because Emily also recorded her dreams and related events, I had a written document (which she later sent to me) of her part in all of this. Too bad the others didn't keep dream journals!

I read that 1979 notebook with awe—I could hardly believe my own psyche had done such feats, apparently without effort. Someday I may write a book on one year's worth of dreams—as soon as I can figure out how to provide all the necessary (and rather intimate) background information. But it's probably impossible to confine such a book to one year's time—because, as I'll attempt to illustrate, I think that dreams reference across years, miles, and all *sorts* of probabilities.

* * * *

I will preface this by explaining that in June of 1980, I married a man I'd known since I moved to Dundee: A dairyman who also raised registered Appaloosa horses on his farm just outside the village. That marriage ended after eighteen months (although, as members of a small-town family are wont to do, we remain friends) but much of what I discovered about dreams, and myself, went on during that time—almost without me, or so it seemed. And actually, one of my first so-called psychic experiences in Dundee was connected with Roy and his father more than a year before I really knew anyone in his family.

Soon after I moved to Dundee in 1973, I started buying unpasteurized milk from Roy's farm (which was so spotlessly clean that the local doctor habitually prescribed the dairy's raw milk as a cure for intestinal ailments). I usually took my son to the farm with me and Roy's father always found time to show three-year-old Sean around the barn (where he was most fascinated by the geyser-like streams of piss and avalanches of manure produced with casual regularity by all fifty cows in turn). Old Art reminded me in many ways of my grandfather Baker, even to an eerie physical likeness and similar speech patterns. In fact, I noticed, it was the oddest thing—but Roy bore an amazing resemblance to my *parents*—a strange likeness to *both* of them, as though their mannerisms could come up through his own features like—well, like fish swimming up in a pool of dark water, or like a reflection of memories—or something. (It was one of several impressions that I shrugged aside in the years to come.) It was even a funnier coincidence when I learned from Art that one of my family's favorite stories, about an uncle who used to race his dogs across a Dundee farm in the early 1920s, had actually taken place on Art's property. He and that uncle had been lifelong friends and political wranglers, and not only that—really, it was like meeting my own ancestral ghosts—but one of Art's brothers told me that he'd been the first patient my great-grandfather Baker had taken on after Asbury opened his physician's practice in Dundee at the turn of the century. All in all, there was a strange invisible family-like thread running among us having nothing at all to do with *official* definitions of heredity.

So it was with great dismay that I learned in April of 1974 that Art had been severely burned in an automobile accident on the road in front of his house, and that he was in an area hospital's intensive care unit in guarded condition. As the weeks went by, everyone in the neighborhood kept track of his progress, and I heard that he seemed to be recovering just fine.

On Wednesday, May 8, 1974, I took Sean down to the farm to get a couple of gallons of milk. Here, I'll quote from notes made later that day: "As we pulled into the farm driveway, I decided to make Sean wait in the car for me while I drew the milk out of the bulk tank inside the milkhouse. I suddenly had the idea that Sean might ask Roy an awkward question about Art and embarrass me, although why I should have thought so escaped me later. I stopped the car and turned the keys over onto battery power to play the radio for Sean. As I did this, I reached over and grabbed the door handle—and instantly got a violent and painful shock. I yanked my hands away from the keys and the handle and sat still, stunned; I didn't realize that such a thing could happen in a car.

"Finally, I went in the milkhouse, stuck my dollar bill in the cupboard, and started the process of pouring the milk out of the bulk tank's faucet into my container. I'd become strangely depressed and out of it. Roy came in and made a remark about the weather, but I didn't respond—not even with a question about his father—and he went back into the barn. I felt withdrawn, very *interior*, and melancholy.

"Then I turned the tank handle and let the stream of milk pour into my jar. Somehow, the milk looked funny—I couldn't say how, exactly, but funny nonetheless. I glanced up at the stirring apparatus to see if it had stopped and therefore let the milk separate, accounting for its look—but it was mixing as usual.

"But now the effect, whatever was causing it, was heightened. I then stood up and lifted the bulk tank cover and looked inside, at all the hundreds of gallons of swirling milk rushing in, right that moment, from the cows in the barn beyond. It was like looking into the opaque eye of a dead animal. The usually creamy-white, foamy milk was, simply, *dead*—flat and lifeless and gone.

"I let out a little yelp!, letting the tank cover bang shut. I knew then, with a certainty that closed out even sadness, that Art had decided to die; that I was picking up on that decision because of my memories of my grandfather, but also because of certain *memories yet to occur*—and that Art's life, this farm and his cows, would naturally reflect that decision. I felt great sympathy and understanding, and a kind of consent with his death—a feeling of rightness about it; although, I mused later, since I wouldn't have to deal with the emotional aftermath, I was of course free to indulge in such things as consent, wasn't I?

". . . Art did die of accident-related injuries on June 23, some six weeks after this experience . . . Roy told me years later that although Art apparently improved steadily after the accident, he abruptly lost his eyesight some weeks into recovery, 'and after that, he just gave up'. . ."

I never told Roy about this experience, since it became apparent to me as we got to know one another that he didn't put much stock in such things; and because I believed then that his was the respectable perspective, I simply tucked my own peculiar notions away—and found myself wishing on occasion that they would vanish from my psyche permanently. Still, underneath all of his enculturated beliefs to the contrary, Roy was a natural mystic, naturally prescient; tuned into the Earth and the seasons as naturally as I was tuned into dreams and their waking implications. And in fact Roy later "confessed" to me that he often dreamed in the spring that he and the old man were plowing oat ground together as in days gone by, side by side on the farm's two ancient tractors. In dreams' fashion, Roy said, he could hear his father's voice clearly even though the tractors thrummed and roared as they pulled the plows through the dark soil—and his father would predict with uncanny accuracy the weather conditions of the upcoming growing season.

I never knew if Roy actually banked on this information—he rarely remembered his dreams and attached little or no importance to them—but I could see that he intuitively believed that this was some sort of legitimate contact with something of what his father had been; perhaps my perspective opened that door of possibilities. And I do think that our partnership, brief as it was, gave Roy and me great gifts of understanding and balance, as opposites can sometimes do for one another; bridges, in our case, between eccentric modes of thought and the practical world in which these must exist. Indeed, the environment of our relationship was permeated always with strange, dramatic experiences involving animals, even after we officially separated in late 1981.

It was in the spring of 1982, then—on May 13, to be exact—that Roy told me that he'd dreamed the night before of being attacked by a German shepherd. Roy described the dream as a terrifying nightmare, in vivid color and with gruesomely realistic sensations of pain. The dog ripped up his right arm and he'd awakened holding his arm out in front of him, as if to ward the dog off. "Does that mean such a thing is going to happen to me?" he asked. He seemed genuinely concerned that the dream was a literal warning.

"I don't know," I said, "but offhand, I'd say to watch out for mean dogs."

Roy shrugged, rather sorry that he'd mentioned it, I could see. But later that afternoon, Roy went to a local restaurant for lunch and sat at the counter next to Luke H., who lived down the road from us. In the course of their conversation, Luke told Roy that he'd been attacked the day before by a large, nasty dog, and that he'd had to go to the emergency room in Penn Yan for stitches in his right arm. "Now *that,*" Roy said later, "is the kind of thing that might impress me about all of this dream stuff."

A cute bit of precognition, yes—but something bothered me about it even then (and not just as a matter of hindsight later on): Why would this little piece of foreknowledge come to Roy, who had no interest in such considerations? Why would his dreams hint at the context of a restaurant conversation? Or had Roy actually picked up on Luke's encounter with the dog? Well, I decided, maybe Roy's psyche was letting him in on such things the easy way—by starting with restaurant chatter before moving on to bigger and better things. (Maybe precognitive dreaming is catching, I yukked to myself.)

I thought of Roy's dream again on the morning of May 15, when I drove to the Dundee flower shop and happened to strike up a conversation there with a friend. She was still quite upset about an incident that had happened the day before. A neighbor's German shepherd had leaped over the fence between their yards and attacked my friend's small dog, chewing it up badly enough to inflict a hairline fracture in the little dog's skull. (This woman also lived next door to one of Roy's relatives, though the shepherd belonged to someone else.)

"Maybe it's something in the air," I said, and told her about Luke H.'s encounter with the other dog.

"Well, in his case, it sounds like he accidently did something to make that dog attack him," my friend said, "but what happened to my dog was just plain carelessness. That shepherd should have been tied up tight so it couldn't get loose and cause trouble."

"Dog owners never think that their own dog will hurt anybody," I agreed, but what I was thinking was—Wow! What a *neat* coincidence!

Later that afternoon, Roy and I drove to our horse trainer's farm to help him get some of our horses ready for an upcoming show. Included in this grooming rigmarole is the trimming-off of all hair on the horse's ears, muzzle, legs, and other areas of its body, and if the horse isn't used to the peculiar buzzing sound of the electric clippers, you can expect to have a battle on your hands—especially when you first touch the clippers to the inside of the ears. The yearling filly that Roy and the trainer started on was absolutely terrified, kicking and rearing up and thrashing around wildly at the first buzz. Finally, she threw herself down on the ground at the end of her lead rope and lay there rolling her eyes and snorting with fear.

The trainer, a large man who is comfortable with horses in all their states of mind, sat down on the filly's neck. "There," he said to Roy, "go ahead and finish her up, she can't move." And Roy, in a completely uncharacteristic gesture of overconfidence, stepped in between the filly's front and hind legs, bent forward, and applied the clippers to the fuzz on her belly.

Instantly, like a flash of lightning arching down through summer skies, the filly lashed out with a hind foot and caught Roy squarely on the right side of his head. Roy was knocked right into the nearby fence—and into the twilight between consciousness and coma, blood pouring from his nose and ear.

We called an ambulance immediately—and when it arrived, who should be driving it but *Luke H.'s son.*

Roy was taken first to the *Penn Yan hospital's emergency room,* where a preliminary x-ray showed a *hairline fracture* in the *right* side of his skull. Fearing serious complications, doctors sent him on to an Elmira hospital that specializes in head injuries, though a week later Roy had recovered well enough to go home and after a few more weeks' rest was declared A-okay.

Now, to look at this progression of events in what you might call scientific terms proves nothing at all. At no time did any of us (particularly Roy) dream of getting kicked in the head by a horse. But when you take a look at the progression of dreaming and waking events, the basic elements of Roy's accident are there, peeking out like tiny eyes in the jungle grasses. In Roy's dream, an animal attacked him and inflicted painful injury to his right arm. That dream registered strongly in his conscious mind, in contrast to his usual lack of dream recall. The next day, Luke's story reflected—and in Roy's mind reinforced—that dream. Luke's son later turned up as the ambulance driver on the night of the accident (we had no idea that he drove an ambulance, as he was a member of the Penn Yan, not the Dundee, squad). And my friend in the flower shop, with no encouragement from me for a mean-dog story, described an experience in which the right side of her dog's skull was fractured (and she specifically said that it was a *hairline* fracture) by a German shepherd, the same type of dog in Roy's dream and in Luke's encounter. A dog that should have been tied up with more care. A dog whose actions my friend associated with carelessness by the owner. Usually, this woman was interested in hearing about Roy's successes in the horse-show world, but that day she'd only wanted to talk about the dog attack—and how it could have been prevented if the shepherd had been tied more securely, certainly a truth that paralleled the filly's grooming session.

And in that split second when the filly's hoof connected with Roy's skull, I realized with uncanny crystal clarity how *wrong*—how non-Roy—was his gesture with the clippers against the horse's ticklish belly. Roy has worked with livestock since early childhood, and certain actions around horses and cattle are as much a part of him as breathing. Was the conscious choice made, then, in that *impulsive* move with the clippers? Or had the accident been coalescing around us, like a slow change in the weather, for days before the actual physical event?

But again—if the self has foreknowledge, why not just send a warning dream to Roy, stating exactly and firmly that if he performed action X it would result in a kick in the head from filly Y? I do think that if you really want this sort of warning, you'll get one. So why not always get one? Does precognition work or not? Do dreams come true or don't they? Or does that cause-and-effect reasoning work without an understanding of personal intent? To come "true" in absolutes implies the existence of a "true" event waiting, as it were, fully formed, in the future. And I just don't think that things work that way.

Perhaps for his own reasons, Roy chose that accident; perhaps in the course of his life it was a necessary ingredient and he chose to block out a specific warning. Like my thoughts on Donald's drowning, was this accident set up and ready to go, waiting only for the physical opportunity to emerge? Perhaps what Roy wanted was a vague waft of the event to come; a subtle hint of what is available to the psyche. And, of course, perhaps the progression of "bits" leading up to the incident was a product of my imagination. Tantalizingly, though, it all reminded me of the somewhat more complicated string of "bits" surrounding Emily—and it was beginning to feed into a peculiar notion, or feeling, that "precognition" was an *extremely* stuffy word for something that works . . . sideways. And inside-out. And in every infinity of direction there is.

And such "bits" weaving in and out of a string of dreams and physical events were about to show me that awareness of these associations can stretch the conscious mind (and experience) beyond imagining . . .

NOTES

1 An interesting aside to this dream involves a small farm drama earlier that year, when Roy's golden retriever presented him with a batch of her own fluffy pups. In an odd sort of precursor to this puppy-dream and the attached events to come, I found myself with an almost desperate feeling of responsibility to make sure the pups had good homes, since Roy was obviously unable to keep them. The first puppy I gave away was to Al and Adrienne S.—who made room in their hearts for it even though they already owned two older dogs. (The pups had been born back in a dark corner of Roy's barn, too.)

SIX

Come Back to Grassroots, ESP

The Great Dundee Dream Bazaar

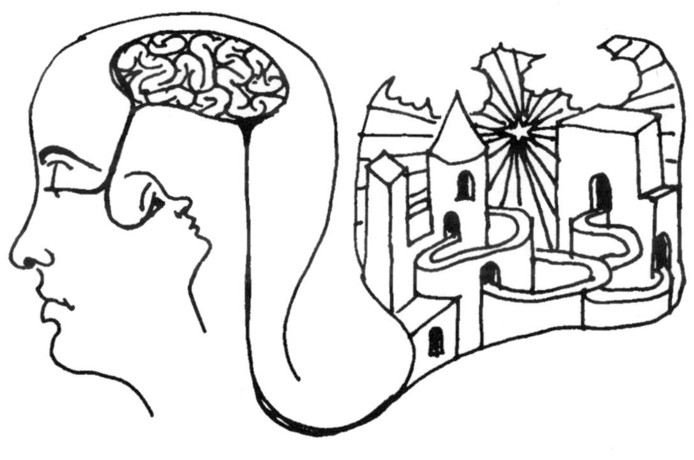

"Now: Nothing is wasted. Nothing is wasted. Creativity least of all. So your thoughts are not wasted, your dreams are not wasted, and neither are the thoughts and dreams of others who have psychological realities perhaps completely different than your own. Nature is luxurious. It uses everything with a grand and riotous display."

Seth in class
December 2, 1978

The moon is full, the wind summer-warm. Far in the dark distance behind me, my bedroom floats silently above the trees, a spaceship waiting for my return. Leaves brush against my face as I fly along above the village sidewalks, glimpsing others moving here and there in the secret windy night, streetlights illuminating like a sky of stars, all possible worlds open to us all. A great yearning nostalgia for this place washes over me, as though I am looking back upon this moonlit village from centuries of time and space, remembering the intimate human experience we shared here; the time of my child's small years; the time of my own growing up. Others notice, leap easily from lawns and rooftops to join me; doors open sideways in tree trunks; houses rise up through the walkways; all of Dundee is sleeping, and alive. I greet friends. Will you remember this for me? Will you?

I wake up, not wanting to leave that other Dundee, the Dundee of Dreams. Always, from one of these, I think, "That's your Dundee dream!" This morning, I recall that the electricity in my Dream Dundee went haywire—fires popped out all along Harpending Avenue, shooting from second-story windows. I write it all down, noting as I do so the great yearning, the pull I still feel toward my own dreams, these Dreams. Do others feel this way, am I the only one? Within four days, two major fires in the area have destroyed a house and barn, and although neither were in the village proper, the owner of the barn is a distant cousin, whose mother's name was Harpending. Is this connected? Does it matter? Nowhere else have I ever felt such—*connection* with a time and place, if there is time and place, in my dreams. I have put roots down through the moments of my life here. Am I the only one? Does no one else remember?

"I should definitely tell you a dream I had the other night," my friend J., then the village mayor, said to me one day in the local restaurant. "It's clear as a bell—I remember every detail. In fact, it's so good I should make a story out of it."

I smiled, ordered another cup of coffee for both of us, asked my standard question as the waitress poured the brew. "Did you write it down?"

"Of course not," J. said, "have you ever known me to write down anything? I'll tell you about it and *you* can write it down, how's that?"

"Fine," I sighed, resigned.

"Well, this is it," he began,

I wake up in the middle of the night, aware somehow that something is wrong. I get up and go downstairs—all of this is as clear as if I were wide awake; as wide awake as I am now, telling you this . . . I go downstairs and look around. It's a moonless night and the only light is coming in from the streetlights outside. I open the front door and look out. All seems well. But I still feel like something's wrong; maybe it's a faint sound that I can't identify.

I walk to the back of the house and look out across my back yard, towards Agway—and then I see it: A huge, absolutely silent parade of men, surrounding the grain storage bins behind the Agway store. The streetlights give the scene a yellowish twilight vagueness, but there they are—a whole army of men, apparently, moving around the buildings.

I walk out into my back yard. As I get closer to Agway, I see that the men are emptying out the grain from the Agway bins and loading it into big cars of some sort—like train cars, only these aren't dependent on the actual train tracks running through town. Then I look up and down the street and I can see . . . from where I'm standing, I see that whatever this army is, it has a guard on every street that intersects with the railroad tracks, and on the nearby corner of Harpending and Edwina, Seneca and Edwina.

I go back inside, figuring that I'd better get word to others that something funny is going on. But when I try to call up the fire chief, I find the phone isn't working—this army's cut off the phone system somehow. So then I call the firemen on the fire phone, which isn't connected with the regular phone lines, and I tell them there's a problem, and to stand by. But I look out the window and see that some of the firemen have apparently figured out that something's going on because I can see Glen M. and Dick P. walking up the street-lit sidewalk toward the tracks.

I go out in my front yard and tell them about the army, and that there's nothing they can do and we'd really better not try to interfere as long as this army isn't doing anything outright dangerous. But Glen and Dick and some others don't like the sound of that; they think we should try to get help.

Well, just then old Albert, you know who I mean, comes riding up on his bicycle and I get an idea. I send Albert out on his bicycle, down the railroad tracks, and tell him to just keep going along until he gets to Watkins Glen or some other community where the phones are working and tell the police there what's going on. I know they probably won't believe him, but it's a chance, see, because I figure the army-guys won't bother old Albert riding along on his bike.

So off Albert goes, down the tracks, and that's all we can hope for. The army is still moving the grain out in these huge bins, off into the darkness of the woods beyond the village. I leave the others on the sidewalk and go back to my house, and go around back to watch what's going on some more.

As I stand there, I hear a sound, and see one of these men approaching me. He is about my size, wearing a dark uniform of some kind. His face is mostly hidden in the shadows, but he seems dark-complected, thin. I realize without really knowing how that this is the leader. I just stand there casually with my arms crossed as he approaches—what else can I do? But he comes up to me and greets me with a funny little wave of his hand.

"You are the head man of this town," he says. "I knew you would see us. Don't worry, we're not going to hurt anyone and we'll be gone before morning."

The man then goes on to tell me that they are extraterrestrials, that they've been monitoring this planet for decades from a mother ship, and that not long ago, some sort of accident involving an emission from their engines occurred, causing a large area in our midwest to be contaminated with a substance unknown to earth. He says his people managed to clean most of this stuff up, but several thousand acres of corn were harvested before these beings could get to it and decontaminate it. They managed to trace the corn through all its various processing procedures and the last of it ended up here in the grain bins at the Dundee Agway Feed Mill. Now they are here to take it away before it can poison anyone, the man says.

"I know that you are thinking of getting word to outside authorities about us," the man tells me. "I understand that. If I were in your position as head of the village, I would do the same. It's all right, but I can tell you now that all of your communication devices have been interrupted—even your radios. Don't try to interfere with us, therefore, and we will leave quietly when we're done—this village as well as your memory."

Then the man explains that any memories I have of the entire incident will seem as though it were a dream. He walks back toward his people and I go back in the house. Just as I get inside, the phone rings. I pick it up and the alien leader's voice says, "You will be the only one who remembers."

And at that point, I wake up. So, lemme ask—do you remember anything about this?

J. leaned back in his chair, grinning, outrageously pleased with himself. "Well? Is that the ultimate fantasy story, or what?"

"That's what I call a 'Dundee Dream,' all right," I said. "No wonder you like science fiction! Or maybe aliens really did land here and clean out the Agway corn bin," I teased him. "Did you go check it out?"

"But of course the thing is," J. replied, "nobody at Agway would remember anything about it—they'd forget they had any corn there in the first place."

I laughed. "I see. Well, how about this: Maybe you feel like an Alien Leader yourself, in this place, eh?" Like me, J. and his family had moved to Dundee only a few years before. "Maybe the guy in your dream was your Alter Ego, cleaning up the town, ha-ha! Think about it!"

J.'s eyebrows went up. "Maybe," he said, stubbing out his cigarette. "Well, gotta go." And with that, he stood up and walked out the door.

A strangely abrupt reaction—though I was getting used to odd behavior from people these days. My interpretative remark to J. had some background to it, though. Several years earlier, he'd told me that he dreamed a recurring "series of three" at regular intervals throughout his life, and that in one of the three—the only one he would describe to me—he always found himself chasing *himself* across a parking lot, into a large building, up flights of stairs and finally into an office—from the window of which he then observed himself, back down on the parking lot below, swiftly disappearing into the crowd. A very powerful vision of a sense of elusive-self—or an alien self, perhaps. Later, I wrote J.'s dream down from some notes I'd made and gave him a copy to check, since I wanted to use all of this rich, remarkably detailed dream here, a one-of-a-kind in my village collection.

All in all, I eventually collected about 100 written dreams from Dundee; and while none of them matched the astonishing stuff that came to me in sidewalk and coffee-shop conversations (simply because most people just don't write down such unofficial things as dreams, I suppose) they make up a kind of tourist brochure of the village psyche all by themselves.

A municipal official who approaches those duties with humor and warmth sent me dreams that were playful, filled with descriptions of color and light—and were the only dreams that actually mused among their dream-characters about what my experiment might turn up. She also dreamed of me a couple of times, with some interesting quasi-"hits" on details of my life, and I was especially intrigued to notice that a metal clanging noise appeared in the background of a dream or two of hers. That odd sound rang through my dreams too on occasion, and usually on the same nights that Sean also dreamed of it. In Sean's case and mine, the noise was almost always associated with nightmares—though in the municipal officer's dream, it was only the sound of playground swings banging into the poles. Well, that made sense—her husband was a schoolteacher and all of us lived within earshot of the playground. Still, it was an evocative similarity.

There was E., a person pleasantly skeptical about all things, who turned in a series of dreams that were nearly exact duplications, so she reported, of her waking life. (E.'s initial comment to me about this dream experiment was characteristically literal: "But how can you sort out random thoughts from dreams?" she demanded one day in the post office. "How can this be a scientific experiment if you don't sort out all the random thoughts?" "But I *want* random thoughts, if anybody's got any," I answered—to no avail.) However, E.'s dreams frequently interconnected with those sent to me by G., a local artist—whose works E. had often admired.

For example, both G., the artist, and E., are excellent cooks, and both have that cook's fascination with the planning and preparation of food. It was amusing to notice how often these two dreamed about cooking—usually on concurrent nights, and with strikingly similar details. (Both sent several days' dreams per week, not just Friday records.) On April 6/7, 1979, both G. and E. found themselves sitting in dream-restaurants, where a "white substance" was spilled on the wooden furniture, bleaching out the finish. In both dreams, vehicles are brought to the restaurant scene via ferry; in both dreams, the main menu is lobster. And in another connection made later that month, both G. and E. dreamed of alligators living in the sewers and waterways of Dundee (maybe they'd both read similar news stories or watched the same TV movie on that strange urban myth).

It's interesting to note that although E. admired G.'s works of art for a number of years while both lived in Dundee, they had never met in person and G. had no idea who E. was (I asked G. about this). Neither knew the other was sending dreams to me either, which was true of all my respondents, as far as I know.

Of course, like all psychological states, dreams reflect one's personality and life expectations as well as the daily routine. W., a woman in her eighties, sent dreams filled with some witty and rather scathing character observations of folks in town, revealing imagination and a rich talent for metaphor. In the course of our correspondence, W. also displayed writing abilities that she later put to use in area newspapers.

Forthright person that she is, W. censored nothing from the sometimes lengthy dreams she sent to me, and so these frequently included romantic scenes with a man whose unexpected death, in another state, followed a vivid conversation-dream between the two of them. A few days afterwards, news of his death reached friends in Dundee.

Actually, I should add here that when I first started telling people that I was interested in what they were dreaming about, the reaction was almost always embarrassment, as though *all* dreams were sex dreams and as wicked as a dirty joke. I'd say, "Write your dreams down and send them to me," and people would often smirk, glance at one another, even giggle. "You couldn't print any of it!" was a typical comment; or, "Oh, no you don't—you could blackmail me!" For many, the act of dreaming as a *category* seemed all wound up with forbidden masturbatory fantasies and punishment for same—a common-enough thought habit, rising, I knew, from the old belief that subjective experience is by definition false, or forbidden, or insane. This attitude disappeared or softened as time went on, however—at least among the people who made it a habit to talk and write to me about their dreams.

Only a few wrote down any sexual dreams, which didn't surprise me—people in a small town learn soon enough to be wary of seeding gossip with such irresistible personal tidbits (though to this day, I've never revealed the identities of my dreamers). Some would talk to me about sex dreams, though—usually when the dreamer was worried that such a dream represented an attachment that might threaten to disrupt home life. For instance, a woman called me up to tell me that she'd had an explicitly erotic dream about a mutual friend of ours. She was quite worried about this—what did such a thing mean? Why should she dream something like this? She'd never imagined being unfaithful to her husband, she said. What was going to happen now?

I responded as best I could to these worries by first admitting to this woman that I'd had erotic dreams about the same man—he was attractive, after all, and so what—a "confession" that immediately made my friend feel much better. "I guess there's nothing so wrong with it if you dreamed that sort of thing too," she said—a statement that left me somewhat nonplussed, so I went on to tell her that in my opinion, such dreams were fun, and they let you indulge in fantasies. And anyway, I added, she couldn't tell *me* she'd "never imagined" sex with men other than her husband—this dream said otherwise, if it said nothing else!

Privately, I thought later that my friend's declared attachment to her husband must be more tenuous that she wanted to admit, if this dream could upset her so much. On the other hand, I had no way to gauge the impact of religious imperatives in these areas—what was that about committing adultery in your heart? Wasn't it taught that such thoughts were as sinful as the act? My friend had grown up in a religious family, so these beliefs were probably the real source of her worry. It was pretty clear how afraid she was of her own thoughts and dreams, as if these were the product of the Biblically evil self that she must really be. Our phone conversations couldn't do much to change that, of course—and she avoided casual conversations with me for a long time afterwards, perhaps out of fear she'd revealed too much.

And then there was H., who said that she hated the idea of being "just a housewife," but would I please tell her why she had these dreams about screwing her washing machine all the time? (Is this what you call feeling married to your household chores?) Still another woman, whose domestic life was in a state of chaos and turmoil, dreamed constantly of catastrophe or of lying unharmed but in total silence in the center of wrecked cars and smashed furniture (in fact, not long afterwards, she left the situation and started divorce proceedings). But at first, she'd considered such tumultuous dreams more scandalous than the act of seeking a divorce from an abusive husband.

All kinds of dreams, including bits and pieces of precognition showed up among my written Dundee dreams—along with some other crafty little tidbits of inner knowledge peeking out here and there. For instance, there was S., an adaptable, intelligent jack-of-all trades who held many jobs and owned several different types of businesses in town and was just as adventurous in the dream state—reporting a dozen little precognitive "hits" and coincidences. A few days after I'd published the essay on K.'s February "pit" dream in the May 10, 1979 *Observer*, S. stopped me on the street to tell me that he, too, had a dream that February about a "pit" with antiques at the bottom, also protected by male guards—details that correlated with both K.'s dream and mine of the same night.

"Must be pit dreams were 'in' that month," S. said. I pulled my trusty pen and note pad out of my pocketbook and started writing down S.'s dream as he stood there. Watching me, S. said after a moment's contemplation, "I had another recent dream that came true, you know."

"Tell me, tell me!" I urged, turning the notebook page.

"I was dreaming about this weird closet that's in the dePlano house," S. began, referring to an old family homestead in the area. "I've shown that place a few times this year [*as it was up for sale and S. is, among other jobs, a realtor*] and there was always something about that closet that I noticed. This dream was really clear and real. Then my telephone rang and woke me up—for real, I mean. It was some stranger, calling to ask me if I could tow his car into town for him—he thought my number was to the local garage, see. The funny thing is, I sold that garage to the dePlano family two years ago, but my phone number isn't anything like theirs or the number at their garage."

Another fascinating precognitive-connective dream series that involved house fires—a series that reminds me of the jigsaw-puzzle element in the community dreams of Donald's death—came out when I read the dream recorded by G., the artist, for the night of March 29/30, 1979. In the dream, G. saw ". . . on the road uphill past my neighbor's barn, a building with people and horses (a school? a stable?). It is afire, but the people won't move, nor the horses . . . again, past the top of the hill, on the Pre-Emption Road, fire breaks out in a campground of buildings . . ."

Reading this, I remembered that about a month before the date of G.'s dream—on February 15, 1979—I'd had a long and vivid dream concerning the fellow who was then chief of the Dundee Fire Department. In my dream, I saw Chief R. rush into a burning building without the precaution of a Scott air pack; predictably, in the dream, he had to be taken to the hospital for treatment of smoke inhalation; and in the dream his lungs were badly injured.

This dream struck me so forcibly that for weeks afterward, whenever the Dundee firemen answered a call, I checked the news the following day to make sure the fire chief hadn't been hurt. Then on Saturday, April 7 (according to the April 12, 1979, edition of the *Observer*), about sixty firemen responded to a house fire near the barn described in G.'s March 29/30 dream. On that occasion, the fire chief did indeed dash into the burning house without his Scott air pack, and ended up in the local hospital's intensive care unit for treatment of smoke inhalation. The chief's lungs, already affected by many years of fire fighting, sustained even more damage as a result.

It's interesting to note that G.'s dream contains a reference to the *site* of the fire (near his home), while mine seemed to pick up on a specific *person* (whose duties as Chief were often the subject of *Observer* articles and photos). Together, the two of us apparently foresaw pieces of an upcoming event—in minuscule form, much like the precognition displayed by those who picked up on Donald S.'s drowning.

Of course, G.'s dream and mine came more than a month apart, and my particular dream-information was exactly two months old when Chief R. was actually injured. But the force of my dream was clear to me: I *knew* that the information was correct. And the chief is such a dedicated and enthusiastic fireman that I also knew a dream warning—if he gave it any credence at all—wouldn't slow him down if an emergency arose.

Also, G. later recorded a dream for the night of April 13/14, 1979—after the April 7th fire where the chief was injured—in which he saw his wife struggling with a rocking chimney on a small house. In the dream, his wife fixed the chimney so that it would eject more smoke and clear the home's interior. (This dream is alluded to in Chapter 7.) Just a night or two after the dream, a chimney-fire disaster in G.'s house was averted only because G.'s wife happened to be home when trouble started. She called the fire department, which arrived in plenty of time, later diagnosing the cause as a thick build-up of creosote from too-smoky fires.

Perhaps G.'s awareness of the fire connection with his March 29/30 dream (connections he notes in his dream journals) helped push his own impending tragedy close enough to conscious levels to avoid the worst. His wife stayed home that day "on impulse," he told me later. Coincidentally, the cause of that other house fire on April 7, according to the Dundee department's report, was a faulty stovepipe in the building's second story.

Again, my Dundee dreamers didn't "prove" anything that would hold up as scientific treatise—which wasn't my intent anyway. But I do think that the attention my experiment drew to the subject served to start many people thinking about their dreams as something more than shadowy memories of half-remembered dramas, or as things of no consequence, or suspicious dirty jokes of the night. People who insisted that they never dreamed (which isn't true, as everyone dreams—some simply recall them and some don't) later told me that they'd remembered a dream for the first time in their lives, expressing genuine wonder at this previously unknown portion of their psyches. Others made intuitive waking connections on their own with impulses and coincidences—such as in this note mailed to me in November, 1979, from W.:

Fact not dreams . . .

The other night I sat at the kitchen table eating my supper as relaxed as you please. All at once I thought, I want some ice cream. I keep it out in the freezer in the barn before I open the package. I told my self I did not need ice cream with all its calories and I had enough to eat without it. But that idea was so insistent it was like a full rolling boil in making jelly that you can't stir down.

I gave in and went to the barn and you will never guess

> what I found, I HAD LEFT MY CAR DOOR OPEN AND THE DOME LIGHT WOULD HAVE RUN THE BATTERY DOWN. I had an app't with my dentist in Bath the next morn at 9:15.
>
> Don't tell me I don't have a little "Seth" looking out for me. Once before I left that door open and I did not write it down but something told me to go to the barn and it was dark, too. I was saved by something, someone. I wish I knew more about such things.

As for me, the Dreams of Dundee served a purpose that *I'd* never dreamed: I discovered that my interest in such things was an important, practical part of the fabric of this little community; that people were eager to talk about their dreams and "odd" experiences (even, or especially, if they were reluctant to write these down); that the standard dream interpretations (whether Freudian or "New Age") did not satisfy people's curiosity or intuitions; that dream recall was always accompanied by a sense of awakening and excitement; and that people naturally knew that they could have faith in their dreams, even when dreams became nightmares or were shrugged off as objectively worthless. Again and again, people said such things to me as, "I had the feeling that my dream was trying to tell me that, but I needed to hear somebody say it."

So my eccentricities weren't so awry after all. I served a purpose, like the fire chief and the town policeman and the municipal officials and the school personnel: a representative of dreams, the caretaker of peculiar notions, the shaman of the tribe.

---

from the Bazaar:

A Sampler of Dundee Dreams

* * * *

From Jeanette, municipal official

Friday night-Saturday morning, April 13/14, 1979:

I was at a house with 3 ladies, including Sue Watkins; it appeared to be Betty L.'s house (who wasn't there). One lady (in her 60s) was vehemently after Sue to leave the house because her old boyfriend, a policeman, was coming and I guess there was something not good for Sue. Something hurtful. [*Note my dream, included on pages 97–98, of the same night and the connection with the "hurtful" incidents of Chapter 5.*]

In the meantime, I finished my business, which was to

deliver rummage for a sale. I went to get my car—which my son had driven off—however that is interesting because he only took the top half. It somehow had acquired wheels and he had it home by the time I got there! End of dream!

Are you leading up to finding out what's *really* going on in my family?? Or just in little ole Dundee??

Saturday night-Sunday morning, April 14/15, 1979:

In the dream I had been shopping and it must have been in NYC because I kind of remember having been in a motel—but somehow my husband & I ended up at a TV show, something like "The Price is Right." I had on a bright blue wig that exactly matched my bright blue dress. Very nice, I thought!!! As we sat there the announcer chose me to come on stage—I remember being at least 6" to 8" taller than the M.C. & looked down & wondered if my spiked heels weren't a bit too much!

Then I remembered my wig was not completely covering my own hair, so I began tucking it here & there. The M.C. started making jokes about this & I didn't know if I was on camera or not—and then I thought maybe I'd better wake up!

Do you suppose this had anything to do with my husband finding my 2 *first* gray hairs the day before???!!

Saturday night-Sunday morning, April 21/22, 1979:

I dreamed about L. [*a teacher in the Dundee school system*]. We were all at the American Legion and someone there started an argument with L. about school policy (this actually did happen to L. the next week after this). The person who later started this argument was not the one who did so in this dream, however.

My part was the real heavy. I interfered (in this dream) and told the person to leave L. alone! (I wasn't there when this actually happened, though.) I did see the person who started this argument the day after this dream, however.

Monday-Tuesday, May 7/8, 1979:

I was seated in a church, quite a few people I recognized. I kept hearing the clang of metal all through the sermon—clang, clang. It turned out to be playground equipment! Is that a message? Finally, two of the men got up and carried the stuff out, piece by piece, and put it together outside! The minister kept right on talking as though nothing were going on . . . his sermon was all about being patient and concentrating on doing what one needs to do and staying with it 'til it's done! Then when we all left, we were no longer all scattered, but rather were a close, cluster group.

* * * *

From E., domestic engineer, craftsperson, gourmet cook

Friday night-Saturday morning, March 30/31, 1979:

Teasing the hooded characters from "Star Wars," threatening to expose their "faces."

Husband decides to stop & visit an old friend whom I don't know without consultation first.

A great number of jagged rocks which someone is trying to dissolve. Toward morning, a similar dream with a whole cliff.

A palace-like place & the announcement that an execution is planned that night.

A conjugal romantic interlude (in the palace?) interrupted at 2:30 a.m. by teenage son coming in to tell of the book he's reading. Much scolding for staying up late.

Henry Kissinger announces he'll become president of Harvard.

A display of cakes & souffles that rise with a little side-nudging—Kissinger announcement coincident with this scene.

A phone number to call—contained all low numbers.

Saturday night-Sunday morning, March 31/April 1, 1979:

A church supper in town has been serving duckling (which I love) & I find out that they're caught right in Dundee. You just go down to the creek that runs east midway between Seneca & Hollister Streets & if you can catch one of the alligators in the stream it will have a duck in its mouth. [*Note G.'s dream of the same night.*]

We wait & wait but don't see any, and are told it's not considered fair to put stakes across the stream to catch them. Some people think you shouldn't eat these ducks as the water is likely polluted. All this time I never knew there were ducks and alligators in Dundee. The stream runs into the Mississippi.

Friday night-Saturday morning, April 6/7, 1979:

It's night & there's a large warehouse-type building ahead. Large trucks keep delivering what I take to be food or food products. Closer & to the right is another building where we're cooking up large quantities of soup (I made a lot of chicken soup Friday). There's talk of live lobster and of capturing the local market.

Then about three of us are in a restaurant and some of the lobster is being served to us. The lady of the establishment is pouring white wine, although there's already milk (in an opaque wine glass) on the table. This spills on the table and makes a bleached spot. When the white wine is gone, the lady serves red, although one of the diners objects. A man takes her place: he's slight, dark-haired & boyish-looking, and speaks with just a bit of a lisp. He's jumping up and down with excitement, saying he can't understand how he got this job after being out of work for two years. I can't understand it either.

[NOTE: This was another of E.'s dreams corresponding with G.'s on the same night.]

Tuesday night-Wednesday morning, May 1/2, 1979:

A group of us from Dundee is shopping in some city (Buffalo?) and someone suggests that we visit a mutual acquaintance from Barrington who lives up there now. I wasn't aware she'd moved, but we go to an address in the suburbs but are told that she now lives in a highrise downtown . . . I'm waiting for an elevator to the 4th floor when I wake up. (Pointless, eh?)

* * * *

From G., painter, sculptor

Thursday-Friday, March 29/30, 1979:

I am to join a club or some organization. On the road uphill past Carl G.'s barn, I see instead a building (a house?) with people and horses. It is afire, but the people won't move, nor the horses. Boys sit in a row. The edges of their straw hats begin to char and burn. Again, past the top of the hill on the Pre-Emption Road, fire breaks out in a campground of buildings. People rush in to save the horses, which are panicking.

Saturday-Sunday, March 31-April 1, 1979:

Alligators in the sewer. But how? There is a connection with New York City. Underground migration of animals? I tell someone this could be a food supply in case of disaster.

[NOTE connection here with E.'s alligator-in-the-sewer dream of the same night.]

Friday night-Saturday morning, April 6/7, 1979:

I have an old model car (model T?) but it is new. I drive a friend and my son someplace. We go on a car ferry. A restaurant in the country. We sit at a big table to eat lobster. Nearby is a cupboard on which has been spilled something white that bleached the wood. Nobody seems to know how to remedy this.

Something ails a little dog who lives in a stairwell beneath a porch. I go to him. He has a small pile of boxes arranged in a corner of this sleeping place.

[See E.'s dream of the same night, with coinciding spills and bleaching.]

Friday-Saturday, April 20/21, 1979:

There is a list of ten families. I go through it looking . . . for what? Three couples are united by a sewer tube, a sewer system. They share the sewer.

I am backstage painting some object blue for a play. Mac Davis, the singer, watches me, curious. He drops a fleck of tobacco into one of the paint cups and throws the whole thing away. Now I am obliged to mix new paint. I am in a hurry and try a short cut. This involves mashing up some water-soluble spongy stuff. It doesn't work. I wonder if Mac Davis thinks he knows what I am doing, since I don't.

I am in a kitchen with somebody. There is a rapping sound and a cat-sized horse prances out from under a counter. The other person is afraid and runs away.

* * * *

From A.S., businessperson, domestic engineer

Saturday-Sunday, April 21-22, 1979:

The whole dream started out with myself feeling very frustrated and determined to drive my car like a bat out of hell down Rt. 14 where the snow had been scraped up in sections about 50 ft. apart like gates.

I was driving faster and faster not having a bit of problem, it was still and quiet, then beside one of these snow fences stood Ray Z., the highway superintendent, with a shovel and this terrified look on his face. I couldn't hear him but I know he was pleading with me to slow down. Then I decided this car was going to flip end over end and I wasn't the least bit frightened, then it started, and I wondered if I should hang on the steering wheel or column. Then I was going round and round and it was impossible to hang on. The next thing I knew the motion stopped, then like in a delayed-action cartoon, the sounds of glass came crashing down from what sounded like a million pieces to that one final little piece that had stuck.

I layed there on my stomach, knees up, with a heavy feeling of glass upon me. I raised my head, feeling no emotion but wondering if I was getting wet from the snow. Still no one was around.

Friday-Saturday, April 27/28, 1979:

1st: Husband and I are driving through some city all over the damn place, seeming like just going around the same old blocks [*a concise dream-observation of this couple's waking life*]—after a while we are going up & down steep hills and finally we are on a horse, well, I am but he's there, but not visible. Anyway, got on this swinging bridge over this huge body of water, the bridge was swaying and the horse started to rear up—now I was scared out of my wits but also mad because at that point I told myself to stop—I hate bridges over water and I *wasn't* going to be thrown in that water.

2nd: THE NEXT DREAM—I'm in the Super-Duper buying cigarettes but they aren't where they're supposed to be; finally I find my self picking 6 cigarettes from the hood of an old man's sweatshirt. It's hazy from there, but something weird was going on about the Super-Duper . . .

* * * *

From W., organizer, writer, widow

Dear Sue: A dream! Went to see B., a neighbor 'cause I had some kind of old book, scrapbook-size. She wasn't where they are now but in a house like below the road. Walls were low—room was large and barren. An old man there in a wheel chair. B. wasn't at all interested in the book or me—true to life! He, though, was very interested in the book as it had carvings raised up (bas-relief?). Pages were of wood. He rubbed his fingers over it & then told what it was.

B. went to another room and sat at a table-like desk. She said I better take the book back as my own family might like it. So I picked up some plants I had there and got out! B. is about the last person I'd think to dream about! She isn't friendly at *all.*

Friday-Saturday, October 5/6, 1979:

Some unidentified person and I walked around a building looking for an entrance. Finally we found one but a dark, yawning pit was in front of us. That person jumped down about 6 feet. In doing so, he stumbled. I remarked that I would not dare as I might break my foot. So I finally found a recessed set of steps. [*Interesting similarity to my "pit" dream earlier that year—which W. hadn't known about.*] I was then in a room and a friend, C., stood there. He beckoned for me to come closer. We sat on a hard wooden bench, similar to a Deacon's bench with spindles on the back . . . He said, "I don't know what you are going to do, but I am going to burn coal." My mother was hovering in the background, a very indistinct figure (she died in 1961). My cousin Graham (a doctor who died in 1963) was there and the two men began talking about "developing their own pictures . . ."

Then C. turned to me and said, "It is good-by for now, I guess. I'm sorry." And that was all.

[NOTE: Not long after this dream, C. passed away in another state. W. had not known that he was ailing at the time of this dream.]

Friday-Saturday, November 12/13, 1979:

It was summer and I was sleeping outside. When I awoke there were small flames of fire licking all around me in the short grass. I got up and started for the house, which was on our old farm. I evidently had been sleeping where we had set some fruit trees.

As I went to the house to hook up the hose I thought that I had slept outside all summer. I went into the house to tell my husband [*long deceased*] that I would be hooking up the hose, so the noise would not disturb him. He was snoring so loudly that I thought, "Anyone could carry off the whole place and he would never hear it!" He roused up and I said, "There is fire outside where you burned grass last night." He stood up quickly—he had on a long white garment.

As I went back through the living room, I glanced out of the window and the grapevines were not full grown, as the top wire was bare. The rows were full of yellow rocket and I thought, we must get those grapes plowed at once. I must have gone back into the early thirties. This was all so vivid that I woke up and I just could not get back to sleep.

Sue, there are just too many dead people hanging around me. Are they trying to come to my aid or are they hanging around to help me go from here to there? It really causes me a lot of thinking and I get nowhere. I feel there is something just out of my reach, out of my comprehension.

[NOTE: As of this date in 1988, W. is very much alive, still writing for the local paper and organizing senior-citizen activities & groups . . .]

* * * *

From N. K., county legislator

Friday-Saturday, April 20/21, 1979:

Dear Dundee Observer editors: I dreamed last Friday night that I was walking arm in arm with a certain cousin. We came to a bank and had to jump down. It was about six feet, but we jumped and continued our walk. He's 78 years old now and I'm 71. But aren't dreams wonderful?

* * * *

[Here's a most evocative case of a dream that seemed to connect precognitively and clairvoyantly with aspects of my private life]:

From M.B., as told to me by her daughter-in-law, R.

Saturday-Sunday, November 28-29, 1981:

In her dream [*according to R.*], M.B. was in Ken's Luncheonette [*a Dundee restaurant*]. A strange woman walked in the door, obviously very upset. This woman was petite, with salt-and-pepper hair and a heavily lined face.

The waitress asked her why she was so upset and the woman replied that she was Sue Watkins' mother and that "Sue Watkins died from eating bad liver," which had affected her [*my own*] liver, and also her mother's liver. M. felt in the dream that it was her job to comfort this woman, and called on daughter-in-law R. to help her do this. M. said she woke up sitting straight up in bed, very upset, feeling that she had dreamed something that would come true.

[NOTE: This dream has some fascinating connections with my mother and me, especially in light of the fact that M. is but a casual acquaintance of mine, knows nothing about my family, and to my knowledge never met my mother; although it's possible that she saw my mother and me together on one of the few occasions when my parents visited me in Dundee.

[At the time that R. related this dream to me, I felt that it was precognitive, though not of my own death. M.'s dream description of my mother is very accurate, which leads me to think that M. might indeed have seen her with me at some point and consciously forgotten it. But what is most intriguing about this dream is that four years later, in January of 1985, doctors discovered that my mother had cancer of the liver—this diagnosis following surgery the previous October in which a malignant sarcoma was removed from my mother's stomach. In 1981, at the time of M.'s dream, there was no indication that these particular symptoms would beset my mother's life, though she had been plagued by increasingly serious—and progressively more internalized—physical problems from a relatively early age. Possibly M. perceived this on levels beneath ordinary consciousness for reasons of her own.

[This eerie precognitive thread carries with it a whisper of the questions I ask myself about the hereditary factors involved with lupus erythematosus, which both my mother and *her* mother suffered from . . . and the fact that there are questions about the carcinogenic side effects on the stomach and liver from the medicines prescribed for lupus control and for severe stomach ulcers, another condition my mother suffered. My mother was handed the lupus-test finding in the spring of 1981, a fact that M. couldn't have been aware of and very likely would not have associated with liver problems had she known.

[Moreover, in late November of 1981, Sean came down with mononucleosis and was out of school for several weeks. The Dundee Medical Clinic physician who diagnosed the mono also said that Sean's liver was "slightly enlarged," a common side effect of that illness. At the same time, a mix-up in pediatrician's records eventually forced me to concede to the school's demand that Sean be inoculated against mumps, even though he'd *had* mumps at age three. I objected strongly to this, my contention being that Sean's immune system now contained natural antibodies for the disease and the vaccine was not only unnecessary and redundant, but possibly dangerous, considering the fact that mononucleosis and mumps similarly affect the glandular system. School and health officials refused to see my point, though, and threatened with legal repercussions, I gave in.

[Within 24 hours of getting the shot, Sean suffered an (-officially diagnosed) allergic reaction to the vaccine along with a recurrence of mono symptoms, and missed another two weeks of school. Health officials would say only that such a reaction "might have involved" the mix of natural and artificial antibody components—exactly as I'd initially argued. The incident left me with a resolve to *never again* accept "official" medical thinking that runs against my own experience, and to take legal action *myself* should a similar situation occur again. It didn't.

[Of course, the question again is—if this is indeed a precognitive dream, as I felt it was at the time, why did M., a relative stranger, pick up on difficulties that would befall *my* family? It's interesting to note here that at the time of the dream, some members of M.'s family were involved with alcohol-related problems, including a string of DWI arrests and other matters. Perhaps the image of liver ailments and substance effects upon that organ provided a symbolic forum for M.'s emotional turmoils (like K.'s dream); perhaps her natural empathetic concern for others reached out in some way and made the connections between our family experiences. And again, my announced dream-study most likely helped M. make those particular kinds of associations.]

* * * *

[Here's a page of dream notes mailed to me by my friend Ellen's daughter, then aged nine, who said that her dreams "come true almost every time."]

	Dream	**What Happened**
1.	I got a Chinese doll	I got a Chinese doll
2.	That there would be a man swimming	There was a man swimming in the Washington accident
3.	(twice) My brother talking from certain angles about certain things	It happened
4.	That I had seen people I didn't know	It happened

Sue—I can't remember anymore. I just dream something and when I see it I kinda freeze or stop and remember seeing it before. *T.E.*

* * * *

A couple of my own "Dundee Dreams"

Friday-Saturday, April 13/14, 1979:

Woke up thinking, "That's your Dundee dream." A strange dream that is like a memory. Susan B. and Al S. and Carl K. [an old boyfriend/policeman] and I are sitting at an outdoor cafe table on Dundee's Main Street, downtown, outside Ken's Luncheonette. Dundee is bright and charming, like a French or Swiss village; awnings over the sidewalks, etc. Carl K. seems to be somehow attached to a political bigwig [*note Jeanette's dream on pages 88-89*], like a Kennedy, or attached to the Kennedy family, although he is somehow locally political too. Susan and I are still doing the newspaper together. We are involved in a conversation about municipal business. All of this radiates a kind of safety, as Dundee does, which I bask in (and once awake, I long for this, which seems long ago and far away).

Something is said about the trees in Dundee. I fly up into the trees to cut down dead wood. An old lady watches this from the porch of her house. The streets are full of people, going on about their business in peace. There is a tremendous feeling of nostalgia for days gone by—a view from vast old age to golden youth. A *safe* youth.

Then I half wake up, without opening my eyes, and can't remember if I'm in Dundee or in my parents' house, which is where I was actually sleeping. I seem to be in both places, actually—I feel as though I'm flashing from one place to the other. I clearly hear my grandfather Baker say, "Let's all start all over again, in all our own old neighborhoods." I wonder if I will ever really achieve that mixture of innocent determination and understanding that you do live in the world that you concentrate upon.

[NOTE: See Appendix 4, in which I've put together a collection of precognitive and connective dreams from my records and from others' recollections.]

* * * *

Addendum

More Dream Ads and the Tail of Fire

[Here is another example of how people are connected on many levels in the objective and subjective worlds—this time from inside a megalopolis! Peter Danison, a fan and friend, is working on his own book about dreams and related matters; he sent me this excerpt from his manuscript at my request. Entitled, "Community Dreaming," it's an account of a fire that destroyed several buildings near his former home in Anaheim, California—and the dreams preceding that event. I include it here because of the interesting "community dreaming" parallels involving *feelings* rather than straight, so-called "precognition."]

"On a sunrise in late spring 1982, a Santa Ana wind that had begun suddenly the previous night knocked down several power lines around the city of Anaheim and environs. The sizzling wires ignited nearby palms and foliage, which then spread fire to their adjacent buildings.

"A depressing-looking, crowded apartment building was destroyed. Fortunately most of the residents had left for work by the time it started. Several business establishments around the city were destroyed in the same way. No one was seriously injured. Local news reported a fireman suffering from smoke inhalation.

"Attending these unusual fires were some usual brush fires in outlying areas beyond city limits (Brush fires are a seasonal event in southern California. Occasionally nearby housing developments are threatened by these; so far there hasn't been a mass catastrophe.) But national news media treated the event in the spirit of Great Chance Disaster: TV screens around the country blared with clips of America's latest tribulation. That day, distant friends and relatives called us up, checking to see if we'd been burned to a crisp.

"We hadn't been, of course. Video close-ups combined with TV's typically deadpan narrative made the event appear ubiquitous. It gave folks back east the impression that our whole county was literally up in flames. In the local reality, most things were business-as-usual. I set my callers straight, uttered some wry comments about news sensationalism. But a day or two later, the Big Fire served to catalyze some sensations of my own.

"I keep dream notebooks. Paging through my current records, I found this scrawled in my large and sleepy cursive: 'Santa Ana burns down.' It was the headline of a dream I'd forgotten, written down thirty days earlier.

"My headline wasn't exactly sensationalism, considering the dream—which was long, strange, and ended up this way: My sweet old collie was trotting down a neighborhood street in the dark with her tail partly on fire. As she wagged it along down the street, flames set fire to the bushes and trees overlapping the sidewalk.

"A few dream-moments later, I stood on an Anaheim street looking out toward the direction of Santa Ana, now in my dream's dawn light. The entire county seemed to be in charred ruins in the sunrise. I thought back to my dog in the dark a few moments before and connected that her flaming tail had burned the area down. I woke up.

"Amazing. I had been writing down my nightly dreams as an intimate personal project for some time. While I'd often found similar—and more accurate—instances of 'precognition' in my notes, this one led to some speculative questions that, I thought, might provide some fascinating speculative answers.

"I ran an ad in a local paper: 'Did anyone dream about the Anaheim fire before it happened?'

"No one answered for a few days. Finally, I got a call from a high school senior named Alex. This young man told me that he did dream his neighborhood burned down. (His neighborhood was called Rossmoore. In the summer of '84, we heard on the local news that there was a big fire in Rossmoore, just like Alex had dreamed two years before.) He said he dreamed it about a month before the fire occurred—as I had.

"We chatted a while. Neither Alex's neighborhood nor mine had actually 'burned down.' Why had we both dreamed of massive fires in this area a month beforehand? Alex wondered if he might be a psychic.

"Maybe so. But I noticed something more obvious about Alex and myself, as we talked on the phone, and about my dog too, for that matter. Each of us had been in pretty sorry frames of mind for months, for our own reasons. My dog had chewed her tail to a fiery red in a losing battle with fleas. My part-time job as a musician had been bringing me nothing but aggravation about money and art all year. And Alex had been so 'burned out' (his words) with school he wasn't sure he wanted to wait around to graduate.

"Very likely, our personal frustrations precipitated fiery dreams (though I can't speak for my dog). And just as likely, our dreams reflected a mass event that was about to reveal similar feelings for a lot of people.

"After this I began paying more attention to the dreams I wrote down; and I found that my dreams certainly did 'predict' local events in the same way. For example, dreams of huge floods in the area reflected my natural feelings as much as they heralded actual events that took place within a month or so in reality. Some were exaggerated, some specific.

"My conversation with Alex inspired a search for overlooked values in the nature of nightly dreaming. Very few people take notice of their nightly dreams. Most seem content to leave this very personal subject to the realms of peripheral science, psychology, or perhaps occultists. Few consider that there may be very practical advantages to recalling their dreams . . ."

SEVEN

What IS This Thing Called ESP...?

(from the *Observer*)

"What sea is this?" asked Clumly, with a comfortable sense of authority. The sailor looked down, inspecting its texture. He smiled again, a man perhaps not to be trusted. He said thoughtfully, "Metaphysics."

—John Gardner
The Sunlight Dialogues, (Clumly's dream)

(May 31, 1979)

What is precognition? Instances of "seeing the future" whether through dreams or in "hunches," visions, or other means, have been treated generally throughout history in one of two ways: either as the unfounded mutterings of those who are in the business of preying on human superstitions; or as a mysterious (and usually evil) power controlled with great difficulty by a select and weird minority, almost always women.

Within these polarities—represented on the one hand, generally, by science and on the other, generally, by religion—lies one basic message, which in modern times has been neatly exploited by movies, television, and the Best-Seller list. And that message is that you are a repository of evil—swim at your own risk. Rarely are instances of precognition (or any other form of what is lumped under the catchall term ESP) acknowledged, let alone regarded, as the underlying sensory data structure upon which our physical lives depend.

One of the things that I've been looking for in my dream study is a verifiable collection of precognitive or future-telling dreams. So far I've received some and one of them, as we'll see, appears to be connected with a national event. But I suspect that what we think of as precognition, in dreams as well as in waking life (manifested in coincidence and in those little urges to follow impulses or hunches), goes largely unrecognized because we've been trained to see only the huge, astonishing, exactly replicated incidents—if we see them at all.

Nearly everybody can tell you of precognitive experiences—from the fleeting, ghostly feelings of déjà vu to the telephone call from the friend you were just thinking about to those "lucky breaks" and "close calls" we pin on Lady Luck and the Fates. But what goes unnoticed beneath the (enculturated) eerieness of such occurrences is how intrinsic the facility of precognition *is.*

Few people plan out in advance how they are going to say a sentence and make it go from start to finish, convey the message, contain all the necessary words (in grammatical sequence, we hope), and maintain the symbolic and literal part in the conversation at hand, all at once. Yet almost every human being in the world does this every day, usually without effort, and often with great unconscious eloquence. The act of talking is so completely a part of our logical existence that it never occurs to us to wonder at the feats of mental gymnastics made by *some* part of our psyche—and a part that we tend to pass off as non-existent.

Looked at in the light of their normal relationship with our waking lives, then, the *pattern* of our dreams becomes more like this unconscious pattern of speech: There exist entire sequences of personal symbols, background settings, archetypal guideposts, and past dream events that may themselves be the sensory structure for the circumstances of our lives. You may say you've never had a precognitive dream; but if you kept dream records over a period of time, you would most likely see connections between waking and dreaming life that are like the pre-staging of conversation; the nouns and verbs and adjectives of life, performing the underlying mechanics of your "objective" world.

One of my respondents [to the dream study] had a series of dreams over a two-month span that dealt with fires and a chimney that rocked back and forth, emitting large amounts of smoke. The fire dreams at one point involved a building near his home and one that specifically showed his wife tending the rocking flue, eventually fixing it to let more smoke out of the house. At no time did G. dream of *his* house catching fire. Yet one day after this dream series had stopped, the built-up creosote in G.'s wood stove did catch fire, and it was his wife who was at home, discovered the blaze, and called the fire department soon enough to prevent the worst.

A precognitive dream? Or a neat bit of hindsight interpretation? Or maybe, with some kind of insight into dream data, and the basic assumption that we receive such data all the time, and for our own good reasons, G. might have checked the chimney more often—or maybe he will from now on!

In addition, on the night of March 23/24, 1979, G. had the following dream: "Something has happened to the city, but what? People sit around—no transportation. There is a lack of water, yet the electricity works. A disaster. I look at a deserted candy store & see an ad for a science-fiction book entitled IF, and I take a copy. There is a story inside this pertaining to the disaster." Four days later, on March 28, 1979, the near-disaster at Three Mile Island nuclear power plant developed: the near-meltdown that was almost exactly depicted in the movie, "The China Syndrome" (which wasn't presented as science-fiction but certainly could be considered as such), released just weeks before the Harrisburg, Pa., incident.[1]

I'll add a dream of mine here from April 27/28 in which I saw a friend, D., in the advanced stages of pregnancy. This woman wasn't actually expecting, but the next day, I learned from mutual friends that her *horse* had given birth on the evening of my dream.

I hadn't known anything about the mare's condition, but I do like horses and I did know that D. does most of the work and training with her small stock.

I purposely chose these dreams because they seem to have no great significance as far as actual, definite, spelled-out precognition goes—as we're trained to think of it (again, if we think of it at all). The fire/chimney dreams aren't extraordinary and didn't help G. avoid the near-disaster . . . except that, according to G.'s notes, his wife decided that day to stay home from work "on impulse," an unusual thing for her to do. (G. and his wife discuss each other's dreams at breakfast, incidentally.) The "disaster" dream could refer to Three Mile Island or not—certainly disaster dreams are common enough, and G. has definite anti-nuclear opinions. In my dream, D. was pregnant, not her horse—and what difference did it make even if I did pick up on the impending event? It didn't affect the foaling one way or another.

But I think that this is the point: Precognition is not something available to a few so-called "psychics" who have the power to foresee disasters; and it isn't just an early-warning system any more than our physical brains are "just" fancy hunks of meat designed to march us through our lives. Precognition is as natural and as biological a function as breathing or digestion—and, in my opinion, the ground of all our functions.The appearance of tiny little "bits" of precognitive material in our dreams or in other ways is, I think, simply a matter of our conscious awareness of what goes on all the time beneath our multi-layered existence. In a very real way, all the world is contained in any given dream—and vice versa.

So my premise here is to illustrate how natural and generally unspectacular the underlying sensory data is that we depend upon; how easily we communicate with all layers of circumstance—including the interior design of time (precognition) and space (telepathy and clairvoyance). I mean to say that such data are not the result of an attack of Freudian hysteria or Stephen Kingian chills; that such knowledge is basic to all consciousness and that we could quite easily teach ourselves to recognize it and expand our perceptions of the world we choose to live in.

NOTES

THERE WERE FOREWARNINGS AT THREE MILE ISLAND!

A dozen residents in the area of the March 1979 nuclear reactor accident in Pennsylvania, according to Larry E. Arnold, director of the Harrisburg, Pa., ParaScience International, ***INDEPENDENTLY "EXPERIENCED THE SAME PROPHETIC NIGHTMARE IN WHICH THEY SAW THE COOLING TOWERS OF THREE MILE ISLAND GLOWING DEEP RED, WITH LIGHTNING CRACKLING ALL AROUND."***

1 This "Ripley's Believe It Or Not" squib appeared in a 1982 Sunday newspaper supplement. I didn't check up on the information myself, and I had no idea there was a "ParaScience International" institution in Harrisburg, but the community-dream aspect here is certainly fascinating—though I have to say that if I lived near a nuclear reactor, I'd probably have a *lot* of dreams like this.

EIGHT

The Day That Stretched Out Into Sideways

(Obits, Coincidence, and Balances)

The most elegant timing is involved in each individual's birth and death.

Jane Roberts
The Individual and the Nature of Mass Events

Wherever I sat, there I might live, and the landscape radiated from me accordingly.

H.D. Thoreau
Walden

In hindsight, it all seemed to start on Thursday, August 9, 1979, when I was guest speaker on the Dundee radio station's noontime talk show. I was extremely nervous about doing this—terrified, in fact. Not only was this the first time I'd ever been on the air, live—it was the first interview I'd given about my upcoming book, *Conversations with Seth*, and about my Dundee dream project. Waiting in the control room for the show to start, I felt woozy and faint with fear. The only reason I'd agreed to do the show at all was because the host was old friend and former ESP class member Joel Hess, who was then working part-time at the station and had talked me into this. But Joel would make it easy for me, I reasoned. Understanding the subject matter, he'd bail me out if I got stuck for words. I was wrong. Uncharacteristically, Joel spent the entire half-hour interrupting me mid-sentence, incorrectly rewording whatever I'd just said, and making weirdly inappropriate analogies that took up more time than I, the guest, did.

By the end of the program, I'd forgotten my fear and was exasperated enough to start stating my case in aggressive, forthright terms (which turned out to be valuable training for dealing later with inept or hostile interviewers). But I was miserably convinced that I'd ended up just sounding confused and stupid. And I couldn't understand Joel's bizarre on-air behavior toward me, either—it seemed almost as though he'd been acting out of resentment, or some old unresolved issue that neither one of us was consciously acknowledging. Still and all, the focus of the show had been the "you create your own reality" concept, so in whatever form, that notion did get out on the airwaves of Yates and Schuyler counties that afternoon.

The next evening, Friday, August 10, Roy and I decided on the spur of the moment to go to the races at the Dundee fairgrounds—the first time I'd been to this weekly event. The stands were full of people, and we chatted briefly with Ryan McCall, who was Roy's full-time farmhand, and Ryan's best friend Duane Day, who'd been discharged from the Army two months before.

That night's dream, for Friday-Saturday, August 10/11, 1979, was a vivid story about a probable me—a version of myself who was at such irreconcilable odds with my father over philosophical issues that he'd thrown me out of the house at age eighteen. (Though my father and I did have the usual trying times, things never approached this sort of extreme in *my* universe.) In this probability-dream, I ended up getting myself an apartment in New York City and living in pretty desperate financial straits. And when a probable version of Joel Hess asked me to marry him in this dream, I refused on feminist political grounds. "Marriage is always detrimental to the female," my dream-self told him, expressing a belief of my own here-and-now that *seemed*, on the surface, quite logical (and which I would later experience).

That same morning, I was pleasantly surprised when Roy told me he'd remembered a dream of his own. In it, Roy asked the Dundee Police Chief for directions to the home of James M. (who owned a horse we were interested in buying, though we didn't know exactly where he lived, rural addresses being what they are. This fellow and the Dundee Chief shared the same last name and both lived in Yates County, so we'd previously assumed the two were related).

"In my dream, [Chief M.] gave me this whole long maze of directions," Roy said. "All I remember was something like, 'Go to [a nearby village], drive up the hill, and it's the third road on the right and the third house on the right.'" Roy said that his dream-Chief then added, "He works days and his wife works nights, so I usually charge a dollar for sending people up there"—implying the usual small-town assumption about a woman's proclivities if left alone all day—or so I pointed out; and Roy and I immediately got into an argument about what I called the male-defined idea of what women "should" be.

Our quarrel faded out of the picture, though, as friends and relatives started calling up one after the other—all with bad news. It turned out that an entire series of death and disasters, all involving people we knew, had taken place during the previous twenty-four hours (and were later confirmed in news reports, which I saved). And it seemed to me, contemplating this list of events, that a maze of coincidental threads was not only tying together the personal experience of those affected, but was also connecting disparate *yet affiliated* experiences and associations of my own.

Here are those events and synchronistic threads, as excerpted from my notebook:

1. Duane Day, whom we'd seen at the races Friday night (Aug. 10), died in a fiery one-car accident as he drove home about midnight from the Dundee fairgrounds. Firemen estimated that he'd hit a culvert at more than 100 mph; they had to pry him out of his overturned car with the Hurst "jaws of life" tool, reports said. We later learned from Ryan McCall that Duane's *mother* had died ten years before this in the same sort of accident—while driving home from the Dundee races.

Upon hearing of Duane's death, I immediately connected it with the 1974 crash (already described in Chapter 5) that caused fatal injuries to Roy's *father*. That mishap had involved a fiery collision between the father's car and a motorcycle, the accident occurring right in front of Roy, who had just gotten out of the car and was standing in his driveway. The motorcycle driver, who was killed outright, had been on his way home from a moto-X race on a track a few miles from Dundee. As I've said, it was during the time of this tragedy that I discovered the connections between Roy's family and mine—for one, that Roy's Uncle John had been one of my great-grandfather Baker's first patients in Dundee. "He did a fine appendectomy," John would say, patting his side. "He saved my life. It wasn't everybody who got over an operation in those days, you know." And in fact, my great-grandfather was rather a medical renegade in his day; one of the first in his generation of doctors to strictly follow Dr. Lister's "new" techniques of hand-washing and disinfecting *before* operations and childbirthing.

2. Also on that 1979 Friday of August 10, two local teenagers—I'll call them Roger Bryce and John Pearl—were badly hurt when the motorcycle they were on, Roger driving, went out of control and flipped into the air. According to reports, Dundee Police Chief M. (who was in Roy's dream), had been chasing them along the village railroad tracks when the cycle crashed. The teenagers had been at the races earlier that evening. Reports said that Roger was admitted to an area hospital for treatment of a concussion, lacerations on his shoulders, and extensive bruises. Pearl was treated for cuts and bruises and released.

Now coincidences seemed to multiply before my eyes. Not more than a year earlier, Roger's young wife—who was John Pearl's sister—had been killed in a head-on collision on the nearby state highway. She was eight months pregnant at the time; she and Roger were both teenagers and hadn't been married long. In fact, she was on her way to Syracuse to pick Roger up at the time of the accident—he was coming home from the Army (as Duane Day had just come home from the Army).

It was Roger's father, Alvin Bryce, who told me that afternoon in 1974 that Roy's father had been hurt in the car-motorcycle crash.

Furthermore, something here touched eerily upon my probability dream of August 10/11—I remembered that John Pearl came from a strict religious family who had told their daughter to get out of their house upon learning that she was pregnant—an obvious clash of philosophies and circumstance. She and Roger had lived for a while with Roger's parents, and were having their share of financial troubles.

3. Another of the phone calls to Roy that Saturday morning was from a cousin, telling him that his 75-year-old aunt had died unexpectedly during that night of August 10. This woman was the wife of Roy's Uncle John, the fellow who liked to reminisce with me about my great-grandfather, Dr. Baker. Coincidently, this aunt's maiden name was the same as one of my other ancestors on Asbury's side of the family.

It also "happened" that Roy's two sisters were visiting him just that week, the first time the three of them had been together in many years. One sister had come back east from California to attend her high school class reunion; the other had driven in from New England. So the family began to gather at the homestead in response to unofficial knowledge—the upcoming death of their aunt, who was much loved by everyone in the family.

4. Also dying unexpectedly on the 10th was Dundee resident Martin Gallway, a man in his seventies who'd been driving Susan Benedict and me slightly crazy for years. Martin had retired from a New York City public relations firm and worked part-time reporting on local government issues for the Penn Yan newspaper. Being the self-proclaimed media critic of epicurean tastes that he was, Martin never passed up the chance to tell Susan and me what a "shitty-looking publication" the *Observer* was, and how "crummy" the reporting, despite the Press Association awards we won every year. During board meetings, he'd light up huge cigars and scrutinize municipal goings-on through clouds of stinking smoke, usually without taking a single reporter's note. Of taxes and budgets, he once told the Dundee board of education, "You people suck the public dry and then bite off the tit." He was colorful, outspoken, irritating, eccentric, and fascinating. Unknown to us, he was writing a book on the English language when he died and was married to a medical doctor—one of the first women to practice medicine in the state; a renegade, therefore, in her time—who survived him.

5. Listed in the Elmira paper's obituaries that same day was Brad N., a friend who, I learned later, had succumbed to leukemia—at the age of 35. Jane and Rob Butts and I had known Brad and his wife Clara for several years. They owned one of the first "health food" stores in the area, and did well with it after overcoming quite a bit of local prejudice about "organic" and "natural"

products. Brad was also a fine cabinetmaker, and the *Observer* had once carried a story on his building restoration projects.

But when Brad and Clara decided to join the meditation-oriented religious sect of a man they were obliged to call "Master," their lives changed drastically. Following this sect required them to deny all worldly pleasures—just minimal food, for example, and no sex, no music, no card-playing or movies, no fun, period. "We really try very hard not to 'do it,'" Clara said to me once. It was really a depressing sight to behold. When I first met Brad and Clara, they'd been in the throes of passionate love, and the two of them had an earthy, bountiful approach to life that was a delight to be around. Now, under "Master," they were like shrunken-head dolls of themselves, cowering from all exuberance as though they must be allergic to sunlight itself.

Sadly, Brad seemed to lose himself in the complete physical denial that his "Master" demanded, though Clara broke away from the sect—and her husband—altogether. It was about then that Brad discovered that he had leukemia. He died within a few months.

And why not—why bother to live at all, under those conditions? Pudgy old Martin Gallway, smoker of rotten cigars, consumer of good whiskey (so he periodically announced), obnoxiously unapologetic, outlived Brad's ideas of "purity" and "goodness" by some forty-five years—though the two shared this death date for reasons of their own . . . *Counterpart* reasons, I mused; like statements of contrast in the experience of Earth . . .

Interesting, I noted, that Clara was thrown out of her parents' home when she was a teenager. Several years after Brad's death, I heard through mutual friends that Clara had been injured in an automobile accident and needed physical therapy to recover. (So too, just incidentally, and at about that same time, Joel Hess's wife was in physical therapy as a result of an auto crash. Speculatively speaking, at least, connections seemed to be rippling out across the years.)

6. Rounding out my notes for that Saturday, August 11, is a description of the drive that Roy, his sister Cathy, and I took that afternoon to see if we could find where James M. lived by following the directions given in Roy's August 10th dream. We ended up lost in the wilds of western Yates County and finally had to ask passersby where the place was. It didn't help. Five people gave us five different sets of directions. "You can't miss it," each person said.

When we did find the house, both James and his wife were there—and it was embarrassingly obvious that this was a couple on the edge of divorce. He was meek and silent; she was hostile and rude. He remarked how much he liked it up here in the hills; she snarled about living "in the damn sticks." So Roy's dream-comment that James "worked days" while his wife "worked nights" was quite apt—they *were* "working" like day and night to one another, and finding their house *had* involved a "maze" of directions and wrong turns. Regardless of any such psychological correlations, though, I thought that the real importance of the day's drive was Roy's urge to see if his dream was "true," an acknowledgment of possibility he hadn't previously expressed. In fact, we discovered driving back down the road that the M. house *was* on the "third road on the right," and James did turn out to be related to the Dundee Police Chief. But Roy was looking for a literal re-creation of his dream, and would see no other creative nuance. (We didn't like the horse, either.)

7. In my mailbox that afternoon was the edited copy from Prentice-Hall of my *Conversations* chapter on "counterparts," the Sethian idea of several personalities springing from the same entity, or whole-self.[1] According to Seth, Joel Hess and I are counterparts (or at least were relating as such during class years), a facet of that idea I'd actually forgotten until I looked at the edited pages and thought of the radio show two days before. Then I checked my dream records and noted that in my August 10/11 probability-dream, Joel had asked me to marry him . . . odd, I mused, that when we met in Jane's class in 1971, he had been in the process of breaking up with his first wife and had indicated a lot of interest in me, which I'd rejected even after I'd felt some initial mutual attraction.

Funny, I thought, as I drew myself a nice, hot bath—funny that Roy had turned on his radio to listen to my show that day just as Joel had made what I thought was an extremely clumsy analogy for "you create your own reality"—he'd interrupted me to say, "Wait a minute, Sue, do you mean that there might be some people who would look up and see an old farmer standing there where nobody else would see an old farmer?" Roy said later that he'd felt so embarrassed by my stumbling attempts to respond to this that he'd shut the radio off . . . but funny how that radio show, and my clumsy explanations of the interconnections between dreams and waking reality, had become a sort of prelude to the coincidences about to unfold . . . like an introduction to the threads running through the fabric of events, weaving out and around and in and out of life and death and dreams, the stuff of existence itself.

I'd written that May 31 *Observer* column [*Chapter 7*] about the "natural" biology of precognition pretty much off the top of my head (a habit you develop with newspaper work, even on the small weekly level). Now, looking at the ganglion of associations clustered around one August day—associations central to me, though I wondered what other coincidental material could be added by each individual (if all could speak)—I could see that my own top-of-the-head thoughts about all of this were widening out into sideways, into considerable and very evocative speculation on the line between dreaming and waking. What if you looked at your waking life as if it were a dream? What if dream-like associative thinking *is* the natural framework of daily life, thus accounting for the nature of dreams in the first place? I'd congratulated myself more than once on how my dream experiment might be touching and changing some people in Dundee—but how much had Dundee's dreams touched and changed me back? And how far was I willing to go with this "natural biological knowing," anyway?

Again, I asked myself—as I would many times over the years—how far does knowledge reach? If there are no limits to what we know, then how much *is* there to know—and in what form? How complete is any given moment, or any given day full of moments? Where—if anywhere—does intuition stop? Where does intuition leave off and speculation begin?

See Appendix 1 for another type of interconnected dream-series, there involving my friend Jane Roberts and my parents. Since this series runs through my mother's death in 1985 and is therefore somewhat out of this book's context, I placed it in with other Appendices.

NOTES

1 That chapter appears in *Conversations with Seth*, Vol. 2, as Chapter 18: "Who Else Do You Think You Are?—Counterparts Are Comparatively Encountered."

A more thorough explanation of counterparts appears throughout Jane Roberts' works, particularly in *The "Unknown" Reality*, Vol. 1 and 2 (1977, 1979, Prentice-Hall, Inc., Englewood Cliffs, NJ 07632).

"Quite literally, you live more than one life at a time," Seth says of counterparts on page 463, Vol. 2, of *The "Unknown" Reality*. "You do not experience your century simply from one separate vantage point, and the individuals alive in any given century have far deeper connections than you realize . . ."

(p. 464) "The greater self 'divides' itself, materializing in flesh as several individuals, with entirely different backgrounds—yet with each embarked upon the same kind of creative challenge."

Elsewhere in the Roberts works, Seth alludes to the fact that counterparts can "alter affiliations" or change that relationship—hence my remark regarding Joel Hess and me. He and I do share some interesting background and course-of-life associations. According to Seth, Jane Roberts and I are also counterparts, and I think this further applies to Susan Benedict and me. Someday I hope to write more about this idea—from the inside out.

NINE

Dreams That Watch and Listen

Natural Knowing and the Caretaker Self

Brighter days are ahead

(Fortune cookie fortune left unscathed in the ashes of Gloria's parents' house—everything else had burned, including the cupboard, the box the cookie was in . . . and the cookie.)

There it was again—a funny little coincidence involving the newspaper. Just that morning, I'd been talking with my friend Gloria about something I'd dubbed "our natural caretaker self." She'd told me about a vivid dream; one of those that you know you'll never forget; and even though its meaning was obscure to her, the dream had given her comfort in a personally trying time.

"See, it took care of you," I'd said. "I think we always take care of ourselves, even when things seem at their worst—I think your dreams take care of you even when they're nightmares. You get appropriate information, tailored to your needs and capabilities. You're your own caretaker self." We'd gone on to talk about childhood comforts, specifically the religious symbols that had given comfort to Gloria throughout her early years.

"Too bad I outgrew them!" she said. "They sure did work for a while."

"I never had them," I said. "Sometimes I wonder if I missed out on something. I never believed in anything!"

"I sure did," Gloria sighed. "I remember praying to my personal guardian angel as a kid—and the thing is, it worked!" She laughed. "Then I figured out that there wasn't 'any such thing' and it didn't work anymore! Like believing in Santa Claus, I guess."

"Now you have dreams that help out instead," I pointed out.

"True," Gloria replied, "but my guardian angel was a lot simpler. I wouldn't have had to ask you what he was talking about, for one thing! And I can't pray to my dreams, can I?"

"Sure you can," I said, lightly, half joking. "Why not? It all comes from the same place. Ask your dreams anything, they'll tell you."

"Well . . ." she hesitated. "I'll send you a copy of my dream. Tell me what you think—unless it's embarrassing!" Gloria smiled, but she was serious—even a little scared. As though I'd see something awful in her dream, or guess some deep terrible secret she didn't know was revealed there.

I remembered the woman who'd handed me a few of her dreams one day in the local coffee shop—she'd pulled some crumpled, ripped-out notebook pages out of her pocketbook and said, "Just don't tell anybody where these came from," then quickly walked away and out the door. Out of the half-dozen dreams written there, two of them were scenes in a confession booth. "I know these dreams happened because I've been praying to my [*dead*] father instead of God, and I felt so guilty," the woman had scrawled in the margins. Though the dreams, not to mention the prayers, were innocent enough, the woman had been afraid of my reaction—while at the same time realizing the dreams were important, at least enough to show them to me, even furtively. And the dreams *were* important—and caretaking, offering as they did the solace of her childhood religion in a trying time.

Now, sitting at the kitchen table that evening, I'd opened the newspaper right to the classifieds—and there it was, leaping out from the pages:

NOVENA TO ST. JUDE—Oh Holy St. Jude, apostle and martyr, great in virtue and rich in miracles, near kinsman of Jesus Christ . . .

Oh, *brother*, I thought, look at that! Right out of my conversation with Gloria this morning—praying to saints in newspapers! Who wudda thunk it! Ugh!

. . . faithful intercessor of all who invoke your special patronage in time of need, to you I recourse from the depths of my heart and humbly beg who God has given power to come to my assistance . . .

"Aackk!!!" I squawked, rattling the paper impatiently. "Don't hold your breath!! Sheesh!"

. . . Help me in my present and urgent petition. In return I promise to make your name known and cause you to be invoked. Say three Our Fathers, three Hail Marys, and Glorias.

"Sure," I smirked, "let me grovel and beg in print for a few crumbs from the gods! Sure!"

. . . Publication must be promised . . .

I rolled my eyes—Heavenward. "So *that's* the secret of getting published!" I snorted.

"What is?" Sean called from the other room, obviously wondering what in *hell* his mother was muttering about now.

"Promise 'em salvation and they'll put you in print!" I yelled. "Ha! How about putting God on the cover of PEOPLE magazine?! Phooey!"

. . . St. Jude. pray for us and all who evoke your aid. Amen. This Novena has never been known to fail. Publication as promised. Say nine consecutive days . . .

"Humph!" I sneered. "Don't you just wish it were all that easy!"

Yes, a small, snotty inner voice hissed . . . *don't you just wish it were that easy? Don't you?*

"Of course not," I retorted, after a second's hesitation. What kind of nonsense was that, praying for something in the classifieds ads? For one thing the damn ad probably cost $35, and for another . . .

I stopped, annoyed.

"Yes?" Sean said, grinning from the doorway. "What's on your strange little mind now?"

"Nothing!" I growled, slamming the paper down on the table.

The cat, a specimen of perfection, yawned from his perch on the windowsill.

"Fart!!" I yelled. "Why does *my* belief system have to be so god-damned complicated? Why can't *I* just put an ad in the god-damned newspaper and have some god-damned saint pay all of *my* god-damned bills? Huh? Why can't *I* just pray to some guardian angel for what I want?"

"Maybe," Sean offered, patiently, "because you don't really think it will work, and if you did you'd have to be a different person and it wouldn't be irritating you in the first place."

"Oh, shut up," I said, throwing the paper at him. But of course, Sean had caught the question by the punch line. There I was, griping about religious baloney while secretly wishing that I could go along with it! There was something rather sweet and innocent about that newspaper ad; something that I found I craved. Easy, tender answers, maybe. Guileless help, for sure. Knowing that in times of need, we're taken care of by *some*thing, somewhere, that's bigger, wiser, and (ouch!) a whole lot nicer than we are. God, Jesus, St. Jude, modern medicine, astrology, anything . . .

Except that whatever it was, you had to believe in it to make it work.

I thought about the conversation with Gloria that morning. That phrase, "the natural caretaker self," had come to me on the spot—and it fit. It was a good enough term for something people seemed to intuitively understand about a particular dream or dream-series, though they were often hesitant about accepting the idea on their own. My woman friend with the sexy dream, for instance. Or there was the thirteen-year-old girl who'd called me up, very upset, about a dream the night before in which she'd stabbed her older sister with a fork. "Does that mean I'm going to do that?" she'd asked, voice quavering.

"Well, maybe you're mad enough at her to *feel* like stabbing her with a fork," I'd answered, "but knowing you, I really doubt that you would! So instead of actually stabbing your sister, you dreamed about it—sort of like getting to wreak revenge without hurting anybody, see? Like your dream gave you a way to blow off steam."

"Yeah, I see," the girl said. "You know, I thought that was what it was, but I was afraid to tell anybody that I dreamed about murdering my sister! I thought people would think I was crazy or something, because it did make me feel better."

"Naw, you're not crazy," I'd said to her. "There's never any reason to be afraid of your dreams. They helped you out, see? What was the worst you could do to your sister? They let you do it and not do it, see? And since you feel badly about even dreaming it, you're obviously not some sort of monster. Anyway, why don't you try *telling* your sister that you were so mad at her you dreamed about stabbing her with a fork? Maybe it'll break some ice between you."

"Yeah, I kinda thought I would," the girl said. "But I wanted to make sure first it was, you know, okay to dream like that!"

I reassured my friend that almost everybody I knew dreamed at one time or another about eliminating other people, and that unless such dream-scenes became an obsession or were misread as commandments to follow through in waking life, they performed a natural and benign function—and who knows, I thought as I hung up, maybe the stabbing-dream was telling my friend something about her sister's frame of mind, too. (She didn't get back to me, though, so I don't know any more about it.)

Gloria's "caretaking" dream, which had started my thoughts in this direction, had troubled her only in that at first it seemed unfathomable. She'd awakened with a vivid recall of the details and the *feeling* that it was a turning point of some kind, but, she said, she didn't understand it. "It's kind of a mish-mosh of stuff," she told me. "But then I hardly ever know what my dreams mean.

"And maybe," she'd added, humorously anticipating my next remark, "that's because I *think* they're a mish-mosh, huh? Right?"

We laughed together at my own predictability. Later, Gloria handed me a copy of her dream, which I read with utter fascination. All sorts of connections within what little I knew of her private life leaped out at me. And the "caretaking," pivot-point thrust of the dream was indeed right THERE, even for an outsider reading it. I was so enthralled that I wrote up some comments and sent them back to Gloria. All she'd ever say about my remarks was, "That's pretty much what I thought was going on in there," and later she gave me permission to use her dream, and my comments (both in edited form), here:

Gloria's Caretaker Dream

"My dream began with several American citizens, including my mother and myself, being held prisoner in what appeared to be Cuba during a revolution. Our captors planned to use us as slaves, yet we were not actually locked up or treated badly. We were held at gunpoint in regular houses along a beach.

"I remember feeling that only a minority of the prisoners actually understood the severity of our situation, with most of the group acting as if nothing were wrong.

"One slave job, which everyone seemed to accept with no need for force, gave three of us a chance to jump off a shuttle boat to freedom. I called for my mother to join us, but she refused to leave the boat, acting as if she didn't believe she were a prisoner. My companions and I soon learned that our port was also occupied by the revolutionaries. They chased us into some type of stadium where we took a series of very strange escalators to a level deep into the earth . . . We traveled down thousands of steps before we reached our destination: a Victorian house. Once there, the revolutionaries who followed us shot my companions . . . but I was saved by an American CIA agent.

"I wandered around the house and came upon a Christmas party, of all things . . . I saw several young girls having a pajama party. They too were prisoners, although they were not aware of it either. All the girls wrapped themselves in afghans and quilts, preparing to sleep. I noticed that each quilt and afghan had a first-prize ribbon attached to it. I felt very tired and tempted to join them, but before I could, revolutionaries bolted into the room and shot one of the girls. I remember this very clearly, because she had just wrapped herself in a brown and beige afghan and flopped on the bed, the exact thing I had been tempted to do. But as soon as the revolutionaries left, this girl popped up off the bed with no injuries—she was apparently protected by the afghan.

". . . In the next room, a young man sat in an easy chair holding a small (2-3 month) baby. I knew immediately the baby was a boy, and that he was very special, since he looked at me and communicated a peaceful, loving feeling . . . I stared at the child for quite some time, as he communicated with me. The baby performed at an adult intellectual level and moved and acted emotionally older. He emitted an aura of love and peace.

"I walked out a set of French doors to a patio facing the east coast. I could see that I was not in Cuba—was I ever? I was on the eastern shore of Seneca Lake, near the edge of the Seneca Army Depot [*which in recent years has been the site of demonstrations against nuclear arms*].

"I walked a distance and saw several bus loads of prisoners being taken into the depot. I felt they would never leave the depot once they entered, and I sensed the threat of imminent nuclear disaster. As I walked closer, I saw my mother and my sons [*both under five years of age*] on the bus. I then voluntarily joined them . . . Later, a diplomatic corps arrived and I explained the circumstances of the American slaves in Cuba. I was driven to the border of Switzerland and Germany, where a trade was made of depot and German prisoners. I took my sons and mother in one of the black cars owned by the government and went home.

"As soon as the prisoners were exchanged the fear of a nuclear war was gone, but I thought about that infant who seemed to inspire me to help . . .

"Some impressions: I have a fear of nuclear war and of innocent U.S. citizens being caught in political crises in foreign countries. I have some trust in 'G-men,' but I have little regard for upper-echelon diplomats who carry on with life as normal while others are suffering. I am concerned for people who don't heed warnings. And perhaps I have some belief, primitive or otherwise, that something greater (the Lord, a God, some higher Being) will appear and resolve mankind's troubles. The extremely strong feeling of calm, understanding, love, and complete loss of fear after 'communicating' with the infant, for example . . .

"Overall, I experienced a feeling (from this dream) that I can do something to help others in a crisis.???"

My response

"Gloria—I liked your dream. Interestingly, it fits in with a chapter I am working on now for my book.

"I think that at regular stages of one's life, dreams of . . . something like summing-up and forecast . . . are given. You may or may not remember them, but they're there nonetheless. I think it's a way for the person, the personality, the soul and body or whatever, to see where it's 'been' and where, given the ideas, attitudes, and circumstances of the moment, you are headed. Since I think nothing is predestined and each individual is always the center of his reality, I also think that these dreams are a method the individual has of keeping on course; of following one's own purposes and desires. You get a message, in other words, from the part of you that knows what's up.

"I think that's what this dream of yours is. I try not to interpret dreams along the lines of . . . this object means that thing, etc., because number one, I don't think symbols exist in an archetypal sense except in the largest context; and number two, your dream symbols are yours and yours alone, and very intimate, and nobody else can know their true origins (Freud was full of crap in a lot of ways). Also, I know a little about your personal background, so that can get in the way . . . but your dream is obviously a milestone for you, with world-class meaning (fear of nuclear war, contemporary events, re hostages, political strife, etc.). But there is a strong sense of you and your present place in your life and family . . . most of it hidden between the lines for an outsider.

"A dream can be 'about' a world event and at the same time 'about' a personal event. In fact, I think that events are mass-and-private at the same time, one reflecting the other. The part in your dream in which all these people seem to be prisoners without acknowledging it . . . makes me want to say, look at your family life, and your role in it as the woman.

"I remember the first time I met you: A bunch of us reporters were all at the village hall, listening to that assemblyman speak about election-year issues. You were there with both your boys and right in the middle of the assemblyman's speech, your oldest one yelled out that he had to make pee and the baby started to cry, and you had to leave . . .

"I thought you were very brave and I felt great affection and sympathy for you, and for women in general trying to do what they find interesting and also be mothers, wives, stay sane, etc., etc. . . . Anyway, I thought of that scene right away when I read your dream.

"Are women in your mind 'political prisoners' of a sort and don't even know it? Is the CIA man (the 'secret' man, the man whose true intent, or occupation, is unknown) the sort of male you think would be most sympathetic to the 'prisoners?' Remember also that people in your dreams can all be yourself. I also got a feeling about your relationship with your parents, especially your mother, when I read the dream, and I wasn't surprised to see her there . . . getting on the bus calmly, you see, as if nothing were amiss. *You* knew something was wrong with the whole scene and yet you got on the bus too (to become a prisoner of the 'good guys'—how much different is that?) . . . and then fear of war stopped. Does compliance with a womanly role offer the security of avoiding a larger war (like having to buck established attitudes)? The little girls were protected from harm (and from 'revolutionaries,' yet) by wrapping themselves in homemade afghans—in woman's work, maybe.

"The feeling of love and peace from the baby—from the innocent male—is similar to dreams I've had: the hope of being bailed out by wiser beings. I used to have UFO dreams like that (and I think this hope is the origin of some of the UFO sightings, too). That can all be a world hope and a personal one, too.

"I don't know what your relationship is with your husband, but my impression is that you're quietly content but in the usual struggles to maintain your identity. Nothing outrageous in that, but the dream seems to reflect defiance, too. Like I say, interpretation from an outsider is tricky. How does your mother feel about your being married? I always sensed from my mother that she considered marriage to be dangerous—nothing to do with the specific man involved, just the state of marriage itself as a destructive one. I absorbed this belief from her almost without question, and I am still affected enough by it that most of my adult life has been spent without any male partner at all . . . of course, I *chose* to accept that idea for reasons of my own . . .

"The slave job, you see . . . and your mother won't get out of the slave bus . . . and you end up getting on the bus with her (going along with her), where she has your children. A real sense of the inevitable there.

"But aside from flat interpretations, I think this is a dream that you should use in a direction-finding way. I think from the psyche's point of view, you're *meant* to do this. I think it's also reassuring for you; maybe it gives you a sense of rightness and hope, while at the same time showing you where your inner life has come to, or evolved to; where it *could* go . . ."

Not long after this dream, Gloria took a job as a social worker ("helping people") in a nearby county, an occupation unlike anything she was doing at this time.

Fascinated with my "caretaker self" idea, I read back through my collected Dundee dreams and my own dream records and notes I routinely make on the sometimes mind-boggling maze of connections that weave among physical events and dreams. It was fun, if nothing else, to read these over with the thought that there *is* a knowing "caretaker" portion of the self—everyone's self—peeking out from the invisible world with an umbrella perspective on the whole and the sum of all its parts. And that idea seemed to make sense, when I spoke of it, to my Dundee dreamers, too. The old guardian angel tale in different clothes, perhaps—though it seemed like an awfully good tale to tell, refuting as it did all the shopworn dungeons-of-the-Id and evil-of-the-soul hoopla we've fed ourselves for so long.

I wrote up some notes about all of it, feeling pretty smug about my observations. And at that moment, I never would have predicted that my own "caretaker self" would soon burst upon my private life and its bottled-up tangle of unrecognized beliefs and doubts with the force of a *very* impatient hurricane.

TEN

Peculiar Notions, Odd Goings-On

Wayward Windows and A Jolt from the Blue

The nature of reality can only be approached by an investigation of reality as it is *directly experienced* in all levels of awareness: reality as it appears under dream conditions, under other conditions of dissociation, and as it appears in the waking condition. Most studies even dealing with the conscious state are extremely superficial, dealing with only those upper layers of egotistical awareness that are immediately concerned with the manipulation of the self within physical reality.

Seth, speaking in session #211,
November 24, 1965

And so my dream-collecting days marched along, following a natural course of interest and enthusiasm, as I'd assumed they would. I am not a documentor by trade or inclination, and neither were my dreamers. Eventually, the small stream of written dreams appearing in my post office box trickled out and vanished, as all of us went on to other pursuits. The dreams filled a typing-paper box, and I read them over and over, adding my notes and the accounts of things people continued to confide verbally about their "secret" inner lives. It was almost like having a magic lantern, that box of dreams and notes—something seemed to be waiting inside the sheaves of paper, and all I had to do was learn how to pay attention to it, turn my thoughts just *so* towards it, and it would spring into a life of its own. Mentally, I kept polishing my dream-collection, turning it over and around and every which-way, waiting for the good objective reporter's book to leap out and grant my wish to get *going* on it, and soon.

But November of 1980 was a strange and transitional time for me, and somehow my attentions kept getting scattered. I was having great difficulty adjusting to my five-month-old marriage, trying to organize my time around two divergent lifestyles—writing and farming (not to mention showing horses, a whole other world of distractions). For me, the farming side of things basically meant cooking—an art I find annoying and burdensome. As the months went by and my dream notes yielded up nothing in book form, a nasty panic began to tighten its grip and I fell prey to the creative death knell of self-recrimination. Maybe I'd never write anything worthwhile again; maybe I didn't really have it in me; maybe I was just another mediocre talent; maybe I'd wrecked my brain putting down floor-tile cement that time in 1978; maybe I was just a big, stupid, worthless blob of glue myself. Worse, *thinking* these thoughts made me feel stupid—I knew I should know better; knowing I should know better, I recriminated myself. I started to gain weight—a *lot* of weight—fueled by my own frenzied cooking for someone else who, working ten to twelve hours a day at farm chores, could afford to eat the stuff.

To me, it seemed that I'd suddenly (though not without warning) taken on two full-time jobs, and "mine" was becoming more and more expendable; though in fact I did have several hours a day in which I could have been writing, had I been able to quiet the racket of my own internal chaos. Even my dreams, those constant companions and helpmates, felt obscure and dead-ended. "Compact and heavy dreaming," I noted in my records, "a certain *type* of dreaming I haven't experienced before; so many simultaneous layers of dreams that recollection is jumbled and nearly untranslatable. Many people appear who are inappropriately pregnant, especially women who for one reason or another are now sterile." On November 13, part of one of these dreams included this: "Roy and I are scientists of some sort. I see the vast array of such equipment as bottles, beakers, bunsen burners, etc., that we use in our research lab. All of this seems to spring out of some other layer of relationship between us—some connection that doesn't exist in my life as I know it, but could—a definite probability.

"This possible relationship seems to me expressed now in our easy partnership in showing horses, where we operate smoothly and flexibly, trading roles off on one another without needing to explain what goes on. This particularly when we're matching wits with the so-called wheeler-dealer type, who tend to see newcomers in the horse world as the proverbial minute's sucker. We've even managed to make some very profitable sales to these old-time sharpies by using our collective skills in concert. In almost all other circumstances, Roy and I are simply unable to do this." In several other dreams during that time, I'd discover that I had various lethal diseases, but would refuse to deal with these through standard medical techniques; I decided instead to rely on myself and whatever cures I could bring about in my own way, bucking established modes of thought at their roots.

In the midst of this and assorted daily horse, cow, and crop chores, Roy started a complete renovation of the farm's 100-year-old tenant house. This lovely, square-roofed farmhouse was structurally sound and basically intact, but it had been empty for years and needed the works—plumbing, electricity, heating, sheetrock, siding, you name it—to bring it up to date.

That seemed like a big investment until you looked at the place. It was on a dirt road bordering the south edge of the farm, framed by the junction of two creeks and a cattail-swamp; and even though Dundee was less than three miles away, the house inhabited a world all its own in the midst of rustling pines and the calls of herons, ducks, redwings, frogs, and all the other birds and animals populating the creeks and swamp and forested hills beyond. So rather than let such a picturesque place fall into ruin, Roy and I decided to fix it up and rent it out. And even the hazards of rental property had been solved for us by a friend who offered to wire the whole house, put in plumbing, and help with the rest of the work in exchange for a couple of rent-free years there, which was certainly agreeable to us.

That November Monday, the 16th, I decided to walk over to

the tenant house with some soft drinks and see how the work was going. I put on a light jacket and started up the side road that passed by the swamp. It was about 3 p.m. on a mild late-autumn afternoon, the sun golden on the stalks and stubbles of harvested fields and yellow willow trees. Here, I'll copy from notes made in my journal a few hours later:

"As I walked over to the tenant house, I stopped on the creek bridge to look down into the dark green pool formed there by the endeavors of local beavers. As I watched, something beneath the water's surface rippled the pool, sending bubbles and lines wiggling across its dark expanse without revealing itself to me at all. I remember thinking—maybe even speaking aloud—'How like life that is: events just under the surface rippling the moments of your awareness, and you never see those events as they really are.'

"I stood there for a while watching a late-season heron stalking fish on the far side of the swamp; then I went on across the bridge and up to the house. Roy was working inside with our neighbor Ethan Sanders, replacing the worn and ragged window frames. To do this, they had to take the frames out of the casements, place them on sawhorses set up inside the house, and then cut window glass to fit the new frames. Most of the original, 100-year-old glass was still unbroken and Roy had decided to match it with the new. Altogether, a tedious job.

"I want to add here that I paid no attention to the house itself as I approached it—I was too busy looking for birds in the thick creek willows. Later, I would connect the house with the pool of dark water and wonder about the progression of symbolic events—about prescience immersed within the progression of moments, and in apparently meaningless, random thoughts. But walking along then, I wasn't alert for anything except the possibility of seeing an interesting animal or bird cross my path.

"Anyway, I walked in the back door and into the living room, where Roy and Ethan were working ankle-deep in sawdust, old lath knocked from the walls, and general ancient-house clutter. Our friend was down cellar putting in a circuit breaker. 'We're almost done with this part,' Roy said, motioning for me to put the soft drinks down on the floor. 'We'll take a break in a minute but I want to get started upstairs before dark.' Obviously they didn't want to be interrupted, so I wandered upstairs to inspect the progress of lath-bashing there.

"The front bedroom of that house looks right out into a huge old pine tree. It's wonderful—you can hear the wind rushing through that tree from anywhere in the house. So I went into that room first and looked out into the pine branches.

"It was in that second, that instant my gaze hit the windows, that IT happened. I was staring out through a completely different set of window panes. The windows I saw at that moment were shaped like this:

"*BUT IN MY MEMORY,* in my knowledge of that house—and most certainly in my experience as it jolted through me then—*THE WINDOWS WERE SHAPED LIKE THIS:*

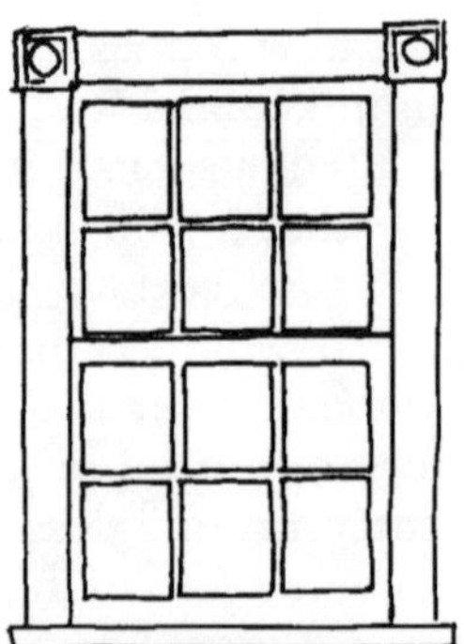

"It was quite possibly the most shocking moment in my life. I stood stock-still, poised on a knife's-edge. The two window-pane shapes were *as one* in my mind. There was no doubt whatsoever that I had looked many times out these windows, into that pine tree, through little square panes of old glass lined with pencil-thin bars of frayed wood. There could also be no doubt that I was now looking through large rectangular panes of old glass lined with thick bars of frayed wood. That simultaneous factual knowledge was so overwhelming that I began to feel dizzy and sick. I ran my hands along the window panes, thinking: It can't be; these windows are *not* like this, never have been, yet—they *are.* The floor seemed to yawn and tilt like a cartoon funhouse. I lost my balance, caught myself—and then ran out of the room and thundered down the newly-built staircase. Roy and Ethan looked up, startled.

"'Roy,' I said too loudly, trying to act nonchalant, 'did you replace all those windows up there already?'

"Of course I knew he hadn't. Roy scowled at me. 'No, I told you we hadn't been up there yet,' he said, but I couldn't let it go—because by then I'd noticed that all the windows downstairs had . . . done . . . the same . . . *thing.*

"'Did you change all the window panes?' I asked. 'Didn't these all used to be a lot of little squares? Didn't they?'

"'No,' Roy said slowly, 'they've always been like this—what's the matter with you?'

"By then, I was really disoriented. I was actually staggering with this whirling assault on my logical underpinnings. I went into the back room and the same dual memory enveloped me: the windows had . . . changed. Momentarily, I had the crazy idea that if I ran outside fast enough, I'd catch those windows before they 'changed' into this pattern—that I'd find the nine-group panes. I *KNEW* those windows had been made in little squares and had been in that house for a hundred years, looking out over the valley. Yet of *course* the windows had always been as I saw them now. *And I remembered both sets of windows being there! Both sets at once!* I felt as though I were falling forward, into a liquid landscape swirling like viscous water, around and around, funneling toward—toward what? Toward the reality I already inhabited?

"Of course, I knew what the official explanation had to be for all of this: That I'd somehow confused these windows with some other windows and transposed that memory onto this house. An unconscious transference, for some hidden reason of my own. *But the emotional impact of what I was seeing*—the overwhelming, disorienting impact of two simultaneous, co-existing memories—sent another recognition through me. I *knew* that I had somehow caught an intersection of probabilities; an intersection literally and symbolically reflected in those old windows; and that it had started with, or sprung from, my musings over the dark green pool in the swamp-creek moments before.

"I *knew* this was what happened—yet as I stood there, feeling as though I'd just stepped off a playground carousel, my mind raced two ways at once. I thought, I'm confused, the dairy barn has some small-paned windows in it; that's where I got that image. But on the other hand, I *knew*—I knew with that sure, gut knowledge that *knows*—that I wasn't confused; that I'd consciously experienced something that goes on naturally, beneath our recognition, all the time.

"Also, I realized that I was beginning to feel something else going on: the fading-out of the 'history' included with those nine-paned windows and the 'intrusion' or fading-*in* of the 'memories' associated with the wider-paned windows. *I felt the intrusion of 'always,' of the 'history' connected with the wide-paned windows,* and I *felt* that intrusion building up into the logical sequence of events as it affected my personal memory. Of *course* these large-paned windows had always been there. *But I still contained the 'other' set of facts around those tiny window panes.* Yet I realized that to insist upon their existence at this point would be tantamount to slipping some major mental gears. Already, Roy was watching me with a strained look on his face—had his wife gone nuts? And I had to ask myself: were my powers of observation fractured, *was* I running on half a track? The previous few days had been loaded with emotional turmoil, including the on-farm butchering of a young cow that couldn't stand up after calving. (I hid in an upstairs closet the whole time, crying, vowing never to eat meat again, cursing myself for being a member of the human species; while ten-year-old Sean, fascinated by the procedure, delivered periodic enthusiastic reports: "Boy, Mommie, you should see what they found in her stomach!" and "Wow, her intestines were long enough to wrap around the *whole house!*") Briefly, it flashed through my mind that all of this was interconnected; that this thing with the windows was an answer to . . . to what? Some buried, unfaced darkness in my psyche? But no other facets of my daily life were shattered—only this weird window superimposition, like a TV program melting in from another channel.

"I remembered that this sort of thing happened once before—a minor thing, many years ago. I'd come home from college to find a different doorknob on my parents' kitchen door (hmmm, entranceways . . .). Naturally, they insisted that it was the one that had always been there. I finally gave in, of course—I shrugged it off as a transposition of the knob on my dormitory room door, or something.

"Still, then—as now—I'd always felt secretly that in fact—in some realm of 'fact'—*it really was a different doorknob.* And that little incident had also been preceded by a time of powerful emotional turmoil. I'd been obliged to spend that summer in college making up for the spring semester, which I'd missed because I'd been seriously ill with meningitis . . .*

"Humph. It occurred to me, as I stood there in that old house, that this whole experience was exactly like a double dream.

---

*Other such experiences are described in Appendix 2.

I had two sets of information, two sets of experience, two sets, in effect, of existence, both with sequential histories—all focused on those windows. The disorientation I'd felt was fading, although it still washed over me in waves. Roy and Ethan kept glancing my way. What in *hell* was I doing, wandering around muttering about windows? It was funny, in a way—what language existed to explain this? 'Don't mind me, I'm just watching a couple of probabilities intersect here; apparently the molecules multiplied by division right where the windows happened to be and then one set flew off into inner space and left us here with the other set, and so the four of us just broke off from our other selves and took a right-hand turn in reality . . .'

"I left for home, my brain in a buzz—and as I put distance between me and the tenant house, the existence of those little nine-paned windows took on the feeling of a half-forgotten dream. As soon as I got back, I opened our photograph album to pictures taken that summer of the tenant house. As I expected, the windows were the large-paned ones. Just to make sure, I dug out some photos taken of the old place when Roy was a child on this farm. Yep—large-paned windows. The official history of the house was what it was. Either I was knocking around inside some rather loose circuits, or the past had changed, backwards, in that shocking moment I'd looked out the upstairs windows, an explanation that would be regarded by most people as pure science fiction, at best."

But I trusted my intuitive responses, and had never known them to lead me astray . . . *if* I paid attention to them, that is. *Something* had happened that afternoon; and if it were a pivotal turn in probabilities—if this was the physical expression of how probabilities emerge—then where did I *go*? Was I the same "me," but now living in a parallel physical world? Or was I a different "me" altogether, my conscious self now focused in a parallel Sue? (Had the world come to an end while I was standing in the tenant house; had the new furnace blown up and sent us all . . . somewhere; was death really just the blink of an eye and there you were, whole and only slightly dazed?) I felt like the same me—certainly similar enough to the previous me to give all of this an abundantly unconventional explanation. Was I now taking a "wider view," literally and symbolically; had the upsets of the past few days pushed me toward a less constricted "outlook?"

As I sat there contemplating this—one eye on the clock as dinnertime approached—my mind reached magnet-like back to the last time I'd seen Jane and Rob Butts, a day or two before Roy and I were married. Jane and Rob and I sat in their living room for several hours, drinking beer, reminiscing about class years, talking about her forthcoming *God of Jane* and its ideas and impulse experiments. The evening was filled with ghosts of myself, with whispers of things that part of me—the scared part—wanted to ignore. I kept telling myself that I was choosing a marriage in which I'd be safe; where I could write and be eccentric and psychic and peculiar and the farm would give me a strong framework to rattle around in, satisfy my powerful love for animals, and protect me from . . . from what? I skittered away from the question. At that point in my life, I was weary of such questions; I wanted to give up asking them, and just be safe. (Safe from . . .??) The answers were often too painful and embarrassing, for one thing. And as I got up to leave that evening and turned to say good-bye to Jane and Rob, something happened to the room around us. It seemed as though the circle of light given off by the table lamps scoped to a tunnel; and as I looked at them, Jane and Rob receded, back and back, smaller and smaller, into a tiny circle of light far away at the other end—at the other end of the world. A huge rush of sadness washed through me, as though I were saying good-bye for longer than a few weeks . . . as though I were leaving them in the truest sense for good, for the rest of my present life. A strong impulse to call off the marriage zipped through my skull like a laser. I immediately disregarded it as a silly case of nerves. In fact, I shrugged the impulse off without even mentioning it to them or consciously considering its meaning—something completely uncharacteristic of our friendship, to say the least.

It was the last time the three of us would gather together in that exhilarating, exuberant playfulness that I had once taken quite for granted. And so I wondered, that November afternoon as I looked aimlessly through the photo albums at pictures of horses and foals and fields and flowers, what might have been if I'd followed through with those impulses in Jane and Rob's living room. Certainly I wasn't blaming the marriage, or marriage in larger terms, for this vortex of swirling, unnameable feelings—but my present state was most assuredly involved with my *choices*, and subsequent directions and assumptions; and with my just-dawning sense of my own peculiar characteristics and abilities which often *seemed* to isolate me so painfully—up until that Dundee dream-collection experiment, that is. And in some way it was all connected to the windows in the tenant house. Something was pushing up through that afternoon's events; some . . . natural knowledge that I didn't want to deal with, but which was moving into my consciousness nevertheless. The thought came to me, as it would later many times, that urges and desires break free from you even if "you" don't follow them.

Somehow or other, the tenant house windows were *mirrors* of possibilities and directions uniquely mine; mirrors of the dichotomy of denial and recognition with which I treated myself. And if you do indeed create your own reality, then mine had been marked that afternoon by a display obviously meant to rock me to the core of my senses.

"I get the feeling," I wrote later in my dream journal, "that each moment is much *fuller* than we sense, even in 'ordinary' physical terms; and that people, places, and events exist within our experience that we simply don't perceive because we've taught ourselves to look straight ahead, as it were. But our senses are really equipped to experience *fatter* moments, or more data in a sideways fashion. Except that our heritage has trained us to blank out the 'unofficial' portions of our sensory apparatus, we could live in a more inclusive physical moment, with more going on inside it.

"Sometimes, usually in dreams, I get the feeling that there exist scores of people and events that I knew in my past—except that they aren't part of officially recognized history; that they dwell in those portions of the moment lying just on the edge of my perceptions and so exist now only as memories in dreams . . . and in those powerful convictions I have upon awakening that these people and events *did* exist in my life as I know it . . ."

I can't say that my life changed direction from that November day on, although during the next year or two, I would face some deep, difficult, and often frightening belief patterns that ultimately led to the healing-up of my most basic psychological rifts. (For one thing, as far as I can tell, The Woman vs. The Writer dilemma is now mostly done with.) In other words, I believe that one of the reasons—perhaps the main reason—I propelled myself into my second marriage involved the intense daily interaction, literally and symbolically, with issues that I think I either had to solve or die, in certain terms. And the turning point in my inner decision to face these issues—which concerned not only my womanhood and my creative abilities, but also my (very complicated) ideas of worthiness as an individual and as a human creature, and, yes, my "vision" of hope and possibility—materialized in the months that followed that odd dissociation in the old tenant house.

Whatever else that experience might have been, it served to jolt me loose from a kind of somnambulistic framework I'd taken on—rocking me right off my mental feet in that respect, opening the *windows* in my psyche that I'd attempted to close for the sake of what I believed, then, to be an irresolvable conflict between my most "peculiar" self and the "practical" world.

It's this kind of experience that I looked for in the "random thoughts" of my Dundee dreamers (much to the dismay of E., as you recall). For I think that many clues to one's *natural knowing* can be found in events we normally ascribe to random, silly thoughts sliding through our heads like childhood fairy-tales or (*gasp*) dreams.

Of course in daily practical terms, such thoughts, peculiar momentary notions and funny, eye-catching goings-on (if we perceive them at all) many times seem to go nowhere and mean exactly nothing. And common sense *is* the final arbitrator; we *do* have to maintain a solid, practical framework. But if we could learn to at least momentarily suspend our ideas of how things *are* and examine subjective experience with a playful sense of adventure, I think that it is the recognition in *itself* of these quirks and oddities (like the recognition of impulses) that matters—and that may even be at the root of a complete change in conscious awareness, both for us as individuals and on a larger scale.

Because for me, at least, such oddities were about to shove me into the path of conscious self-awareness . . . whether I liked it or not.

ELEVEN

Messages from the Deep

Animals and the Unconscious Exchange

On May 28, 1978, four fishermen—Kobus Stander and his son Barend, from Boston Estate; Wessel Matthee, from Parrow; and Mac McGregor, from Maitland—were lost in a dense fog off Dassen Island, South Africa. Four dolphins appeared and swam around their boat until they changed course—just in time to avoid running into rocks that protruded above the water but were invisible because of the murk. The dolphins nudged and bumped the boat until it reached calm waters, where they blocked it from going further until the men dropped anchor. Then the dolphins swam away. When the fog lifted, the men found themselves in the very bay from which they had set out earlier.

—from *"Nine True Dolphin Stories"*
collected from the AP wire service

When I learned to invent music at eye level with a gobbling tom turkey, I seem to have stumbled upon a basic reality of the natural world. This I now call *natural wisdom.*

Jim Nollman
Animal Dreaming: The Art and Science of Interspecies Communication

Roy's oldest mare had given birth that spring to a handsome blanketed bay colt. Except for the fact that she was blind in her left eye, old Suzie at 22 was strong and healthy, the undisputed top horse in the pasture pecking order. She was wily and stubborn, too—and as far as we knew, nobody had ever tried to put a saddle on her in all the years since her undated birth out on the Colorado Platte River basin. Riding her wasn't important to us; she was halter-trained, and that was enough. It was precisely this gently wild, streetwise nature that attracted me to the old girl—I found myself spending a lot of time coaxing her to a bucket of oats, and before long she was calmly munching grain while I patted her neck and sides.

Had I not managed to nudge Suzie into this oat routine, I suppose I wouldn't have noticed a few days after her foal's birth that her good eye was clouding over just like the other one. (Later I wondered what the course of events would have been if I'd just left her alone.) I yelled at Roy to come take a look at her, but I already knew what it was. The old-timers called it "Moon Blindness," and however it was caused, it was permanent.

There was still some color left in the mare's good eye, though, so hoping against hope, we rushed to the house and (quite on impulse) called an area veterinarian who was, we'd heard, a horse specialist. He told us to get Suzie in the barn, out of the sun, and that he'd be there in a couple of hours.

A couple of hours! I was sick with fear that poor Suzie would be stone blind by the time he arrived, but rather than hang around her stall worrying, I decided to go sit in my workroom, calm myself, and see if I could send her some healing energy—anything was better than staring into that dimming eye.

Within seconds of relaxing in my desk chair, I was flooded with an uncomfortable, sweaty-humid sensation, as though it were a sticky July afternoon. Mentally, I saw myself standing on the shore of a vast, opaque lake. No birds sang in the nearby trees; no insects or fish rumpled the absolutely smooth surface of the water before me. Somehow I knew that the lake was *too full*—those words were emphatic—and far too warm.

And my image-self knew that this lake was my interpretation of Suzie's eye. So I then saw myself touching the edge of the water with a sharp stick. Instantly, warm, milk-like water gushed out of the lake and the ballooned appearance of its surface began to relax. A blue jay screamed out a warning and I came to—blue jays screaming in the trees outside my window. I looked at the clock. Not even five minutes had elapsed.

"Well now, wasn't that cute," I mumbled to myself. At least I hadn't lost my imaginative abilities where the Alpha state was concerned.[1] But could such a thing actually heal a nearly-blind eye? Intuitively and intellectually, I understood that healing energy was capable of fixing anything. But what I *felt* was distrust of something so phantasmagorical as meditative dream-tales. Not only was that just too easy, but who in their right mind would call the vet back and tell him never mind, the horse had been fixed up with brain waves? Not me! I was still terrified for Suzie—vivid Alpha hadn't changed that. If the mare went blind, that would be the end of this sturdy, proud old lady, because we'd agreed that we wouldn't keep a blind horse alive just to get foals out of her—we wouldn't force her to live as "less than a horse," as we put it. I wanted the vet there, and I wanted him there *now*.

Finally, the veterinarian drove in and parked his big truck up next to the barn. We ran to greet him. I noticed right away that he was young, bearded, hip-looking—everything that I automatically associated with unofficial philosophies. Until he opened the truck door and swung out. Following him from his radio like a river of corn syrup was the sappiest piece of religious music I'd ever heard in my life. My childhood upbringing woke up in its crib and screamed bloody murder: An *educated person* was listening to this slop??? Yuccckkkk!!!

Yet, Doc was confident and compassionate, and over the seasons we found that he'd drive to the farm any time of the day or night, no matter how busy he was or how minor the problem. That day, he took one look at Suzie and declared that yes, she was indeed going blind. But rather than do nothing, he injected her with a massive dose of steroids that might, he said, disperse the fluids in her eye and bring back some vision in it. And within a few hours, her eye did start to clear up. Later, I would connect my Alpha experiment with this remedy and wonder—briefly, feeling silly—which technique had really been the effective one? How could you tell for sure? But for all practical and logical purposes, the miracle was Doc's, and his religious persuasions—he announced right away, and many times thereafter, that he was a Born-Again Christian—were entirely *my* problem, as it were.

The puzzle for me as I got to know Doc during the next few years was that he really had no faith at all in anything that you might suppose would be God's. He didn't believe that anything could heal itself unassisted—particularly not animals; in his book, creatures without souls. ("I'm put here to be kind to the dumb beasts," he said more than once; and only because Farm Rule #1 says that you *never* piss your veterinarian off did I bite my tongue and smile.) Doc's true faith was in the medicines and chemicals brewed up by humans (most of them not even born-again, I thought wickedly) in some distant laboratory—and most of all in two of the newest laboratory developments: steroids and the "miracle drug" DMSO.[2] He injected steroids into everything, including himself, at the slightest provocation; and in his life, there were many provocations. One medical disaster after another sent members of his family rushing to area hospitals, where Doc was always in a wrangle with the M.D.s about diagnosis and technique, mainly because everybody else was too chicken to use steroids. I think that in his way—and out of honest convictions—Doc regarded the body—anything's body—as a kind of petri dish, where all you had to do was spread the problem a little thin with one miracle drug and then annihilate it with massive doses of another. Natural healing capabilities could not compete with disease. And he treated any such possibilities with great sweet disdain. "Oh, you girls," he'd admonish with a smile whenever I brought the subject up. If his religion was indeed an answer to a mechanized universe, Doc had ironically found a mechanistic lore all his own.

I did have to ask myself what kind of curmudgeon I was turning into, though, panning Doc's Christian sweetness as I did. At least his disposition was predictably cheerful, which was more than mine would have been, confronted all day with animal suffering most often brought on by human stupidity. But then for the hell of it I'd turn the TV to the Christian network and watch, fascinated, while one bright, cheery, sweet person after another told bright, cheery, sweet stories about miracles afforded them by God. All they'd had to do, said these happy, happy, happy people with the perfect hairdos and mannequin makeup, was just stop making decisions, turn their brains over to the Lord, and that was that. Everyone smiled. Everyone smiled and smiled and SMILED. Nastily, I thought of Faith Godwin and hubby smiling like greasy Cheshire cats while selling us their pre-packaged psychic answer-sheet . . . how rude of me to compare, of course, with the CBN minister's cheerful speech admonishing his audience to pray for his network, the world, and themselves—IN that order. After all, Christians were pure of heart and motive, were they not? Doc himself had informed me, cheerfully, one afternoon, that born-agains were the only people he considered trustworthy enough to hire as office help. Well, I thought, chances are his employees would at least smile all the time and not do anything silly like use their own brains to make decisions . . .

Still, Doc had expressed some pretty outlandish Christian-hierarchy animal-worthiness notions, including the sternly-delivered statement that he wouldn't minister to any of the "lower primates" because monkeys "gave diseases to humans." Apparently, this rose out of a highly charged religious extrapolation that made monkeys evil and disgusting by virtue (so to speak) of their association, by default, with evolutionary premises—even if you weren't supposed to believe in the theory of evolution to begin with. "Then what about humans who give diseases to animals?" I asked, trying to tease Doc into some sort of playful dialogue. His response was to hand me a righteously indignant look and his bill for the day's farm call.

But later that day, alone in my workroom, I had to ask myself how much "faith" *I* really had in natural healing abilities and in the validity of my own subjective experience. About as much, I had to admit, as I'd accused Doc of lacking from the other direction. I'd shrugged my Alpha-healing efforts off as a waste of time and looked frantically to the steroid injection as the only practical avenue left to all of us—Suzie included. The thing was, I didn't really believe that outside solutions worked unless the individual involved had solved the difficulty from its internal source. Except for explicit emergency fix-ups, medical procedures offered no security to me whatsoever. And unlike Doc, I had absolutely no use for Theism and attendant myths. So what was left?

I stared down into the void of that question and realized with a thump! of cold terror that there was *nothing* left—nothing but that small whisper of intuitive *knowing*, partly mine from birth, partly learned from ESP class days, vaguely reinforced in dreams and in my writing, that the only answer possible was the natural knowing authority of my own stubborn self.

"Shit-too," I sighed. "Who the hell am *I*?"

Nobody answered. The next morning, we found old Suzie dead in her stall, her poor blind eye, thick as milk, buried in the sweet straw's darkness; her orphaned foal standing forlornly beside her. Sometime in the night, she'd caught a leg in between the stall slats and apparently thrashed about wildly, eventually twisting a gut. A terrible death, trapped in the stall where we'd taken her to be "saved."

"We should have left her out in the field with the others," Roy said miserably. "She'd be blind but the end wouldn't have come to her this way."

"Maybe she did it on purpose," I mumbled. Roy didn't respond. He felt terrible, of course. And how much worse an end can artificial efforts bring upon a creature, I wondered silently. What if—just imagine what if—things were such that we'd relied upon the energies in my Alpha-trance and we *had* chosen to leave

Suzie out in the pasture—left her alone, as it were, to decide for *herself* how the Moon Blindness would affect her. Could the results have been any worse?

But of course you can't do that, I told myself—of course you have to go for help when a crisis arrives; of *course* you have to turn to veterinary (or medical) science for help. Like my disgust with religion, my suspicions about technology were my own, after all—and I couldn't force suffering on any creature to prove my own half-formed notions. And nobody but (I suppose) a complete idiot would advocate turning a collective back on the benefits of 20th-century medicine. Still, I couldn't get over the feeling that we'd interfered in a natural process that Suzie had agreed to with an understanding we didn't have (or refused to see). There was no way to know, however. You chose an action and experienced the results. "Natural" and "unnatural" processes became meaningless—the action was always a part of the creatures involved.

Why do you make everything so complicated? I groaned inwardly, echoing a gripe I'd heard before from family and friends. *Things are just the way they are, and that's the way it is. Why look for all this hocus-pocus??*

I found myself thinking that now I was the only untamed critter left on the whole damn farm—no wonder I'd loved that old mare so much. She'd never apologized for what *she* was, however.

And besides . . . and besides. There in my notebooks, like cracker crumbs in my bedsheets, was another of those odd, entwining progressions of events involving Suzie, and Sean, and . . . eyes, and all sorts of emotional issues. Just a few weeks before Suzie's foal was born, I'd noticed that several of the fish in my tank had developed revolting cataract-like growths on their eyes, something I never saw before, or again, in my aquarium.

Five days later, according to my notes, Sean, then twelve, accidently snapped his friend Jeff in the eye with a slingshot—fortunately not hurting Jeff seriously, although that was the end of slingshots around the house. But two days after that, *Jeff* accidently hit *Sean* in his left eye with a bicycle flagpole—landing Sean in an Elmira hospital, blindfolded and totally inert for ten days, while his iris, hemorrhaged by the blow, healed up. I'd felt a certain understandable panic upon seeing Sean's injury, of course—I'd never imagined that the *blue* part of his eye could fill up with blood as it did—and, feeling glum, I stopped over at Jane and Rob's on the way home from the hospital after admitting Sean and having to leave him there, alone, it seemed, in the clutches of philistines. The three of us talked at length about it and my fears lightened up a bit. A day or two later, Jane called me to describe an intriguing Alpha-type image she'd gotten on Sean's injured eye—along with the feeling that everything would be just fine.

". . . I saw a sparkling clear . . . image, though at first I didn't know what it was," Jane later wrote of the incident in *The God of Jane*. "The visual data itself simply showed many dark red-brown clumps, rather large, interspersed with strings of the same color, surrounded on the left by a curved white area. In the beginning I thought I might be looking at red clumps of foliage that formed islands; but viewing them from above. Then I realized that the clumps were blood clots, seen as if through a microscope . . . the white curved area somehow advanced on the red clumps and strings, and they began to disperse. They looked as if they were being eaten away at the edges. As I saw this happen, I 'knew' that the necessary healing process had begun . . ."[3]

Doctors said it was "amazing" that Sean didn't suffer a detached retina; but his eye healed without complications. I don't believe I ever had a chance to tell Jane and Rob about the quite similar imagery I'd picked up in the Alpha state on Suzie's eye condition, or the strangely related series of incidents that gathered together that spring like clouds before rain. While Sean was recovering from that mishap and Roy and I were trying to maintain a round-the-clock feeding schedule for the orphaned foal (which we soon gave away to folks better set up than we were for this sort of thing), Roy's golden retriever, Goldie, ran in front of a car and was knocked end over end into the ditch—but upon examination by the veterinarian was found to have no injuries other than *a detached retina in her left eye.*

A few days later, another note was struck in this strange concert of associations when one of my Dundee dreamers confided some highly charged personal history to me over a cup of coffee in the local restaurant. The information involved an inherited optic disease and its effect on the person's *left* eye. My friend had known about Sean's accident (which was the take-off point in our conversation for these revelations) but wasn't aware of the other incidents.

A fascinating coincidence of event and image—all of which I noticed, in silence, wondering (as I would again, later, in the swirl of other, even more startling animal coincidences) what subtle communication was going on here; what messages of birth and death, in healing and loss, in trust in what the Self really *was*. Two days after Sean returned from the hospital, Roy woke up to discover his right eyeball mysteriously swollen to such proportions that it bulged from the socket. The condition disappeared by itself within a couple of days.

I'll add here—just for the sake of speculation—that soon after Goldie's accident (and partly because of it), I gave one of her puppies to Al and Adrienne S., an incident I connected as an "aside" in the footnotes for Chapter 5 with the "puppy" dream involving reassurance to me that the universe *can* take care of itself . . . And that (also as described in Chapter 5) it would be the *right* side of Roy's head kicked in the accident-to-come involving the horse; his *right* eye that bulged in such terrible anger when the filly's hoof connected with his skull . . .

Again, how far does coincidence reach? How complete is the webwork of our days?

I'd always noticed a strong connection in my dreams (and also in the dreams turned in to me by my Dundee dreamers) between animals and precognition. Of course animals have a long-standing symbolic heritage in the psychology of dreams and personality. But when I came in daily farm contact with animals of various temperaments and personal importance (particularly our horses), I began to suspect that something else was going on here; some odd sort of *exchange* that, once again, our linear-logic thinking automatically makes invisible. As I watched, and let my mind ramble along the piquant relationship between my dreams and my association with the animals, I began to pull together some notes about this . . . exchange. I couldn't help but notice how the daily contact and crises with the animals fit right in with all the other galumphing goings-on, not to mention my personal hassles—how they always *had* fit in that way, in fact; creating a strange balance in which the creatures around me seemed to give and take, symbolically and literally, in an intricate cooperative network.

At least in my hopeful moments, that's how I interpret what my records evoke.

Waneta was a big, rugged seven-year-old mare that I considered "mine" even though she and Missy, her half-sister, had been Roy's first Appaloosa horses years before I came on the scene. Nearly seventeen hands tall, Waneta was gentle and placid, colored like a copper penny with a big copper-spotted white blanket on her rump. Roy loved horses and understood them with a quiet confidence—he and his father had used workhorses on the farm up into the 1950s—but I was less sure of myself around them: their knife's-edge readiness to bolt and run radiated to me likc a fire siren, and I could never quite relax. But Waneta—well, Waneta was special (every horse lover finds one that is). Besides her quiet temperament, Waneta was a natural pacer, which meant that riding her was as comfortable as sitting in a gently swaying train seat. (In

Appaloosas, this pace is called the "Indian Shuffle" and for some reason is considered undesirable by the breed registry.) She never jumped or shied at anything while I was riding her, and she tolerated my non-existent equestrian abilities with dignity. But she and the more fiery-tempered Missy provided Roy and me with far more than a couple of nice riding horses. We poured all of our emotional energy into them. They (and the show horses we later purchased) occupied our thoughts and conversations to the exclusion of nearly everything else. And whenever a discussion began to border on certain "dangerous" areas—particularly those areas involving my "peculiar" interests—we would smoothly slide back into the horse world, often repeating word for word to one another dialogues we'd had many times before, like a reassuring litany of avoidance.

On cool summer evenings, crickets rasping in the grass and frogs honking distantly in the pond's mist, Roy and I would walk out into the pasture and call the mares' names and watch the two of them burst out of the creek willows and gallop directly for us, pounding the earth like a herd of hell's own demons. Roy would stand absolutely still, as I would beside him; and in those moments that it took for the mares to thunder down upon us, a whirlwind of emotion would roar through us like the wind, and I knew without doubt, knew with a certitude that ripped the nonsense from theories of multitudinous lives, that other selves of Roy's and mine were alive, now, rising up within us, and that we were acting out some lost time and place, like an echo of those others from long ago; and I would think, "If only we could take off across the plains and brave the unknown together, everything would be all right." And the mares' strong, dark odor would hit me in the face, and they would be right on us—and every time, they turned aside at the last second, brushing our clothing as delicately as a whisper, kicking and biting at one another in a frenzy of excitement that never once touched us. It was the only mystical experience that Roy and I ever shared, and we could never acknowledge it. The horses symbolized everything we would never be able to articulate, and in particular, they symbolized our own relationship—what existed between us, and as emphatically, what did not.

I couldn't see in those days how the horses acted as lightning rods for my beliefs—beliefs that I was forcing myself to face at last. Ultimately, it was a follow-all-impulses experiment that brought all of this interior business to light, but only recently have I fully understood how the farm tragedy that befell Waneta gave me the insight to extricate myself from an overwhelming identification with the horses—with the *female* horses—and start mending the congenital rip in my psyche that had consumed so much of my energy for so long. And it is Waneta's story that comes to mind when I speak of the "unconscious exchange"—hers and the others I've included here—and of the notion that we have to throw out our old ideas about animals, and by inference, about ourselves. We tend to think of animal consciousness—if we think of it at all—as an easily definable thing, with some minor divisions by species: one cat, you say, is basically like any other cat; any horse acts in a certain way under certain conditions, so the pony in your backyard is just as horsey as the Lippizaner performing its fancy disciplined dances. Or: You can't change human nature, so why try? And so we apply the same rules to ourselves, and erase hints of an earthy exchange system that goes on, perhaps with great mutual tenderness, beneath our preconceived rhythms of activity.

We bred Waneta and Missy to our old stallion, timing things so they'd foal in the spring of 1981. At seven and nine years, they were somewhat older than most maiden mares at first foaling, but they were big and healthy and the veterinarian gave us the go-ahead; nobody expected any problems.

By early 1981, I was also busy with galley edits for Volume 2 of *Conversations,* due out that September. To free up some extra time, I hired a friend of mine from the village to clean house for me once a week. Nora was 25 (just ten years younger than I was) and expecting her first baby in late March. In many ways, Nora reminded me of myself at that age—and uncomfortably sometimes, of myself in the present moment. She was an aspiring writer who worked diligently at it; and though unpublished, she had tremendous perseverance and had managed to strike up a regular correspondence with a respected editor at one of the larger publishing companies. He encouraged her to keep sending him material for comment. I was impressed by Nora's coup—it was far more "establishment" encouragement than I'd ever received (witness those disgusting book reviews for Volume 1 of *Conversations,* I grumped). But herein was the rub: Nora confided to me that her husband resented the time she took out of her day for writing, and she'd had to pack most of her work away to keep the peace. I flew into an instant rage over this, roaring like a wounded lion in her defense; but Nora shrugged it off as all part of "learning to be a wife and mother," a statement that sent me into such paroxysms of anger that I nearly threw up. Later, I had to ask myself where such an extreme reaction *came* from, for god's sake. Why should Nora's problems send me into such a tizzy? (Even then, thinking about it, I was furious all over again.) Could it be that some unresolved beliefs of *mine* were involved? But I wouldn't go any further with it; I didn't want to face it. Face what? I stared into my typewriter keys, near-strangers to me these days. Were women *never* free from this sort of thing?? Was the mind forever trapped by the womb, and vice versa?

On the morning of Tuesday, January 27, 1981, I recorded the following dream: "I am with Nora M. in her house when she starts having labor pains. At first they are 20 minutes apart, although they seem to strain her a lot—dreadfully so, in fact. I tell her to relax and breathe with them, but then the contractions come faster and last two minutes at a time. This seems all wrong, all bollixed up and unnatural. I realize that she is not at all prepared for the ordeal of labor—and that she has to get to the hospital *fast,* or she will die. I make a long-distance call to her husband, and then I get Nora into a car and get to the hospital.

"But when I get there, they won't take us into 'maternity emergency,' whatever that is; they make us wait at the regular admissions desk, in a long line. Nora curls up on the floor in agony and starts to thrash around. I'm pretty disgusted with bureaucracy and I crab at everyone until they finally take her into the delivery room. She's having an awful time . . . the baby is way too big and is ripping her. Her husband doesn't show up. Finally, after much pain—which I also begin to feel—Nora gives birth to a girl."

The next morning, my friend D. stopped by unexpectedly to pick up some horse transfer forms. She brought along her two-month-old son, whom I'd never seen. D. had suffered a terrible delivery with some rough handling by doctors after many hours of agonizing labor, all culminating in a C-section; eight weeks later, D. was still in a kind of delayed shock. She sat at the kitchen table for nearly an hour, drinking coffee and talking about that experience.

"Nothing I read about childbirth could have prepared me for that," D. stated. "Nothing could have helped—it was just incredible."

"It certainly was," I agreed, thinking guiltily of my previous night's dream with its—aha!—apparent foreshadowing of this conversation.

The next day, January 28, Nora came to the house and said that she'd have to forgo cleaning that week, as she'd fallen downstairs the day before, (January 27), hurting her back. She'd immediately called her doctor to ask if she could come in for a checkup, but the doctor reassured her that as long as Nora wasn't spotting or having cramps, she was okay. Then Nora and I somehow got into a lengthy discussion about the details of childbirth; and listening to her, I thought—awake, this time—that she seemed completely and innocently unprepared for it. Well, I mused, maybe that's the way it has to be. If women *knew*, humans wouldn't have gone beyond the first generation.

It was funny, though, how the incidents with D. and Nora tied into my dream of the 27th—another of those little tidbits of precognition; a little witticism from my unconscious, showing me how clever dreams can be.

As the time approached for Missy and Waneta to have their foals—due respectively on the 7th and 21st of March—our anticipations, and my dreams, boiled over with speculations. We spent countless hours ruminating on what color the foals might be, what we were going to name them, how we would compete with them, et cetera, et cetera, et cetera. Oddly, at this same time, Sean's dreams turned into hideous nightmares, populated with black furry monsters and terrifying metallic clanging sounds. "But lots of times the black rabbit comes," Sean told me. "He's a giant black rabbit with cat's eyes, and when he's there, he looks at me and I can wake up any time I want to. Sometimes I just see his ears, like from a second-floor window, and I can wake right up."[4] But his nightmares went on and on. Maybe it was a stage; they eventually stopped. However, Sean's feelings about the horses were exactly opposite from mine: he disliked and feared them and expressed great disgust at the energy that Roy and I burned in the horse world.[5]

On Friday, February 27, 1981, I recorded a grisly dream from the night before in which I saw Waneta standing up against the wall of the horse barn, straining to push her foal out. In the dream, the foal was coming out backwards (hind legs first), with one leg caught sideways. The foal was solid black and covered with blood. Somehow, Waneta walked across the road by the barn and up into the tenant house driveway. At that time, Roy was renting the house to Ethan and Aileen Sanders, who kept a daily watch over the horses from the picture window that looked out over the pasture. In my dream, Waneta finally pushed her foal out onto the driveway—only by then, the foal was marked like the tortoiseshell cat that lived out in the barn. My dream-self, watching all of this, felt disgusted and sick.

Writing this dream down, I began to feel some alarm—was this a precognitive coincidence of dreams and conversations circling around us here? I knew that horses don't usually survive foaling complications; that even the strongest mares easily sicken and die from difficulties that would hardly faze a cow: breech births, for instance, or twins (which rarely live even if they do manage to be born). Even the minor dream-detail about the solid black foal was disheartening: solid-color Appaloosas weren't allowed in breed competitions then, and their appearance in a foal crop was regarded as a *human* failure.

We checked the mares out daily, patting their bellies and watching for milk droplets or "wax" on their udders. The veterinarian looked them both over too, and even though Waneta was huge with foal by the end of February and both mares were acting irritable and unfriendly, they checked out fine.

"Mares carry for eleven months, but they can foal with no problem anytime from ten months to a full year's term," the vet reminded us. "Waneta *[due March 21st by our breeding records]* will probably foal before Missy *[due March 7th],* that's all."

That's all it is, I told myself; of course that's all it is. But both mares' due dates came and went, and nothing happened. Roy went in the horse barn first thing every morning before chores, and there they'd be, calmly munching hay and getting bigger and bigger. "They're going to explode," Roy said, grinning away his anxieties. "They'll blow up like bombs and splatter spots all over the damn place." But on the morning of March 25, Roy found Missy in the pasture with a nice black-and-white-blanketed filly, everything an Appaloosa breeder could ask for.

Except that Waneta was still trudging around the pasture like a bus on stilts, so uncomfortable and surly that when I tried to pat her rump one day she lashed out with a kick designed to knock my teeth out. I'd stumbled on a rock and staggered backwards just in time; *but what was my Waneta doing,* trying to kick me? Shocked, I wondered angrily if motherhood was going to ruin Waneta's disposition and take her away from me forever.

"Damnit, we shouldn't have done this," I told Roy. "We should have just left them alone to romp in their pasture, what the hell."

"But if we sell their foals, they'll have paid for themselves," Roy explained, patiently, as he did whenever I expressed this sentiment. "After all, that's what the mares are *for,* don't you know?"

"For??" I blurted, but I couldn't articulate my frustrations about it all, and we changed the subject.

Meanwhile—weirdly, even humorously (if you were outside looking in)—poor Nora was as overdue as Waneta, and just about as huge. She quit working for me altogether, and I didn't blame her. She was horribly uncomfortable and looked pale and drawn and bloated all at once. April arrived but both unborn babies stayed put. Meanwhile, Missy and her foal cavorted in the pasture, free as the oncoming springtime.

Then on Thursday, April 16, Roy and I decided on the spur

of the moment—*on impulse*—to go away for the weekend and drive to a big horse show in Decatur, Alabama. A nationally-known trainer was going to show our fancy young stallion in competition there, and the warm spring air had made us restless besides. Waneta still hadn't foaled, but we had the vet check her out again and he said everything was fine, just very pending; Ethan and Aileen watched the mares' every step from across the road; the fellow who did Roy's dairy chores would feed the horses every morning and night; and help, if needed, was a mere phone call away at the veterinarian's office. So we told ourselves. I often look back on that impulse and marvel at this rationalization process, so uncharacteristic of either of us in the face of Waneta's condition.

We stopped at the pasture as we drove away from the farm and walked down by Waneta. She was standing by the barn wall, head down. I reached toward her flank and again, she stabbed a quick kick at my hand, this time cracking my knuckles with her shinbone. A sudden impulse to stay home clutched at me: This wasn't right, Waneta wasn't *right.* But I pushed the thought aside and we left, pulling obliviousness over our heads like a handmade quilt.

We drove down through Kentucky and Tennessee into Decatur and watched the two-day show. Business in Dundee seemed far away. And then we called Ethan and Aileen on Saturday for an update on things at home. We were in for a rude awakening.

Aileen was in tears, her voice shaking. Early Friday morning (April 17), Ethan had found Waneta in the barn lying listlessly on her side, her dead, half-born foal hanging out of her bloody vagina. Ethan raced back home and called the veterinarian; together, they pulled the dead foal out of the mare and packed her uterus with antibiotics. But Waneta couldn't stand up. She tried to, thrashing and rolling back and forth across the barn floor, eventually working her way outside into a corner of the pasture. There, Ethan built a blockade of straw around her, kept her supplied with water and hay and even covered her with blankets at night. Aileen said that according to the vet, the huge, *solid black colt* was the biggest newborn stock horse foal he'd ever seen, weighing at least 150 to 175 pounds. And, Aileen added, there was blood all over the barn wall, high up, where Waneta had apparently started to have the foal while standing up.

I listened to Aileen's voice with a terrible sense of doom. I knew what happened to animals that couldn't get up, even when they weren't mares of delicate birth-parts. They died, either slowly by themselves or quickly, by shotgun. We knew that Waneta was done for, but we made some frantic long-distance phone calls to friends near home and arranged to get Waneta trucked to the large animal hospital at Cornell University. And even though Waneta seemed bright and alert upon arrival there, according to our friends, she died of peritonitis sometime in the early morning hours of Easter Sunday, April 19.

It hit us like a fist. We felt responsible, irresponsible, vulnerable. Roy felt that his instincts about livestock had failed him, that he'd betrayed his upbringing and left the mare to die. Could he have saved her, if he'd found her at four o'clock that morning on his usual rounds? He'd never know. And I'd ignored clear-cut warnings from my own set of instincts, including the strong impulse that Thursday to stay home. Adding salt to these wounds was the fact that the whole disaster had been witnessed by dozens of passersby; Aileen said that neighbors, state troopers, several area veterinarians, and even some horse breeders ghoulishly interested in the dead foal's color had been in and out of the pasture to look at Waneta.

My grief was terrible, exaggerated all out of proportion, a loss more irreplaceable than anything I'd ever experienced. That was dumb, I realized, but it was more than the death of a favorite horse and her foal. The incident touched with an icy finger that entire unresolvable territory between my husband and me, and on that same territory within myself. What would we do without her, I thought crazily.

"My father used to say that as long as death doesn't come in the house, you can't feel bad about it," Roy said. It didn't help. "Death *has* come in the house," I insisted, but I couldn't explain. For one thing, there was my dream: that gory dream of February 27, with Waneta straining to birth her foal against the barn wall, standing up. That bloody dream, ending finally in Aileen and Ethan's driveway. It was all too horrible—I was a nerd, a failure. Me, the big shot, always blabbing about precognition and dreams and ESP and—shit. What good had all that done when it mattered? Lying there far from home in the dark of that Decatur motel, I encountered an absolute, bleak despair that was a black monster all its own. How could I believe that the natural world was enough? How could I presume to think that our natural, instinctive, "caretaking" selves could keep us safe? In the animal world I knew with Roy, the veterinarian had become the central figure, gradually replacing old-timers' remedies and potions with the new magic of chemical medicine. And Roy shared my suspicions about that—we believed that nature could basically take care of anything.

Well, we'd been wrong this time. "Nature" had finked out,

my so-called psychic smarts had finked out, and our assessment of Waneta's condition had finked out. If there was a Self that "always knew what you were up to," as I'd said ad infinitum, then what the hell was it up to now??

We came home, not looking at the horse pasture as we pulled into the driveway. Glumly, we sat at the kitchen table, opening mail—and the phone rang. It was Nora's mother, of all people, with some good news. While we were in Alabama, Nora had finally gone into labor and after eight difficult hours had given birth to a girl on Friday morning, April 17.

"She really had a hard time," Nora's mother said. "She said the doctors were very rough and she didn't dilate until the very last. They had to use forceps and she bled something awful." Her voice cheered. "But she's doing just fine now and so is the baby. I thought you'd want to know."

"Fine," I stammered. "Great." My heart was thudding like an overloaded washing machine. A million connections were suddenly connecting in my illogical, sideways brain. Nora—and Waneta—and me. Birth—and beliefs about being female—and my dreams. Something . . . something really weird, some crazy-sounding . . . con-currence; some meeting of intents and purposes and . . . some *lesson* . . . had exchanged in the twilight, some . . . presque-vu. Almost seen. Almost grasped. I don't have any idea what I said to Nora's mother, who probably thought I'd fainted. I hung up.

"What are you staring at?" Roy snapped. I realized I was gazing across the room at nothing. Without answering, I ran upstairs and pawed through my dream notebook. Oh gawd, there it was. First, my January 27 dream in which Nora struggled through a difficult labor, trying to give birth through an opening that was too small, and ripping; *Waneta's* baby had been way too large, and had torn her up inside . . . In the dream, Nora had thrashed around on the floor; Waneta had thrashed halfway across the pasture. In the dream, I made a long-distance phone call to Nora's husband . . . we'd been long-distance ourselves during these births. My dream emphasized that Nora was "unprepared" for the delivery—and in fact, her cervix hadn't opened until the last few minutes of an eight-hour labor. And we'd learned from a veterinarian at Cornell that Waneta's birth canal was "infantile"—or that her labor-signaling hormones had been "immature." She was physiologically unprepared, in other words.

There was the coincidence of the birth dates on April 17, which couldn't have been predicted—both occurred long after the expected due dates. The coincidence of D.'s visit and the difficult-birth conversation the day after my dream about Nora. And

Jeee-zus, that explicit dream in February of Waneta's bloody struggles! How the *hell* much warning does anybody need, I grumbled.

It was like an explosion of births and deaths, beginnings and endings whirling all around me, back and forth, in reality and in not-quite reality. My mind felt stretched—about to give birth itself. In a way, in a really funny way, Waneta had been involved in the same questions of life's purposes as Nora and I were. After seven years of pasture freedom, with nothing more asked of her than an occasional ride through the fields, Waneta was about to turn into a brood mare foal factory—*or at least that was how I felt about it.* Nora was to me like a younger version of myself, caught up in the eternal war between being a woman and being a writer (or whatever; the *what* didn't matter)—*or at least that was how I perceived it.* And I suddenly and coldly recognized what my powerful, overwhelming, and passionate identification with the mares was all about.

An object lesson had been given to me, from myself and from—elsewhere. After all, our own impulses had taken us away from Waneta at the last, opening the door on this grim tale. And it was reinforced in the kind of winding-down process that I'd noticed before in precognitive-type dreams: On May 5, Sean dreamed of seeing a deformed snake "with scaly mouse ears" that "pooped out a little pink crab that waved its bare arms all around—yukky!" On the same night, I dreamed that a mare we'd just purchased gave birth to a hideously deformed foal. The next afternoon, that mare unexpectedly foaled three weeks early, although the colt was perfectly fine; but the same day, one of the *tortoiseshell* barn cats aborted her premature kittens all over the driveway, leaving pink, naked kitten fetuses waving half-formed limbs behind her in the dust . . . and in my dream of February 27, Waneta had finally birthed a tortoiseshell-colored foal out into the Sanders' driveway . . .

In times of great stress, I believe that our psyches turn on full blast, handing us all the information we need to know, on whatever level we care to act. And sometimes the invisible world punches through to us with such force that our present psychological equipment simply can't categorize what's happened. I don't *think*, for example, that there was a literal life-or-death exchange between Nora and Waneta—I don't *think* I think that; it veers almost too far off the old beaten path for me, even; and besides, I don't believe that anything has to die for anything else to live, in those terms. And yet . . . a death in one system is a birth in another, and there are many kinds of midwives; a phrase from ESP class days. Because we see ourselves as the "superior" species rather than as a creature nestled among our fellows of somewhat different habits, we automatically dismiss natural cooperation—even among levels of our own being. And because I was now becoming convinced of this naturally cooperative network, I was running full-bore into its workings in my conscious experience—workings of great give-and-take, great wisdom—and yes, even humor.

See Appendix 3 for "More Animal Tales."

NOTES

1 Alpha, one of the officially-categorized brain waves, indicates that the individual is in a state of relaxed awareness or mild trance. Alpha biofeedback methods have been used since the early 1970s to monitor and regulate supposedly "involuntary" body functions such as heartbeat and blood pressure.

I use the Alpha-level "trance" state myself for a variety of reasons—such as my meditation on Suzie's eye. Beyond that, the state of inner-directed consciousness I'm in while I write is probably an Alpha wave state, though sometimes I feel as if I'm much farther "out." In the early days of Jane Roberts' ESP class, we did many experiments with Alpha, including some provocative healing stuff. Sometimes we'd do a mental "search and destroy" Alpha, imagining all sorts of cartoon-like "cures" for whatever ails one of us was complaining about . . . and we got results, too.

Recently, Sean's sixteen-year-old friend Jeff seriously injured his ankle playing basketball, and spent a few weeks on crutches. As far as I know, Jeff hasn't read any of the Roberts books or mine, but he told me one afternoon during a break from mowing my lawn that he'd "figured out a way" to make his ankle feel better. Jeff went on to describe how he did this: by imagining "a bunch of medics in an ambulance" driving down the veins inside his leg and into his ankle, "where the guys get out and start spraying fix-it foam all around the injury." Jeff's details of this imagery were vivid and thoroughly optimistic—in the face of medical warnings that he might not be able to play basketball again.

Jeff said that his ankle always felt better, and seemed less swollen, after each of these mental exercises. And he's back on the high school varsity team, too. This was the kind of effect I was hoping for with my meditations on Suzie's eye that day.

2 A quick definition of these drugs as used in veterinary medicine: DMSO, or dimethylsulfoxida, is a relatively new sulfa derivative that is used to treat inflammations. Generally, it is rubbed on the hide or skin and its chemical action forces circulation to the affected area and reduces swelling by dispersing the fluids (and any accumulated infection) throughout the body. So quickly is this drug absorbed into the blood stream that within seconds after it is rubbed on the body (horse or human), the animal's breath is permeated with a distinct garlic-like odor.

Steroids, at least as commonly used in veterinary situations, work much like DMSO, but will also suppress the body's natural immunity response—thereby having a much greater impact on the hormonal system, the kidneys and liver, and other organs.

3 *The God of Jane: A Psychic Manifesto*, by Jane Roberts, 1981, Prentice-Hall, Inc., Englewood Cliffs, NJ 07632, Chapter 16, pp. 162-163.

4 Sean's dream reminded me of some of my own from a somewhat earlier age than he was while he was having the majority of his "black rabbit" dreams (though occasionally he still has them)—when I was five or six. I used to meet a woman in my dreams who taught me how to control nightmares and wake up at will by using the trick of rapidly blinking my dream-eyes. This woman always had long black hair—just like a woman who appeared in Sean's dreams and whom he described as "the black rabbit in disguise"—and remarkably large, though round, eyes.

5 A reaction I never tried to talk Sean out of. For one thing, I respected his wariness around horses, since I'd seen too many people get badly hurt by them. For another, I remembered quite clearly a remark that Jane Roberts had made to me years before, in ESP class, out of the blue but with a chilling urgency.

"Watch Sean around horses, Sue," she said, turning suddenly and sharply to face me in the midst of an unrelated group discussion. Her eyes were like dark lasers drilling into mine. "Watch him on a horse farm—a lot of horses." We stared at one another for a moment and then Jane blinked, shrugged, lit a cigarette. "That's all I get," she sighed. "But it's pretty clear."

At the time, I owned no horses, had never owned horses, and had no prospects for ever owning any, since this was several years before I met Roy or even knew of him. Jane's warning, though offhand, stuck with me—silently, for I never repeated it to anyone, including Sean.

TWELVE

Following (Aackk!!) Impulses

A Cautious (and Surprising) Start

Only people who trust their spontaneous beings and the altruistic nature of their impulses can be consciously wise enough to choose from a myriad of probable futures the most promising events—for again, impulses take not only [people's] best interests into consideration, but those of all other species.

Jane Roberts
The Individual and the Nature of Mass Events

The ocean was turquoise, the sky pale blue edged with pink. A warm sea wind ruffled the palm trees outside, fluttered the drapes at the open patio door, and lifted sheets of paper off the table . . . where I sat, inside, typing. Here I was, on vacation in Florida's "fabulous Keys" with my parents and son—and what was I doing all day, every day?

Typing. The final manuscript of my book, *Conversations with Seth,* was due on my editor's desk, and I still had two more chapters to go, and here it was, 9 p.m. already. Sean and I would be flying to New York City in three days, and the pages had to be finished.

What a grind, I grumbled. I couldn't complain too hard about missing those sub-zero temperatures back home in Dundee, but I was getting more than a little sick of typing, typing, typing—especially on these balmy Florida evenings when everybody else was out fishing for who-knew-what-weird-sea-critter off the front pier.

Sighing, I forced my mind back to the current chapter, which involved questions raised (endlessly) in class about drugs and the consequences of using them. Just as I started up again, my father stepped through the doorway and switched on the TV news. At once, I heard the word "drugs." I looked up—right in the middle of typing a paragraph describing a class member's LSD trip. There on the nine o'clock news was former Beatle Paul McCartney, who'd just been arrested in Japan for carrying 7.7 ounces of marijuana in his suitcase. (He was later released, although according to newsmen he could have ended up in a Japanese jail for up to fifteen years.)

Now, that's a funny coincidence, I thought. Just the day before, I'd noticed another of those odd little synchronous blips: President Carter had announced on a television newscast that draft registration would be revived for the first time since 1973. At the time of that newscast, I was in the middle of typing Chapter 12—which includes a lengthy description of a class member's draft-avoidance techniques.

Huh. Oh, well.

I made note of it, of course. (Sometimes I think I'll be taking notes at my own funeral.) And in the next couple of days, two more little connections between my book-in-progress and day-in-progress came to pass. While typing up some remarks directed toward a body rash that my son had suffered when he was three years old, I was interrupted by Sean stomping in from the beach—

he had a rash all over his neck, and it itched, and what was I going to do about it? And later, while I was finishing up some pages on mental events and their role in the creation of physical reality, I was interrupted by a knock on the back door. I was tempted to ignore it, but *impulsively* (the significance of which didn't come to me until later) I got up and opened the door. Two nicely-dressed women in their mid-sixties stood there. They quickly identified themselves as Jehovah's Witnesses, making the rounds of the condominium.

"We have a message for you," one of them said. "God will let you live through the coming disaster if you think that He will." The woman smiled. "You don't have to die to live in a better world," she said kindly. "You can imagine any world you want, and He will let you live there."

I was rather surprised—she seemed to be paraphrasing the lines I'd just been typing, albeit with religious overtones. And even though I usually just shut the door on such occasions, I couldn't help but respond to their sincerity—which was nothing compared with their astonishment when I said, "No, of course you don't have to die to live in the world you want."

Automatically, one woman offered a pamphlet. "No, I don't want that," I said. "I just agree with you—we get what we concentrate on."

The women glanced at one another, probably gearing up for Step Two, when the condo manager walked around the corner of the building.

"Hey! You there! Get the hell out of here!" he shouted at the women. "Take your junk and hit the road and stop bothering people!"

Politics isn't the only thing that makes for strange bedfellows, because suddenly—on impulse—I leaped to the women's defense. "Roger, they aren't hurting anyone," I said. "I can shut the door if I want to and they have the right . . ."

"Like hell they do!" Roger yelled, shooing the women away like barnyard chickens. "Not in my condo they don't!"

I shrugged at the women. "Thank you very much," one said. "God blesses you." And they left, probably thinking that they'd nearly made a convert. Oh, well, I thought; I can't stand their philosophical folderol and they couldn't stand mine if they heard it; but somewhere in between all those juxtaposed ideas, some funny little synchronous messages were whispering about the "reality" of mental events. Again, old questions buzzed around my head. It was one thing to write a book about Jane's ESP class and the practicality of psychic phenomena and all, but . . . something here in my warm tropical days was unzipping the fabric between reality and idea. How visible *was* the invisible world?

I spent the next hour or so gazing off over the balcony at the gorgeous green-blue ocean, thinking about those two women whose religion was the scourge of the condo. Well, I mused, at least Roger was egalitarian about it all. A few days before, he'd chased two women wearing microscopic bikinis away from the pool, yelling about indecent exposure and "filthy soliciting." No sex or God-stuff *here,* by Jove. Maybe I should hand him a copy of my book . . . I was leaving in a few days anyway.

Then I looked up my previous night's dream in my notebook. In it, I'd defended an odd half-human, half-horse creature, keeping it away from an auction block and protecting it from humiliation.

Hmmm—a three-pronged coincidence: the connection between my book chapter and the remarks made by the women unexpectedly arriving at the door, plus the little connection with my dream . . . all held together by the glue of my *impulse* to get up and answer the door. There was a vague precognitive air about it all: my defense of the odd being in the dream (and I certainly consider Jehovah's Witnesses to be "odd beings," at least as far as their religion goes . . . granted that they would consider me worse than odd, and probably destined for Hell), complemented by the little coincidence between my typing and the subject of their call. Or, one had led to the other inside-out: Maybe the dream's message had pushed up through my consciousness and impelled me to argue with Roger . . . or maybe it was all because I was into that chapter on mental events and I was struck by the "you create your own reality" flavor of the women's speech, and . . .

"Don't get so goddamned analytical," I said aloud. Maybe the whole thing was no more than a quirk, something fun to think about. Sometimes, as old Sigmund pointed out, a cigar is just a cigar.

Maybe.

Looking back, I have to say that the minute I started paying attention to coincidental, impulsive oddities in my life, my whole train of thinking changed radically and permanently. A year later, when I started supplementing my dream notebooks with a "record" of impulses, the synchrony of dreams and daytime coincidences occurred so often and in such an endless maze of interrelationships that I gave up trying to keep track of them all. Not only did I start noticing precognitive patterns and "bits," but my waking moments became themselves more like dreams: objects, actions, even ordinary events turning slippery and streetwise, connecting in neat little lineups that couldn't help but get my attention. And none of this clouded my daily life or made it less "real"—in fact, this "impulse perspective" served to *un*cloud a frightened, untrusting, and apologetic climate that I'd unconsciously accepted as "normal" since my early twenties. My impulses literally cleared up my personal vision, with methods peculiar to me—and to what would naturally catch my eye and tickle my heart.

In other words, I think that your impulses are pretty smart.

In the summer of 1981, after reading Jane Roberts' *The God of Jane: A Psychic Manifesto,*[1] I decided to start an impulse "diary" of my own—after a bit of a nudge from my son. While I was immersed in Jane's book, Sean told me one morning about a dream in which he'd seen a "baby blimp" floating in the sky above Dundee. As we were talking, I *impulsively* decided to get in the car and go for a ride around the countryside. About five miles from home, we saw a tiny advertising dirigible floating in the sky above a golf course. "Look!" Sean said. "A baby blimp!"

"Wow!" I said. "How neat—how exciting—how magic!"

How *safe,* I would think, much later.

So, following my (typically writer-oriented) impulse, I stopped at the local drug store and bought a notebook just for this impulse diary.

. . ."*I determined to watch for different kinds of impulses with as much eagerness as I looked for different species of birds at our bird feeder . . .*" Jane recalls in *The God of Jane.* "*. . . to study their eccentricities and emotional plumage, and most of all, to follow their emotional or mental flights to see where they might lead.*[2]"

Splendid. Marvelous. How brave I was, I told myself; from now on, I'd follow my impulses, no matter what. Moreover, I would write them down as they came upon me and then I'd record whether I followed them or not (though surely I would do so), and what happened as a result. I tingled with anticipation. Living as I did then on a farm, where the routine was anything *but* impulsive, I felt that I already deserved a medal for even considering this experiment.

I opened my notebook to the first page, dated it, took a deep breath, and waited.

???

From that notebook, dated June 16, 1981:

"Spent many hours in a strange and amusing state of suspension, sort of waiting for an impulse to follow. Where are they? When are they going to thunder in?

"Maybe I don't have any impulses any more—what if I

don't? Maybe I've squashed them all into nothing. No, wait—was that one? What did it want me to do? Would I actually dare *do* it?? Gawd, now I see the problem with weeding out random thoughts—is there a difference? How will I know?

"Let's see—we'll try it systematically: Do I have an impulse to go for a walk? No. To hike up the hill and look at the horses? No? Well, how about weeding the garden? Forget it—can't even work up an impulse to do that. Well, how about something crazy. Do I have an impulse (long-buried, I'm sure) to roller skate down the highway? No. Throw rocks through the barn windows? Of course not. Take off my clothes and go running around the yard? Jesus, no.

"Well then, where are they, damnit? I thought I'd be seething with them! Of course, I did have the impulse to get this notebook—even (come to think of it) to sit down here and write down this lack of impulses (not bad writing, either). Humph—is this what it's all about? So much mental masturbation?

"Will I feel impulses in my head, like a thought, or in my stomach, like fear? Jeez, my impulses must be so laundered that I can't even remember what they're like!

"Well, that's all I'll commit myself to for now: Giving recognition to my impulses. Then after two or three days I can follow them if I want to—okay??"

Boy, I thought, nobody's going to award me for courage in the trenches. Then it struck me: What if *getting* crazy impulses isn't the problem—it's *not* getting any that does it to you? What if I never have the impulse again to clean house or take out the garbage? Could I be honest enough to be true to that impulse *lack* and let the house be a mess? But on thinking about it, I realized that I didn't have to worry about it—I naturally and, yes, impulsively wanted a clean house. So there are "good" impulses that end in safe, homey results, I assured myself.

For the next couple of days, I jiggled back and forth between impulses that I didn't have and impulses that I wasn't *sure* I had, chewing my mental fingernails and driving the rest of the household nuts. Then one afternoon, the phone rang. It was a fan who'd read all of Jane's books and my own, and decided "on impulse"—yep, she said it—to drive up from (for gawd's sake) *Virginia* to find us. She'd tracked me down through the folks at the local coffee shop, she said. Then she added, shyly, "I've, ah, been keeping track of my impulses for the past couple of weeks, and it's the damndest thing, but I don't seem to have any at all, I mean other than the big crazy one to come up here to see you, and I'd really like to talk with you about that."

I laughed. What a (here we go) coincidence! Or maybe the human psyche tends to go mildly berserk the moment we start taking it seriously, and impulses (like leprechauns) disappear when you look for them on purpose. I had coffee with my fan that afternoon, and we had a comforting conversation about non-impulses, and I returned home feeling that I'd figured everything out once and for all, nothing to worry about, impulses were all natural and seamlessly unconscious and no big deal at all.

Then the door blew wide open, and nothing was ever the same again.

That weekend, Roy and I planned to take our two stallions and one of the mares to a big international Appaloosa show in Massachusetts. We'd spent several weeks preparing for this show and besides a large financial commitment, we'd made a considerable investment in time and labor (as grooming show horses is an exercise in true anthropomorphic craziness). And suddenly I found myself in the middle of these preparations with a great big fat impulse to forget it all and stay home and send the horses out with the trainer—without us.

I dutifully pulled out my notebook, wrote the impulse down, and acknowledged that I'd acknowledged it.

Now what???

This was one of the year's most important Appaloosa shows with the best horses from all around the country scheduled for competition, and Roy was planning to lead the mare himself in her halter class—very prestigious. Was this a case of stage fright on my part? Was I just fed up and bored with all of this equine madness; was the impulse a cover-up for something else?

I considered it, tweaked the impulse on the nose, and tried to get it to turn into something else (hunger pangs, maybe).

Nope. I definitely, powerfully, impulsively, most assuredly wanted to stay home. I wanted both of us to stay right there on the farm and let the trainer do the job of caretaking and showing. And when I allowed myself to follow that impulse, mentally, through my storyteller's imagination, what I felt was odd indeed: a shadowy nastiness and dread—something troubled and uncomfortable and not at all the pleasant weekend we'd been anticipating.

So now what? I'd decided when I started this venture that I was going to be true to it and follow these goddamned impulses and then write up the results (a useful justification in case it led to something awkward, like shooting the next person who interrupted my writing). But how could I follow this one? Roy was not inclined to give credence to such things as impulse experiments, especially when such experiments asked him to stay home from international Appaloosa expositions in which there was a 90% chance of winning at least one class. Oh, boy! I wasn't so sure that I was inclined to go along with it, either. I *wanted* to go to the damned show. Or did I? Didn't this impulse state otherwise? But no, the tricky part was that the impulse hadn't changed my actual desire to attend the show—I loved horse shows and the attendant excitement and drama. No, the impulse was simply and cleanly straightforward: to stay home from the show, regardless of other feelings.

I bit my lip. I chewed my pen. And I chickened out, and kept my mouth shut, and we went to the show.

Here are excerpts from comments made in my notebook after that weekend was over:

June 19-22, 1981

Didn't follow impulse to stay home from the Massachusetts show. Had we done so, the following events would have been avoided—if not entirely, at least by us:

1. We waited three and a half hours at the trainer's place Friday morning for the trucker to show up with the horse trailer and get on to Massachusetts (at least a six-hour drive). We chewed him out when he finally got there, but he acted as though he didn't care *when* we got to our destination. Very frustrating.

2. As we started to load up the horses, the trucker, by now in a rush and angry with us for telling him off, carelessly tied our older stallion inside the trailer next to a mare. Of course the stallion went into a frenzy, sending the mare into a kicking and squealing frenzy of her own, and both had to be taken out and separated until everyone calmed down—a dangerous situation. We decided to leave the older stallion behind in the trainer's barn, even though we'd already paid all entry fees on that horse. At this point, Roy and I seriously discussed going home, but—again—that impulse was denied.

3. Once we arrived at the Massachusetts fairgrounds, I called Information to get my sister-in-law's new phone number. We'd planned to stay overnight with her, as she lives just a few miles from the show arena. But she never answered the phone and we concluded that she and her family must have forgotten our plans and gone away for the weekend. By then, there were no rooms available anywhere in the area, so Roy and I had to sleep in the front boot of the horse trailer—a cold, damp night spent between a layer of straw and a scratchy horse blanket. Ugh! (Adding insult to injury, a bunch of neighborhood cats crept into the trailer in the middle of the night and pissed all over the bedding sawdust—an

inglorious comment from the gods if there ever was one.) Later, it turned out that the Information operator had given me the wrong telephone number!

Had I followed an impulse (discarded because it sounded stupid to think that an operator made a mistake—obviously my in-laws were plotting against us) to re-check the number with Information, that miserable night wouldn't have happened.

4. Our young stallion didn't place in his halter class the next morning (the only time this happened in the years that Roy and I showed him), and we were disappointed, to say the least. This was somewhat mitigated by our mare's third-place win in a large Two-Year-Old class, an excellent placing in that show.

5. As we were pulling out of the show grounds to return home Saturday noon, there was a grinding skreeek! from underneath the horse trailer. The rig suddenly lurched sideways, and a wheel went spinning off into the ditch! Fortunately, this didn't happen on the Massachusetts Turnpike at 55 mph, which would have been a major catastrophe. Nevertheless, all the horses had to be unloaded and another nine hours spent in the business of finding someone to fix the broken wheel hub. In the middle of all of this, who should show up but Roy's sister, very annoyed that we hadn't bothered to call her the night before . . .

And it took all night to make the long drive home on a temporarily-welded wheel hub, the trainer keeping himself awake by blasting old Bob Dylan songs from the cassette player while Roy and I tried to sleep sitting up in the truck cab's tiny benchseat (actually not too difficult a feat, considering the previous night's accommodations in the horse trailer). We arrived home tired, dirty, stinking of old horse straw, furious with the trucker, on top of our relatives' shit list, and more than a little irritated with each other. Only later would we see the humor in it all. But after this—maybe because of it—I finally started to feel impulses; little crystal-clear *blips* of impulse, like psychic needle stabs. Nothing too scary came upon me at that point—and I began to take tiny umbrella-steps toward actually following them.

I followed an impulse to join an exercise class—which took a mightily begrudged hour out of my morning three days a week, but which turned out to be the cure-all for the aggravating lower back pain I'd had for years. I followed a series of impulses that eventually led me to kick a nasal-spray habit I'd had for nearly fifteen years (and I followed this impulse even though it was initially terrifying, since without the nasal spray my nose and throat stuffed up solid for an entire week and I had to sleep sitting up in a chair or suffocate—or so it felt). I followed an impulse that we'd both expressed and bought an Australian shepherd puppy, an unusual move for me as I'm really not fond of dogs. But this also turned out to have unpredictable benefits: something in Oscar's spontaneous puppy-ness helped me begin the process of disentangling my powerful emotional identification with the horses, and brought me to the doorway of my deeply-rooted belief that animals are helpless in the face of blind, stupid human beings (by inference an invisible judgment upon myself).

Sometimes the impulses were more aesthetic in nature, as in these notes from my journal, dated June 25, 1981:

"Followed impulse to walk down the road and stand by the creekbank for a while. The birds and frogs and other sounds were lovely. The longer I stood there, the greater the depth and color reflected in the water . . . A nearby black willow changed from an opaque green to a mosaic of light patches as I watched; a redwing blackbird perched on a cattail and chirred. I felt immersed, scattered beyond memory, in the network of the natural world . . .

"As I walked home, I saw a fox sparrow fly into the side of a passing car and land, dead, in the road. I picked the bird up and stroked its feathers. It seemed a perfection of form and color, and a sense of great tragedy pressed upon me, that there was one less songbird in the world tonight. I placed it in a patch of weeds, and thought that if I could find an answer to the death of this one small bird, I would understand all the questions ever asked about existence.

"I arrived home from this walk in a mild euphoria, filled with the mutterings and mumblings of trees and birds and creek-life. Later that afternoon, still in the throes of this dreamy contemplation, I followed an impulse to go back out and walk down the pasture lane for a look at the mares, even though it was nearly dinnertime. To my surprise, I discovered one of the mares rolling and straining and biting at her sides, all signs of colic. This condition can quickly cause a horse to die a painful death, so I ran back to the house and called the veterinarian, who rushed to the farm and treated the mare successfully."

Now *there,* I mused later, is what you might call a practical impulse, if you had to qualify the damn things. And obviously, I needed to give my impulses some justification, to hook them to specific daily routines; because in point of fact, I was scared to death of what my impulses might bring. Which, when I studied the past few weeks, was really funny: The "worst" experience so far had come about precisely because I'd denied the first strong impulse I felt. But on the other hand, because of that disastrous weekend, we'd decided to buy our own horse trailer and haul the critters ourselves—plus we'd learned a handy thing or two about welding busted wheel hubs.

So things had ultimately worked out anyway, and with some advantageous results at that. Denying impulses, then, wasn't necessarily a psychological death knell, I told myself; people get along one way or another, right? Isn't there a part of you that always knows what's going on, no matter what? Or . . . I wondered: Is our psychological balance dependent upon the *act* of following impulses, perhaps in itself a healing balm or psychic vitamin of freedom and self-confidence?

I was soon to find out—again, despite many previous lessons—that cause-and-effect rationalization about impulses was like trying to catch a fish with your bare hands, because as I continued—hesitantly, fearfully, with nearly all of my bets hedged—to acknowledge and pursue my impulses, my days began to turn inside out, as though my untamed and *very* witty inner self, now set free, was going to shove me back on the road whether or not *I* knew enough to see where I was going.

One evening a few weeks later, I was sitting in my pajamas at the kitchen table, reading, when I was suddenly *struck* (the only word for what was almost like a physical blow) by the impulse to take my son for a walk down the pasture lane. A full moon was out and the grasses were illuminated in that other-world light of ghosts and dreams; but pooh, I thought, Sean's in bed asleep and I'd have to get dressed and the puppy will follow us and bother the horses and . . .

At that moment, as I sat there grumbling about this impulse (which was strange, since Sean and I often take walks in the night to look at the stars), the phone rang. It was my mother, calling to tell me that there was a partial eclipse of the moon at 11 o'clock, and we should be sure to see it.

Had I picked up on her decision to call me? I'd been unaware of the eclipse, as far as I knew. Or had I read about the eclipse, forgotten it consciously, and reminded myself with this sharp, unmistakable urge to go outside? Probably—the self is a good timekeeper that way. (My mother said she'd called "on impulse," neatly fitting in with this inner signal system.) But in any case, Sean and I did watch the eclipse from lawn chairs set up in the pasture, passing binoculars back and forth, the puppy chewing at our ankles and barking happily at the wind.

The next day, I read over some hastily scribbled notes made during the week about coincidences that cropped up around my impulses, similar to the incident of my mother's timely phone call.

Funny . . . these were like precognitive dreams in their way, as though the relationship between impulses and coincidence was creating a daytime dream, or thinning out the line so studiously drawn between days and dreams.

Of course, I'd experienced coincidences before, as everyone has. But what stood out in my mind now was the nature of these little synchronisms. Something more was going on here than just a matter of something happening that was like something else that had happened. These coincidental events appeared to enlarge upon themselves, spreading out in all directions in such a complicated maze of people, objects, and emotional connections that the usual "logical" explanations for "simple" coincidence waxed absurd. And like those quirky synchronisms that I'd recorded while in Florida, these became more and more interconnected and interrelated when I was able to trust and follow the impulses that rose up out of the synchronisms *themselves*. I'll quote here from my notebook, dated July 14, 1981:

"Within the past week to ten days, Roy and I have both experienced dozens of little coincidences, usually in twos. These incidents seem to have all started with my decision to follow impulses, but they certainly accelerated after a near-disaster when Roy flipped the riding lawn mower over but managed to leap away, unhurt. Some coincidences are directly connected with impulses; some don't appear to be; but then, are all impulses conscious? Do we have impulses that go on unnoticed, like invisible beliefs that nonetheless affect our lives?

"Have synchronisms always gone on around us unnoticed until these separate, personal incidents: my impulse-following experiment and Roy's close call on the mower? Did these 'shock' us into using an innate, more comprehensive awareness? (Do the inner senses rush in after such alarms as these go off, like the body's autoimmune system rushing in to attack an invading germ?) I don't know. I do know that I feel a heightened sense of things approaching, moving through us, and whirling on . . .

"I've noted along with these an increase in small precognitive 'bit' dreams that also relate to matters beyond our private world. For example, on July 8/9, I dreamed that the tomatoes in our garden were infested with strange insects, but that if we sprayed them, the tomatoes would have to be ripped up and thrown out because they would be 'unclean.' This was very nightmarish. The next day, I read in the daily newspaper about the medfly invasion in southern California, and the debate there on the spraying program designed to control those insects. There were arguments for destroying the medfly by any means possible before it destroyed the crops, and there were arguments that the spray was more harmful than the bug . . .

"Here is a list of some coincidental incidents—the ones I had time to write down, that is . . .

"1. Early in the morning of July 9/10, I woke up from a vivid dream about my friends Terry and Ann C. (people I rarely see these busy days). That afternoon—on impulse—Roy and I drove to the Yates County motor vehicles department to register our new horse trailer. As we were waiting in line, Terry and Ann walked in. They greeted us and explained that they were registering their motorcycle. Ann then said that they usually go to the motor vehicle office in Schuyler County, as they hardly ever have to wait in line there. But, she said, they'd come in here today 'on impulse' while doing some other shopping. And we 'just happened' to be there when they came in, the day after I 'just happened' to dream about them.

"2. The next day, Roy turned the radio on while working inside the farm's tenant house, and listened to a talk-show host's interview with a London couple visiting the Yates County Fair. The couple talked about moving to this country and specifically mentioned the 'opportunities in America' and the difficulties they'd experienced in getting citizenship papers. Roy told me later that this remark stuck in his mind because he'd always thought that the United States and Britain had some sort of easy-access citizenship agreement.

"That afternoon, a car stopped by the pasture across the road from our house and a man and woman got out to look at the horses. Because a bend in the road at that point makes for short warning of oncoming traffic, we almost never stand around with casual horse-lookers by that pasture fence; but that day, impulsively, we walked over to talk. The couple turned out to be from London—but they weren't the same couple interviewed earlier on the radio (we asked). In the course of our conversation, the woman said, 'You have so many opportunities here—you just don't know!' The man agreed, adding that they planned to move to the U.S. and eventually become citizens. (Newspapers had been carrying stories about riots in the British city of Liverpool during this time, so perhaps this was the source of the coincidental attitude . . .)

"3. On Sunday, July 12, while driving back from a horse show, we *impulsively* took a different route on the last leg home and passed a couple in a red pickup truck going in the opposite direction. (We noticed this truck because of a pair of bull horns attached to the front bumper, which we made jokes about.) We'd been home about ten minutes when this truck pulled in the driveway. The man—a large, beefy cowboy type—told us his name was

Victor Fassett. I immediately connected his name with an old fellow who lives in Fassett, Pennsylvania, a small crossroads hamlet about 50 miles south of Dundee. That old man sold a group of Appaloosa mares to Roy several years before—those were in fact Roy's first Appaloosas, and held a special significance for him. The mares were all sired by an old-time Appaloosa stallion, Missoula War Path, by 1981 long dead.

"As we talked with this couple—who stated that they'd turned around *on impulse* to follow us after spotting our large horse trailer—Victor made the casual remark that many years before, he'd brought a bunch of Appaloosas back to Pennsylvania from Missoula, Montana, where the breed's registry had been organized in the 1930s. One of those horses, Victor mused, was a black-and-white stallion 'named Missoula something-or-other, after the place out there.' Of course, this horse turned out to be Missoula War Path. I hadn't mentioned the connection I'd made with this man's name and the old fellow in Fassett, Pa., and neither one of us had mentioned the pedigrees of those particular mares.

"We spent an interesting afternoon swapping horse stories—sort of a four-legged version of The One That Got Away—and the couple left for home. I then went outside and picked the Sunday paper out of the delivery box. On the front page was a photograph of an old horse barn located in Fassett, Pa. (according to the caption).

"4. On Monday afternoon, July 13, Roy and I talked at lunch about some friends who live several miles down the road from us. These folks also have horses, and in particular, we talked about their Appaloosa mare, which they'd offered to sell us a year before. Not more than an hour later, as I was working in the yard, these people drove up to the house, jumped out of the car, ran up to me, and handed me the registration papers for this same mare—along with a sales pitch. They said—right out loud!!—that they'd decided to come over 'on impulse' and offer the horse to us again. This time, we bought the mare.

"5. On Tuesday, July 14, the mail included a form-letter invitation for me to apply for an American Express credit card, something I'd never received before and had not solicited. Neither one of us had a credit card at the time, though we'd often talked about getting one for the obvious travel conveniences.

"To my astonishment, Roy—who so rarely remembers his dreams that I never even ask him about them—told me this: 'I must confess [*that word again*!],' he said, 'that last night I dreamed that you and I got into this awful credit hassle in a gas station and we had to call up a friend to send us money.' He shook his head. 'Isn't it strange that you would get that credit card thing today? I mean, we were in a mess all night long! And our friend ended up giving us his credit card! I actually woke up worrying about it!'

"6. The next day, Wednesday, we had an unexpected visit from a woman who's been trying for months to sell us an absolutely worthless horse. She brought along her brother and sister, who turned out to be very peculiar. I want to add here that since I've started to keep this impulse journal, the number of daily visitors and interruptions of various sorts has increased dramatically. Oddly, the people are usually strangers to us but often know or resemble one *another*, in sometimes hilarious ways. The day before this—Tuesday—a man we didn't know saw our geese patrolling the barnyard and stopped to ask if we raised them for sale. That fellow had one brown eye and one blue eye, and a shrill, very annoying laugh. The woman who visited us Wednesday introduced us to her relatives by referring to her sister as 'Molly Goose-Girl' for some unexplained reason. Weirdly, the brother had one brown eye and one blue eye and a shrill, nervous laugh. In fact, his resemblance to the goose-hunter from Tuesday was so strong that I had to choke back flurries of guffaws. I could see that Roy was in the same difficulty.

"Moreover, our friend's sister kept asking me over and over if I knew anyone who might have merganser ducks for sale. Finally, our friend said to her, 'What are you going to do—pay for them with the credit card you don't have?' I didn't even know what a merganser duck was at that point—but that night, I found a classified ad in the newspaper offering merganser ducks for sale!

"7. On Friday, July 17, I was ambling around the yard, looking over the flowers, thinking absently about my two typewriters. I thought that I should really give one to my friend Susan, and buy myself a new electronic model. Then, impulsively, I called Susan up and suggested that she try keeping an impulse diary herself. We talked about this and that, but I didn't say anything about the typewriter—until she mentioned that she's been saving money to buy a used one!

"8. On July 22, the members of Roy's country-western band came to the house to rehearse for an upcoming job. Impulsively, I asked several people over and made a party out of it, something I definitely don't do, ordinarily. One of the guests from a nearby town talked about his many relatives in Dundee, and specifically mentioned his grandmother. The grandmother's name was unusual, and stuck with me, although I didn't know her. One week later, the woman's obituary appeared in the July 30 edition of the

Dundee *Observer*. She'd passed away unexpectedly the day after my party.

"So now—how do all these impulses and coincidences relate, and what do they mean to me on a practical scale? They seem to hang on one another's coattails, although I wouldn't say that one 'causes' the other. But I can't ignore the fact that coincidences and eerie, interconnected incidents have pushed up through the fabric of our days and changed the entire texture . . ."

And indeed, the synchronisms went on and on in a grand and dizzying spiral. A feed salesman would bring up a subject unrelated to his product and two hours later, that subject would come up again on the news, or, without our prompting it, in the conversations of friends. We would discuss something privately and later that day or the next, someone involved with the matter would show up at the farm. Or I would follow an impulse to do something and that action would be reflected in something else. More, I began to get the weird feeling that my impulses took on a life of their own. For instance, I'd been toying for months with an impulse to start a writer's workshop in my home—but denied the urge for various reasons, mainly shyness. Then one day I got a phone call from a Penn Yan woman. She'd never read my books, but she'd been told that I was a published writer and she needed some advice. We talked for nearly an hour, and I enjoyed helping her out. Afterwards, I thought about my workshop idea; this woman's call was like a response to an impulse that wasn't. Yikes—could it be that your impulses could get tired of waiting for you to get off the stick and march out there on their *own* to grab at passing opportunities you're too wishy-washy to find yourself?

Because more than leading me through new philosophical puzzles—which was all I'd consciously expected or wanted—my impulses (followed or not, apparently) were busy prying open a collection of emotional responses almost completely alien to me. Instead of having to rummage through mazes of you-shouldn'ts and general numbness I'd always slapped on top of my feelings, those feelings were all at once right THERE, unmistakable and brilliant—and very, very frightening. One of the results of putting a lid on your more difficult emotions is that you end up swimming in a sea of sameness, a stranger to your own feelings. And for the most part this was fine with me: I *wanted* a smooth ocean to sail on. Consequently, I appeared to be the most serene person you'd ever want to meet—and I appeared that way to myself, too, as far as my everyday "normal" mindset was concerned. Which is probably why my first attempts to "find" my impulses met with such a vacuum.

No more.

Suddenly, I was facing a huge balloon of feelings—loud and direct and fiery-hot. And I had no idea what to do with it. I panicked. I also cried quite a bit, in private. But I wasn't sad, exactly—I was many things, mostly confused, pulled this way and that by a brand-new spontaneity that I didn't even like. What the hell was this, anyway? Weren't impulses supposed to be *fun*? I mean, I'd been a good girl—I hadn't had a single impulse to do anything mean to anybody; they'd all been safe, funny little impulses to do this or that harmless little thing . . .

Then what was this burst of strangers in my house, talking away my time? What were all these feelings criss-crossing inside me, burning away my comfortable serenity? My inner space was as crowded as my house. First I'd feel such a strong explosion of anger that I wanted to pound holes in the walls or start screaming and never stop; then I'd feel a tidal wave of love for the thing (and weirdly, it usually *was* a thing—my typewriter, or the dishwasher, or some other object) that had just made me so angry; then I'd feel a blast of self-loathing that took my breath away and reduced me to tears; and beneath *that* were other feelings (and my god, unrealized beliefs) pushing and shoving and trampling each other to get in line . . .

It was terrifying. It was exhilarating, too, in its way, if only because it was so new—and because I also understood somehow that this upheaval was *myself*, my true caretaker self, leading me exactly where I wanted to go—wherever *that* was. And on the heels of this emotional storm came the barrage of impulses that I'd dreaded when I started this whole experiment.

From my notebook, dated August 4, 1981:

"Now impulses fly at me from all directions, like a radio station's signals gone haywire. I get an impulse to do something and instantly get an impulse to do something else. Or am I confusing an urge (an impulse?) to deny impulses with contradictory impulses?? Or mixing up feelings with impulses? Which are impulses, after all: thoughts or feelings? Or both? Or neither? And how do you tell the difference, if there is any? They seem not to know one another, and yet each impulse is absolutely clear, if fleeting.

"I no longer have the tight control over my feelings as I once did. The battle of how to combine being a woman with being a writer seems to have escalated into nuclear war in here. I feel as though I've betrayed both sides by trying to stay in the middle, and that before I'm done I'll blow up the whole planet [me!]. The agonizing rush of long-repressed emotions (and I've found that means not just long-ago feelings, but *types* of emotions long repressed) must be a cleaning-out of stuff, liberated by my decision to live as impulsively as I dare . . . expressed somehow or other in the endless stream of coincidences and strange people (like strange emotions? Have I called them up by sending impulsive signals out into the universe??).

"And I can say for sure that I've come by the following insights: One: The body never lies. It follows your impulses whether 'you' do or not, in its own language and in response to your own desires, repressed or acknowledged. Two: We find ways to carry our denied impulses with us always, like authoritarian guardians of the psyche—especially evident if we fear and disapprove of our impulsive natures. Some of these denied impulses might be expressed in, say, overweight, as I've experienced—nicely taking care of any troublesome sexual impulses I might have (*help!!* my inhibitions holler, and *help* is what I get—even though I don't like the physical results). Or, someone else might be accident-prone, hurting and punishing the self for being too playful or frivolous, if that's what is most feared . . .

"Three: In spite of what looks like chaos sometimes, *the Self always knows exactly what it's doing,* and if you find yourself in physical or psychological difficulty, the Self that got you there can get you out—*if* you trust and use its methods, which are, perversely, the methods used to get into the difficulty in the first place . . .

"We have a lot to learn about the nature of our conscious stance in the world, but we have to step out of our established mode of cause and effect to start figuring out what's going on. Up to now, everything is considered meaningful, or only those things provable under rigidly controlled conditions are meaningful—depending upon the established school of thought accepted by the considerers. Or, if you're a nihilist, nothing is meaningful, an equally limited philosophy.

"But all of these conditions are based on pre-established precepts that lock us in to seeing experience as one set of narrowly defined moments that follow another set of narrowly defined moments, however else the meaning of those moments is interpreted. I think it's time that we tossed out the basic precepts—*impulsively*—playfully, even—and, always keeping our good old common sense, started re-examining and trusting the nature of *subjective* experience, with its own sort of non-temporal moments.

"I write all of this even though I've been in a good deal of emotional pain since I committed myself to this hairbrained notion of impulses. But if the purpose of life is to become as complete and self-fulfilled—and happy!—an individual as possible, then I have to say (not without human qualms!) that the only way to achieve this is through an intimate interaction with your impulsive nature. *It's obvious that this is how self-fulfilled people naturally make their way, and usually without having to figure it all out beforehand.* Self-fulfillment through the impulsive self is a natural gift of life! And impulses may be our direct line to this 'caretaker self' I've been talking about all this time and seeing in my dreams and those from my Dundee collection . . .

"So I think it *is* our nature to follow our impulses; that indeed, we are obliged to do so on some level, or we end up in big psychological trouble. And I think that sometimes your impulses will even lead you in unprofitable directions, perhaps letting you check out once and for all that this is *not* where you 'want' to go—that it's time to clean house and find out where your 'true' purposes lie.

"That takes courage. It also takes a hefty dose of eccentric stubbornness, and, in the beginning at least, a psychological balance that includes a record of 'objective' observations of subjective experience . . . we've denied our impulses too long as a species to go flying without a manual! And this is why the act of keeping a journal is so important . . ."

"Once more I imagined 'the people' making their own determinations about existence," Jane Roberts says in *The God of Jane*. ". . . recognizing, classifying, and identifying not exotic species of plants, but those subjective oddities of thought, impression, or vision with which science and religion refused to contend. I saw all of us together, collecting evidence of a different kind of reality; gently but surely enlarging the range of our experience."[3]

Dream, December 30/31, 1981

Al S. and I walk into my house. The place has "grown" another room and we dimly see someone, a strange sort of being, moving around inside this extra room. We go inside. At once, we are in a different universe. Al puts on a dark cloak and I find myself wearing a sword-belt, leggings, and fur-trimmed shirt. I realize that we've assumed different personality aspects appropriate to a world parallel to ours.

We start walking down a wooded road, following this other creature. "You realize," I say to Al, "that this is a . . ."

"Quest," he finishes. We walk on and eventually come to a small wayside market. We've lost the other creature, and we have to find him. I see a fat man in skins fussing over a display of pots and wok-shaped cooking utensils. He ignores me. I watch him for a long time, wrestling with an impulse to ask him about our destination. Finally, I approach him and the minute I do so, he addresses me by name and tells me where to journey next in search of this unknown Quest-thing.

"Do you mean," I say to him, "that such an important thing as this Quest rested on such a small thing as my tiny feeling that you knew who I was? On my tiny impulse I had to speak to you?"

"It always does," the man says.

NOTES

1 *The God of Jane: A Psychic Manifesto*, by Jane Roberts, 1981, Prentice-Hall, Inc., Englewood Cliffs, NJ 07632.

2 ibid., p. 105.

3 ibid., p. 239.

THIRTEEN

Looking Back

Speculations on A Fieldbook of Dreams

Once in everyone's life there is apt to be a period when he is fully awake, instead of half asleep. I think of those five years in Maine as the time when this happened to me . . . I was suddenly seeing, feeling, and listening as a child sees, feels, and listens. It was one of those rare interludes that can never be repeated, a time of enchantment. I am fortunate indeed to have had the chance to get some of it down on paper.

E.B. White
Introduction to 1982 edition of *One Man's Meat*

"There is a revolution of events that occurs when you have a revolution of thought. Following impulses, trusting hunches, looking to the subjective self, are not so much creating a new method of action as making conscious the natural mechanics of existence. But that kind of attention, turned upon the Self in the moment, literally re-creates the world you experience.

"Ask your dreams! They know!"

I sat back in my desk chair, contemplating the words I'd just written to a fan. How easy it was to write such advice to others—and how often had I made little insightful discoveries for myself while answering letters from people who sought that advice. How often it happened that I didn't have any idea what to say about something until I'd actually written it. Funny, to find myself observing this *impulsive* side of letter writing, as if from afar.

Outside my window, kids on motorcycles roared up and down the street in the relative cool of a summer evening. Dogs barked across a chorus line of backyards; cars squealed by in anticipation of the night's races down at the fairgrounds. People living their lives in small-town innocence, apparently unconcerned about the larger meaning of things; about the inner equations of their experiences. Or so you might think. But in a small way, I'd discovered otherwise; I'd become, for a brief time anyway, the dream-shaman of this tribe and from that started out on an odyssey of my own—one that had shocked and changed me; one that I would have insisted I'd already taken, like a college course that gets you a degree and then you're done with it.

Ha. You're never done with it—never finished with inner journeys. Flipping through my old dream notebooks should have made *that* plain enough: your consciousness evolves no matter what; your life springs from impulse whether or not you acknowledge them for what they really are.

Now I was single once more, living in Dundee with my son in the first home I'd ever owned, a 116-year-old place with lots of "character" (i.e., green and blue woodwork and a furnace that ate twice its weight in gas every day, like a cast-iron bird from Brobdingnag). The events of the recent past were at last pooling around me, as it were; no longer did I feel as though I were swimming in a murky and alien sea. In paying attention to my impulses, in according them importance and conscious trust, I'd discovered this truth: that my impulses are *not* mindless actions, ready to rend me willy-nilly from the path of rational existence—they are in fact the natural roots of my physical life; and that what my impulse "experiment" had actually done was to change the nature of my *beliefs* about impulses and, by inference, about myself.

I was not filled with an uncontrollable self-destructiveness that needed to be kept in line; my impulses were not impish fleeting things to be grabbed at the first blip! or lost forever. I was in fact filled with the impulse and desire to do well by myself (even though this might at times lie beneath a complex of anxieties that had assumed something of an impulsive life of its own). My mistake had been in thinking that because I'd achieved some wisdom about my life, I was set from then on; a finished product circa 1979. More, in interpreting the ideas behind the Seth material in my personal life, I'd invisibly incorporated *blame* into the concept of Creating Your Own Reality. If I were unhappy, I *blamed* myself for it: I'd created the circumstances and they were all my fault—period. I—Susan M. Watkins, author—should know better, so something was obviously *wrong* with me. The result was a learning period of self-recrimination and despair.

"Your dreams will take care of you," I said countless times to people who described nightmares or unusual dreams to me. "You can trust them—they're telling you what you need to know in the way you can handle knowing it."

Not that I hadn't followed (some) impulses before then; not that I hadn't studied dreams or looked into my belief patterns as the source of experience . . . in fact, I was naturally predisposed in that respect anyway. The difference this time had been in my resolution to bank on my impulses—and to keep a record of what happened. Since I already looked to writing, reporting, and dream-record keeping as the physical index of my subjective experience, I had a solid commonsense framework already in place. I had reference points; I could see where I'd been. Later, I would read these records over and see the Me of them as though I were looking through the wrong end of binoculars: myself, all right, but bogged down with old patterns of thought and behavior that just weren't necessary any more. Thus I learned that impulses can be relied upon and turned to in moments of doubt; that they can give you a feeling of sustenance and caring; and that the combination of your dreams and impulses will lead you to the quality inherent in your own life. I was becoming aware of my present moment as the only true authority of the self, and this realization was being won over all sorts of powerful exterior authorities to the contrary.

One summer day not long after I'd finished the first draft of this manuscript, I went out to pitch a load of peat moss into the flower gardens around the front of my house. It was the perfect afternoon for it, and soon I was pitching away, happily engrossed in matters of dirt, when suddenly my attention was diverted by the rumble of the biggest RV camper I'd ever seen creeping down the tiny village street. The thing was the size of a semi, not counting the enormous boat lurking along behind it, and the whole rig looked like a whale wallowing in a trout stream. People were actually coming out on their porches to gawk.

Then I noticed that it had out-of-state license plates . . . that the couple inside was obviously trying to read house numbers . . . and that the camper was slowing down.

Oh, oh, I thought—I bet they're looking for me. And they'd spotted me, too. The RV ground to a halt midstream and a woman dressed in nicely tailored slacks and blazer stepped out and walked up to me with a cautious smile on her face.

"Excuse me," she said, "do you happen to know where Susan Watkins lives?"

There I stood in short-shorts, a red T-shirt that said "Nothing is Ever Quite True," a red visor hat, bright green plastic gardening clogs and a patina of peat moss dusted on me like cat hair on the couch, and don't you think I was tempted to say, "She died"? Besides, I felt cornered and put upon; I love fan letters, but this . . . prowling up and down the street looking for me was something else altogether. The woman just stood there, sneaking quick peeks over her shoulder through the screen door. Claude, my cross-eyed Siamese cat, peeked back.

"Well, actually, I'm Susan Watkins," I finally admitted. "What can I do for you?"

The woman's face lit up like a flash bulb. "Harold!" she yelled in the camper's direction. "Harold, I was right! We found her!!"

"Found me?" I repeated, false-cheery.

"Oh, yes, we drove all the way up from Florida to find you and tell you in person how much we loved your book," the woman said.

"You drove . . ." I sagged against my peat shovel. All the way up from *Florida*? Two thousand miles? To see me? I doubted that, somehow. In fact, it sounded like so much come-on flattery, though admittedly that wasn't a very nice thing to think. Harold, for his part, was doing an outstanding job of backing into the old unused firehouse parking lot across the street, after which he yanked on the brake, shut off the motor, and joined us. I felt extremely conspicuous—my gardening shorts were rapidly getting shorter, or so it felt—and this wide-eyed, sweet-faced woman seemed so *eager* that it was downright uncomfortable.

She introduced them to me by first stating that Harold was a construction contractor who made $185,000 a year (instantly making my little peanut brittle-colored house seem dumpier than it was) and "never read any of the Seth books or anything spiritual." Meanwhile, Harold stared away from us, out over the part of downtown Dundee visible from my yard, apparently lost in his own world. We stood there. The Hollister Street oriole burst into song overhead. I started to itch all over. What was I supposed to *do* with these two? I didn't want to ask them in for fear they'd never leave—and anyway I didn't want to sit around in this gardening get-up. Then I hit on the obvious solution and made arrangements to meet them in twenty minutes at the local bar. We could have a drink and talk a bit if they wanted to, I suggested. "Damn good idea," Harold said. They walked off toward downtown and I reluctantly left my garden, showered, put on clean clothes and denied the impulse to jump in the car and head for Martha's Vineyard—or maybe Mars.

I walked down to the bar and joined them. We ordered beers. The bar was crowded and noisy with the afternoon's local Slow-Pitch crowd. The beer tasted great, and I started to get into a better mood. Maybe it would be fun to talk about my book and dreams and stuff with these two—you never knew what you could learn from strangers' feedback. What the hell, they'd *sought me out*, after all. I should have more humility about this sort of thing, I admonished myself. Dundee folks had revealed fascinating experiences to me during the time I'd collected dreams—why not people at large, then? Why not do the same thing on a wide-open scale, extend the Shaman-of-the-Tribe as far as it would go?

Then the woman—let's call her Annie—looked at me with eyes wide and moist, and said, "So can you give me a reading in here, or do you want to go back to your house?"

I stared at her in surprise. Harold was studying the neon beer sign at the other end of the room.

"A reading?" I said. "I don't give readings—what are you talking about?"

Now it was her turn to stare at me in surprise. "What?" she whispered.

"I don't do that sort of thing," I said. "I've never said I did. What made you think I did?"

"But—but—I thought . . ." she trailed off, genuinely stricken. "I thought all you people involved with Seth and Jane and all, gave readings. Everybody else does," she added, scowling.

"Everybody else *who*?" I asked, getting annoyed.

"Well, all the psychic people," Annie said, just a touch

of whine creeping into her voice. "I thought you were a psychic. You *said* you were, in your book."

Bruce Springsteen picked just that minute to come blasting out of the bar's jukebox—thankfully, for once. The conversation was beginning to embarrass me; the music would keep it private. "I reported psychic experiences in my book, yes," I said to her.

"Well, isn't it the same thing?" Annie demanded.

And then it was that something fell into place in my head with a *click*. It was as though this woman's expectations—innocent enough, really, considering the marketplace atmosphere of the so-called "New Age"—and my own furtive yearnings for self-justification had just rolled together down an automatic coin-sorter . . . and fallen out unwrapped. There just plain wasn't any denomination that fit what either one of us was really looking for—not from my perspective, at least.

"Um, listen, I'm not 'A Psychic,'" I said. "I think of myself as 'A Writer' with some psychic abilities, but . . ." I groped for words. "I like paying attention to dreams and such, and I keep extensive records and I think I have something original to say about it; but I write about other things too—like someday I'll write a book about the horse-show circuit; it needs doing. So if you want a reading, you'll have to go to somebody who does that, but you don't need to go anywhere but your own dreams, you know."

Annie blinked. Her body language clearly displayed how scandalized she was that I might write a *horse* book. On his part, Harold had let go of the fascinating beer sign and was staring directly at me.

"Yeah?" he said, his voice rough with cynicism. "So you're saying you don't charge big bucks to tell people their future? How come?" He smirked, sure I was jiving them.

"I think it's bullshit, that's how come," I said. Harold snorted and shook his head. Yet I liked his blunt disgust—it felt familiar. Annie, on the other hand, seemed like a fragile porcelain doll, all big-eyed and filled with wonder—gullible wonder; wonder without any conscious filtering process on her part at all. This became more apparent as the conversation limped on—she'd somehow managed to talk Harold into stopping at several psychic doorsteps (nicely confirming my suspicions about her "coming up to see me" remark, but never mind—and also telling me that Harold was more interested in this stuff than he wanted to admit). The readings had all given remarkably coincidental details, Annie said, in particular the "fact" that Harold's hardheadedness in matters spiritual was causing their various marital miseries.

Harold and I looked at one another over this revelation.

"You've got to be kidding me," I said. "These people told you that you can't get along because *he* doesn't read the Seth material?"

"Well, one of the psychics channeled a higher consciousness named John, and John said . . ." The waitress brought us another round. I was getting quite a buzz on from the combination of a sweaty afternoon's work, beer on an empty stomach, and this impossible merry-go-square line of conversation.

". . . John told me the same thing, and you know, it was all the exact same information that my therapist had told me, six months before," Annie went on.

"I can certainly see why," I said. "It's about as hard to figure out how you two feel about one another as it is to blow your nose—what in hell do you need a psychic for?"

"Then, you really *don't* give readings or channel for anyone, do you?" Annie said sadly. "I really thought you'd be able to help us out."

Now I felt a twinge of guilt. "Look, the point is that whatever you want to know is already part of your *own* psyche," I said. "I think you've simply been projecting the obvious and these . . . psychics have just been feeding it back to you. Nobody's got a copyright on inner imformation. Do you pay attention to your dreams, write them down?"

"Sometimes I dream about knocking her over the head," Harold put in, grimly.

"Jeeze, I can't blame you for that!" I chortled, the beer working its magic on my big, fat mouth. "Anybody who introduced *me* by telling how much money I made last year wouldn't last long in *my* camper-van, lemme tellya!"

Harold gave me a grudging smile. "You certainly aren't what I expected," he said. "I thought you'd be another of those lah-dee-dah pie-in-the-sky types." He sneered at his wife. "She's a *writer*, for chrissakes," he snarled. "She doesn't believe in any of this shit! She doesn't have to!" He patted me on the arm with good-ole-boy affection. "She's got her own little game, going, right? Selling books!"

"Uh—wait a minute, hold it," I said hastily. "I didn't mean I don't believe in psychic experience." Annie gave Harold a so-there grimace. This was getting nowhere fast. "What I *meant* was that things aren't categorizable under one label or another—there's not a separate 'psychic' world all packaged up, with magic ceremonies and passwords to get in, it's that the physical world *rides* on another type of order and event." They seemed to be listening, so I went on for another twenty minutes, trying to make sense through my beer-lined cloud. "I also tend to over-label myself as 'A Writer,'"

I added at the end. "The fact is, we're all individuals expressing ourselves in whatever way interests us. I *like* to write—I write about everything; it's what I *do*, and whatever psychic experiences I've had go hand in hand with writing. But I bet if you paid attention, you'd see that you get 'psychic' answers to your questions too, in your own way."

Unfortunately, by the time I finished, they decided they liked what I had to say a *lot*—in fact, they liked it so much that they made up their minds to go right over to the local real estate office and see what vacation properties might be for sale in the area—so they could come up every summer and spend *weeks* talking with me! Yikes! Or at least that's what I think they said . . . I left them with the realtors and walked back home to fix some supper. Apparently, though, there wasn't anything for sale to their liking; about a half-hour later, I saw them pull out of the firehouse lot and slowly wind their way back up the street. Watching them go, I tried to imagine the two of them cooped up together in that big tin bucket for weeks at a time, Annie searching for "channeled" satisfaction and Harold dreaming (pleasantly, I supposed) about mayhem.

It must be high adventure for them, in a way, I supposed—like sailing around the world with a crew bent on mutiny. And what was it, really, that they'd wanted from me? Well, I thought, they hadn't really wanted anything from *me*. What they *wanted*—Harold too, despite his hard-nosed posture—was a formula independent from themselves that applied nonetheless to themselves; a formula that would check out all across the psychic wonderland and therefore be safe, tried, and true: like an invisible prescription drug thoroughly tested out by the FDA. In that they were searching for new answers in some form, they intrigued me; but they'd gotten it all mixed up with a belief in systems vs. the individual, another version of the idea that the YOU of you knows nothing of "real" value, on its own, about you. So their visit had nothing to do with who they really were, or with who I really was. As far as Annie was concerned, I was interfering with the important stuff by talking about all this writer-person crap—while in Harold's mind, I'd simply managed to cop a lucrative schtick. That was fine with him; at least that made horse sense (never mind the financial realities). But still, it all had nothing to do with *me*.

Looking back on this incident, I see now that it was like a closing chapter; a true epilogue to the awareness I had been forming throughout my Dundee dream experiment, of just who I was as a writer, as a dreamer, as a person doing these things and as the female I'd chosen to express my personhood through in this time and place. Above all, it was a look at my beliefs about the public face I would present as an explorer in a relatively unexplored field: the public and the private person in the public and private world, evoked. On one hand was the Dundee dream experiment, which, small even though it was, drew my deepest interests out into the tiny and relatively safe public eye of the town (and which in turn drew out of people some of *their* most secret ideas); on the other, there was a marriage played out against all of my own beliefs, and cultural ones, about men and women and myself in the world—myself from the underside, as it were.

While my upbringing—an unusual mixture of Socialism, medical authoritarianism, and an utter absence of any sort of theism—made it easy for me to lampoon, say, Doc's Born-Again nuttiness, there were other limiting belief-modes that I was playing around with just as invisibly in my private life. If, for instance, I looked the horse world square in the proverbial mouth, I had to ask what sort of assumptions I was at the very least going along with in silence. The power of pedigree left little room for the individual, after all—especially tricky when the individual being (the horse, in this case) was judged as a meaty conduit for equine genetic make-up; as a foal or sperm factory with which to propagate *more* foal and sperm factories. Again—an unrecognized judgment on myself, perhaps.

That dream I'd recorded right at the start of my marriage to Roy looms out of my dream notebook with an urgent simplicity: Roy and I working together in a scientific laboratory, performing all sorts of experiments with "chemicals"—with things that mixed and those that never would. (And what, therefore, were his reasons for being there, I wonder.)

Somewhere in the middle of all of this, I'd managed to thread my way through without being caught up in any "schtick" at all (or anyway none obvious to me). I wasn't a "psychic," charging money or making myself famous for giving readings in the media. I also wasn't deliberately writing for the "markets" in the way that many writers can do—and not because I hadn't tried. It was as though Annie and Harold represented the extremes of certain directions my own abilities offered in the commercial world—and both sides held its attractions, certainly. But the fact was that I'd spent most of my "apprentice" years honing my talents in two very specific and peculiarly small-town places: in Jane Roberts' ESP class, and as co-editor of the Dundee *Observer*, circulation 2,000 on a good week. Both places held a certain guileless innocence; for one thing, people came to Jane's class spontaneously—no one, myself included, had any deliberate purpose, such as note-taking for a future book, in mind at all. Both ESP class and the *Observer* were there because the participants loved it. A strong sense of creativity and ground-breaking permeated both, with common sense the final arbitrator. And both in class and as co-editor of the *Observer*, I'd felt a powerful connection with people as individuals, and with the magical sense of community—and the *precision* with which truth tends to emerge from the ordinary events of daily life.

The modern high-tech approach to the "new consciousness movement," for instance, would mean nothing to my Dundee dreamers, naturalists all. The current "channeling" craze would probably offend Mrs. Densig and her sense of propriety and good sense—yet by herself, she'd discovered that information *does* travel between states of consciousness, and in the simple vocabulary of daily life. Thad, my farmer friend, would have heaped a succinct barnyard epithet upon such business as the "personal inter-power products" advertised in one company's slick "New Age Technology" brochure—and this from the same practical stance that gave Thad his natural understanding of dreams' importance.

On the other hand, I had tried out the farm-wife role for myself, almost at the expense of my more intangible characteristics—which I'd believed had to be cut out and sent adrift if I were going to lead anything approaching a "peaceful" life. I'd discovered firsthand, and painfully (through circumstances of my own choosing), that such characteristics as mine were as practical, and as necessary for survival, as any "hard-nosed" approach to the Earth ever was. The point proved over and over to me in both the private and public portions of this "experiment" was that all of us reach out to the mysterious in whatever form we perceive it—we yearn for it, in fact, and we must find it or die, as I'd discovered so vividly.

Intuitively, my Dundee dreamers and sooth-tellers recognized the inner origin of external events. And I think that we all understand this naturally, no matter how cynical we become about inner realms (cynicism seeming quite respectable in the face of current psychic poppycock).

The absolutely miraculous thing about it, though—the crafty, marvelous, and *wickedly* humorous thing—is that the mysterious, in whatever form we perceive it, *always reaches back*. We *do* always get help. The universe *does* always answer our calls—but in the smooth, literal language of the soul. And in the end, our psychological stability depends upon faith in this caretaking universe, whether we call it Self, God, science, or anything else.

So, as I tried to tell Annie and Harold, there isn't a label anywhere that fits the individual by decree, unless you're willing to make some mighty efforts to squeeze your Self inside whatever definitions come with it. And that never works for long. Your naturally knowing self will always push at whatever framework proves too small. You might be suspicious or purposefully ignorant of the process, or even wide-open gullible about it; but you know who you are, and always have. Coincidence, dreams, impulses, and the simple magic of your days are all the sources you ever need to discover it. That is the free and naturally accessible gift of your caretaker self.

It's the discovery of this caretaker self, of the natural knowing abilities within you, and of a cohesive order of things in which all acts have meaning, that is within a written record of inner journeys. A week's worth, a year's worth, several years of dream/impulse records open up self-knowledge that is impossible to describe. I think you will find, for one thing, that the combination of your dreams and your impulses will lead you to quality—in quite practical terms.

All in all, such field notes have convinced me that dreams, natural knowing, impulses, and the rest hint at a quality of perception that simply escapes our current ideas of the workings of the physical world. Because we think we move forward from one moment to the next, leaving the past in cement and groping blindly toward an unknowable future, we are therefore stuck with a similar idea of precognition (if we think it exists at all): that it moves ahead just a bit faster than we do, leaving behind it a photo of the moments to come, like a bright piece of sea-glass on an otherwise deserted beach.

However, there is too much we don't know about the mind, the self and its possibilities, and the evolving nature of consciousness to pin rigid definitions on what little of the landscape we've seen. I'm convinced from my own experience and those of others that your dreaming self—your caretaker self—knows why you're here and what your best intentions are. Encased in dreams, impulses, personal events, and the chatter of your own conscious mind is all the information you need to get where you need to go, and it's all free for the looking-in.

The fact is that you DO know what your dreams mean, and you CAN trust what you believe to be true about them. You get what you want from your caretaker self—and records of that information can give you a method of reflection that will literally revolutionize the fabric of your days. You will find within yourself a wisdom that incorporates, and yet supercedes, fact; a wisdom that can be trusted always; a balanced combination of discernment, intuition, and action.

The act of trusting subjective experience may in itself have a tremendous evolutionary impact upon consciousness.

The record-keeping methods are simple enough. Keep a diary of your impulses, whether you followed them or not, and what occurred that tied in with events or dreams or funny little intersections of coincidence (and do use some commonsense judgment at first—even if you just record your impulses for a while, the emerging pattern you'll see there is amazing all by itself). Sometimes people ask me how they can start remembering their dreams—often insisting that they've never recalled a dream in their lives. I think that an impulse record will automatically open up your dream life to you; but you can also jog your dream-consciousness by pretending that yesterday was a dream! Write down what happened to you during the day and then interpret those events as if you were remembering a dream. Or try writing a description of an outstanding event in your life and the circumstances of your days just before it occurred; then interpret the information as though it were from a dream.

Such exercises should bring about dream recall—which in itself is enhanced by the act of writing dreams down. Dreaming educates the memory; dreams present you with new thoughts and with new looks at your *current* thoughts, or at the way you think about your own means of perception (an intriguing subjective perspective, to say the least!). Dreams also focus the "chatter of your conscious mind" and put mental fingers on beliefs and realizations you may not have known were yours. Associative connections, for example, are important pieces of knowledge and understanding—and truth-telling—that you might tend to discount, or shove away with the learned reaction that such associations aren't "logical" . . . or because you might not want to face what such associations imply.

Dreams discount nothing. They operate from a wider form of what we *call* logic. Dreams are innocent, and have no qualms or "morals," in the cultural framework as we think of it. They know!

One example of this associative dream-process is familiar to most everyone—the experience of seeing different people combined into one dream-person. The implications are as varied as any set of associations, some of which are obvious: someone you know reminds you of someone else. On another level, this sort of person-mix can demonstrate quite vividly the ongoing precognitive and clairvoyant nature of dreams and at the least is never a superficial observation.

For instance, several years ago, within the space of a month, I dreamed five or six times of two men—"A," whom I was dating at the time, and "B," a fellow from high school years—who were merged into one rather frightening person. The two men didn't know one another and consciously I'd never associated them at all. However, a couple of months later I discovered that "A" had some serious personal problems that were almost exactly the same as difficulties that had caused me to break off my friendship with "B" years before. In this case, the dream-mix served as a warning, which I heeded. Consciously, I had no knowledge beforehand of "A"'s problems and they weren't obvious.

Interpreting your dreams may seem intimidating, but with practice and the belief that their meaning *is* open to you, the interweaving of dreams and your daily life will blossom. Keep notes on anything that happens during the day that connects with your dreams—even if that connection is tenuous, or "just a feeling." Dream-waking life synchronisms and their meaning may not come together for a while—sometimes not for years. But again, the act of record keeping in itself serves to bring this type of information into your conscious awareness, not to mention the benefits of keeping such a record for reference. You may see, upon studying your records, certain patterns and phases of dreams, and maybe even dreams coming true by "bits," as I did. You may discover, as I did, that precognition is a quality of the naturally knowing self quite unlike the present connotations and limitations of the word.

You will find that dreams can allow you to "practice" the probable results of decisions—and allow you "emotional" practice in upcoming events. This was involved in Mrs. Densig's death-dreams, for instance, or my worried friend's sexy ones. Or take my Dundee dreamer, E., who insisted that her dreams were straight re-creations of her daily life—except for dreams she "confessed" to me in which her son, who was then elementary school age, was grown-up and gone; a natural, common dream of parents preparing for an eventuality that may be very difficult to consciously face.

Dreams can simply be designed to make you feel good when you need it. Whenever I feel discouraged about writing, I tend to dream about some thrilling athletic achievement—usually ice skating in the Olympics (a childhood fantasy acted out!) or riding horses in some competition. During a particularly difficult time in my life, I dreamed often of racing Niatross, the great pacer, and knowing that the beautiful horse was *my* champion, too . . . winning because of the rapport between us. These dreams never fail to carry feelings of accomplishment and renewal over into my days.

So it would seem, listening to my Dundee dreamers and heeding my own hunches, impulses, and dreams, that this . . . facility of natural knowing and the caretaker self must, in our time and place, rise from a learned determination to recognize and make use of it. It would seem that natural knowing knows true experience from official experience, and knows how to guide the individual with a variety of inner and outer "clues." To experience natural knowing on a conscious, creative level means having the audacity to sidestep safe, preconceived definitions of how things happen; of staying alert to the odd, the peculiar, and the "illogical" moments, and keeping track of them and how they relate to daily events as you ordinarily perceive them.

There is a multitude of theory and speculation about dreams, coincidence, and other subjective events, running the philosophical gamut from the mechanistic idea that dreams are nothing more than the mental gibberish of neural housecleaning to the dungeon-of-the-Id theories of traditional psychoanalysis. In the middle, there is a tremendous amount of research being done that is at least starting with new premises and questions about dreams—the studies at the University of Rochester and at McGill University, for example, looking into the relationship between nightmares and health problems; or the lucid dream experiments being conducted at the Stanford University Sleep Research Center.

However, the fact remains that no one else's opinions, including mine, on the nature of your dreams has more validity than your own experience; and this is, I think, a basic truth that people understand—everyday people in a small rural town understood it; you understand it *now*.

You don't have to seek out a string of psychics or be intimidated by someone else's credentials. You know what you know. There is nothing wrong with you to make right. Listen to your own voices, your own thoughts, your dreams and your impulses. No one else's voice, thoughts, or impulses apply. Moreover, your dreams exist in the open marketplace of your natural creature-self. Impulses, dreams, and private vision are your connection with your idealized sense of what the world should be; and you and I and the world are more than ready for a new order of logic—for the fullness of the moment, for the thickness of events, for the next step in the evolution of consciousness. In that regard, we are all of us scientific naturalists in the virgin land of dreams.

Dream yourself, dream your town, dream your world. Dream a grand dream, indeed. It's the most natural thing there is.

EPILOGUE

(The Dream Goes On)

"I've got a dream for you that makes absolutely no sense at all," the man said to me with great finality.

"No sense at all, huh?" I put my bundle of books, letters, and other stuff down on my friend's desk and prepared to listen. He'd hollered at me from the other side of Main Street to get right over to his office, he had something to tell me, something I'd really be interested in, get over there right *now* . . . all that for a dream that made no sense? I doubted that, somehow.

"In this dream, I saw a bridge being built across the sky," he said, gesturing illustratively. "It was half-done, only halfway across, and covered with hundreds of little tiny people who were working on it—but the thing was, it was being made out of trash. Old appliances, junkyard stuff, old cars, that sort of thing. Flimsy construction, too, like a cartoon—you know, somebody would nail a board down, walk out onto it and nail another board down, then walk out on *that* one, on and on across the sky . . ." He stopped, staring at the expression written on my face. "Naw, you can't . . . aw, c'm*on*."

I felt a little chill, as though the window were open on a March rain. It was so obvious to me—but then it's easy, looking in from the outside. Not quite a year before, this man had suffered a heart attack and bypass surgery; and though he was recovering nicely, he'd had occasional symptomatic setbacks here and there—shortness of breath, chest pains, rounds of general rotten-blah. I suppose everyone coming out of that kind of physical shock goes through that sort of thing, but just then I found myself thinking, oh *please*, people, *stop* telling me this stuff . . . let's have an election and get Dundee a new dream-shaman, okay?

"Well?" he said, challenging.

"You mean you can't see what that is? A bridge across the sky? A *bridge* ?"

No response.

"All right," I said. "It seems to me that your dream is a pretty clear picture of where you are right now. You *are* on a bridge—a psychological bridge, a transition of some sort—between two worlds. Two levels of existence. Where you are and somewhere you're thinking about going. Could be life and death, or maybe

health and illness, or present and future, I don't know. It's *your* dream." Still no response. "Well, the important point is that you're building a flimsy structure," I added. "See, it's made out of trash, built in a haphazard, cartoon way. It's not a permanent crossover, like a 'real' bridge—you can tear it down at any time, or build it better, for that matter. It was only halfway there when you became consciously aware of it. Um . . ." My friend was staring at me the way one might stare at an arrow honing in on the spot between one's eyes.

"Listen, it's your dream," I said hastily. "Interpret it any way you want." I smiled.

No comment. He had apparently entered a state of suspended animation, complete with cigarette in hand. The clock, ticking its mindless way through the hours, chimed four times.

"Well, gotta go," I said brightly, gathering up my stuff and heading for the door. "Just remember—your bridgeworks is a pile of junk, ha-ha! See you!"

I banged out the door and headed home. Jeezus, I thought, I can't believe he was *that* opaque to the meaning of his dream. Well, maybe the encounter would serve to get him back on the physical track a bit; get in shape, stop smoking, whatever his beliefs were about the situation. I knew that if that dream had been mine, I sure would have done some belief-reassessing, and fast. (And in fact, my friend suffered a minor stroke not long after this dream, though he quickly and almost completely recovered.)

The more I thought about it, though, the funnier the whole scene was. Even when you tried to *force* nonsense upon inner knowledge, the important parts got through somehow—how well I knew that to be true. It's our *ideas* doubting the worthiness of subjective information that lead us on searches for the correctly-credentialed authority to approve of our own inner knowing—not the nature of dreams themselves. People kept telling me their dreams because the *telling* is important; people know their dreams are *true* in the same way each individual is *true*.

Sean's friend Jeff, for instance. Jeff at 16 understood his dreams in a way that outshone every supposedly learned "psychic" on the talk-show circuit. Even when his dreams baffled him, Jeff could see that they were "true," whether or not you could define why, in so many words. He'd told me about some "shockers," too, like his dream of the space shuttle Challenger. Many months after the January, 1986, Challenger explosion, Jeff told me that he'd dreamed the night before that his Challenger poster had fallen off his bedroom wall . . . and that when his alarm woke him up that morning, the poster *had* fallen off the wall.

"Then I came home from school to watch the lift-off," Jeff said quietly. A few days after that disaster, Sean told me he'd dreamed of talking with the seven astronauts. "They were in the shuttle, in orbit, and didn't know they were dead," Sean said. "But some of them suspected it, 'cause they couldn't get radio contact. I didn't want to say anything, though—I felt kinda sorry for them."

Truth in dreams . . . it reminded me again of the Dundee-"bits" before-and-after dreams about Donald's death. But of course the "true" nature of dreams is also explicitly personal. Like the retired schoolteacher who'd recently stopped me in the hardware store to tell me a dream that he also insisted was senseless. In it, he'd found himself standing on the street trying to get his point across in an argument with someone (a typical waking characteristic, as this man loves debate and discourse), bothered all the while by the feeling that he was late for a play in which he was performing . . . yet when he finally arrived at the theater, he realized that he didn't know his part at all.

"The manager said that somebody else had gone on for me at the start of the play, but that I could finish," he said to me. "But! I was terribly worried—I didn't know my part! How could I perform when I didn't know my part!

"Now, what does *that* mean," he finished, grinning at me.

"Uh, well, gee," I stammered, embarrassed by what I'd picked up—again, the dream seemed transparent to me. "Just try thinking about how you feel about yourself since you retired—maybe you aren't sure of your 'part' in life anymore, or something."

He blinked, and a look of amazed comprehension washed over him. "Oh-h-h-h, ye-e-e-es, of *course!* " he said. "Yes, yes I see now . . . I don't know my *part* . . . my *PART* . . . sure, sure, my PART!" Hand on chin, he turned abruptly and walked out of the store, still muttering, not even remembering to say good-bye.

But possibly the best epilogue here is really the forward.

After I finished the final draft of this book, I decided that it needed a better title and more of my own dreams added to it. On the interminable impulse, I took my 1979 dream notebook (the year I first asked for Dundee dreams) from the shelf and began skimming through it, looking for a dream or two that might make interesting reading.

And suddenly, there it was.

On Wednesday, September 19, 1979—seven years before this book was finished, before this cycle of . . . realization and growth of mine was done, before any of the impulse experiments, precognitive progressions, coincidences, and attendant revelations—before all of that, I'd recorded the following dream:

"I walk into the Dundee Pharmacy and see on the paperback bookrack by the door a paperback book of *mine*, complete with bright, splashy cover and two (!) photographs of me on the back. THE BOOK'S TITLE IS SOMETHING LIKE, 'DREAMING MYSELF.'

"I stare at the book in disbelief [*as I was staring right then at my dream-notebook*]. I can't remember writing it—yet as I stand there, staring, I *do* remember writing it. The book seems like a reissue of something I wrote several years before this dream—'back when I censored certain things,' my dream-self thinks. I take the book out of the rack to feel its bright, shiny cover.

"Bob H., the pharmacist, walks over just as I'm adjusting all the books so that a copy of mine appears in every slot on the rack (something I frequently do with Jane Roberts' books whenever I see them in stores). Bob grins and we laugh about my self-promotion. I ask him, 'Did I write this?' I'm still caught in a strange juxtaposition between knowing that I did write the thing and knowing that it isn't written yet. The book is definitely about Dundee, however. Just then Judy D., now an *Observer* editor, walks into the store, grabs a book, and asks me to autograph it. I'm flattered. What to write?

"Then I'm in another scene, on the ferry to Martha's Vineyard. Copies of *Dreaming Myself* are floating in the water alongside, although for some reason this is part of its promotion. I'm with a woman who reminds me of Roy's twin sister, L. We all sit down to eat on the ferry deck—and I stare at L.'s plate in horror. She has boiled up my *lycopodioides v. cristata* (a very peculiar-looking variety of succulent, cousin of the cactus) to eat, like a common cabbage! I scream at her, 'How dare you do that to my plant!' But then I see that she's done the same thing with my *Euphorbia flanaganii cristata*! Unspeakable! I yank the plates with these poor boiled plants out from under her knife and fork and push her into the sea, where she makes a big splash and I yell at her for getting my books all wet!"

"Hey!" I said aloud, laughing, triumphant. "Hey! You know what?? You did it! *THAT'S YOUR DUNDEE DREAM!!*"

AFTERWORD

On the Death of Jane Roberts

Jane Roberts Butts died on September 5, 1984, after a long bout with rheumatoid arthritis. For more than sixteen years, she was my friend and my mentor. I met Jane and Rob in 1968, at a New Year's Eve party in their Elmira, N.Y., apartment—at which time I believe I told Jane that she was "really great for 39." Having moved through 39 and out the other side myself by now, I can see that I greatly understated the case.

From the start, Jane encouraged my writing and other abilities and in doing so birthed my artistic freedom, giving me a context in which to express my own eccentric musings. She was a gifted poet, prose writer, psychic, and intellectual achiever. But she was most of all a pioneer—for you, for me, for everyone. She and Rob explored the great uncharted countries of the psyche in ways that demanded throwing out nearly every premise that human civilization, for better or worse, is built upon. The risks that Jane and Rob took in doing that are difficult to comprehend; but by taking them, they changed forever the direction of consciousness in the world as we know it; literally writing new messages on the genetic code of experience.

And Jane's struggles with conflict and pain sprang precisely from the very human nature of that splendid, stubborn, infinitely

gifted self. To ask where Seth is now is to ask where Picasso's paintings have gone; for it is always the human character of the artist, living and dying among us, that creates the artwork for us all.

I would like to think that Jane's work has set us all free here, and that she chose to focus in worlds that need her voice now more than ours does. I think therefore that the best tribute, or gift, that we can give in Jane's memory is for you and I simply to trust our impulsive, eccentric, forever untamable selves—and to demand always that our lives "thrill with quality." For what else did Jane leave us but the awakening of the Seth within each one of us, and the possibility of personhood's grandest evolution?

APPENDIX ONE

Death and Dreams

(The Body Never Lies)

In my mother's last days,
crows marched black dagger-eyed
across the lawn's September heat,
massed in strident cabalistic flocks
the likes of which we'd never seen before—
Oh, crows, I said,
show my mother out of here.
Escort her, if you please,
dressed as you are in cloaks of jet,
dressed as you are to eat her eyes;
come in the door, all cunning as you are,
beckon with your silken wings; come close,
fill her sky with your sharp rapacious tongues,
march her through the shimmer-waves of heat
and take her where she wants to go. Crows,
I said, take her before
the winter comes. She understands
your grinning avarice—
Oh, crows, your predatory dreams are hers.
Your nature is the thing she most desires.

-SMW, 1985

In the spring and summer of 1981, both Jane Roberts and I began a series of dreams that involved past events rising up and emerging into the present—oddly disturbing dreams for both of us. At the time, I was busy helping my husband manage our show horses, and my mind wasn't consciously occupied by people and places from the past. And yet, dream after dream came to me with long-dead relatives who revealed that they'd never "really" died; or past events that had rearranged themselves, making these relatives "not-dead" in my present. Jane told me of many similar dreams, most often of her parents, who were both dead by that time. It was strange. What were we trying to tell ourselves?

I dreamed most often of my maternal grandmother, Lois Templer Baker, who died on her 61st birthday, September 13, 1956, when I was eleven years old. The cause of her death stemmed from the disease lupus erythematosus, discovered in autopsy, and at the time so unusual that my grandmother's case was written up in the New England Journal of Medicine.[1] The disease had caused kidney failure and internal hemorrhaging; and my mother often recounted the moment when she and her sister, my aunt Marie, had made the decision to disconnect their mother from life-support systems.

Twenty-five years later, in March of 1981, doctors confirmed my mother's suspicions—her *insistence*, really—that she, too, had lupus, with that diagnosis made almost to the day of *her* 61st birthday. So maybe, I mused, that unhappy discovery brought on dreams of my grandmother; perhaps I was playing out some worries about my mother's health—and for that matter, my own. There was a two- and possibly three-generation lupus link threading through the women in my mother's family, and according to a strong body of medical thinking, I was now standing in line to pick up the thread. My grandmother Baker's eccentric and rather bohemian personality made a strong impression on me as a child; and even though more than thirty years have gone by since her death, I still find myself missing her—or at least my idea of who she was—and the feeling of *like* that I shared with her. (She came from the same planet I did, my child-self said.) I'd dreamed of her before this, of course, but those 1981 dreams of her—and others—had a whole new feeling about them. In the back of my mind, then, was a knot of questions involving the trustworthiness of my own eccentric characteristics as against standard notions of heredity, family behavior patterns, and the weight of modern medical thinking.

On Wednesday, August 26, 1981, I recorded the following for the previous night: "A strange, oddly comforting dream of inarticulated portent. A huge group of people (maybe everyone who ever came to Jane Roberts' ESP class) has gathered together in my old Elmira high school. I run up the sidewalk, a bit late for this gathering . . . it's apparent that something is afoot; that there are great purposes behind this group's dream—for I do feel that it's a group dream . . ."

Later in the week, on Friday, August 29, I dreamed that I was ". . . riding in a car with my *paternal* grandmother, Marion Disbro Mullin. She is clear and vivid, looking as she did at age 50 or so. She says she is there to impart 'Mullin wisdom' to me, especially 'wisdom of the body,' or something like that—something genetic from that side of the family."

Then on Tuesday, September 1: "A strange, gruesome, and very haunting dream. Beginning with something about the veterinarian's truck, I am led by a woman—is she my mother or someone else, or a combination of the two?—into a small, cold, secret building; one that resembles the slatted orchid houses I've seen in Florida.[2] As I walk inside, I notice an older, white-haired woman working at a bench. At first I don't recognize this woman. It's been so long . . . but then it comes to me: it's my grandmother Baker.

"She looks up at me. Does she recognize me or not? I'm flooded with memories of her creative, funny, and very outrageous self. But is she dead or not? Someone—an outside voice—tells me that she's been 'preserved' all this time [since 1956] by keeping her in this building at less than 40 degrees—that this method keeps her lupus 'in abeyance' and that's why my mother (or this other combination person) is here also. This seems gruesome enough, somehow, but then both women either leave the building or the place suddenly disappears from around them and in an instant, they are reduced to bags of blood with hair and bones mixed in. This happens in an implosion, from their bodies to these bags. I pick these up and leave—it seems my grandmother's remains fill an especially large bag—but I know there's no place else to go. If I could only find the right place, I think, perhaps the remains would reconstitute. I wake up feeling sick and frightened."

That morning, my husband Roy mentioned that he'd had weird dreams all night long in which he'd been dehorning deer, and that officials from the Conservation Department had arrived to analyze the resulting pools of blood. "Gory," was his succinct comment.

Then on Thursday, September 3: "Another dream about my grandmother Baker 'coming back.' This time, a group of us is staying at my parents' home [located in the hamlet of Webbs Mills, just south of Elmira, where my grandmother and grandfather Baker had also lived]. We are making preparations for my grandmother to reappear. It's not clear what this means, but apparently she is returning from her state of death to re-insert herself into my life—*specifically* my life, and no one else's. We sit in my old bedroom, which is as it was before my parents redecorated the place in the 1960s.

"This dream seems to be connected with the August 26 class/group dreams, and with the August 29 dream of my grandmother Mullin—and especially with the September 1 dream of my grandmother being 'preserved.' Are they a continuous dream? Do they mean a literal emergence of past events into the present? But how? And why does this involve my grandmothers, both many years dead?

"Whatever they symbolize, these dreams all have a feeling of great importance to me personally and in some larger sense, having to do with some 'whole new way of thinking' about physical events, as Rob Butts recently described it . . ."

Later in the morning of Thursday, September 3, I received a phone call from Beth Dennis, daughter-in-law of my "first fan," Emily [see Chapter 5], who had some shocking news: Emily had died early in the morning of September 2, of a massive heart attack.

Even though my friendship with Emily had been entirely by telephone and letter, I felt a sudden fist of loss at her death. Then Beth went on to tell me some of the details: Emily had been just 55 years old and apparently in the best of health—until Wednesday, August 26, when she was suddenly struck by a minor heart attack while at home. She was rushed to the hospital, where she seemed to be recovering. Then in the early morning hours of September 2, Emily suffered a violent cardiac arrest. "They said that her heart just exploded, that was the term they used," Beth said. "She didn't have a chance; there wasn't a thing they could do—and nobody knows why it happened. She'd never been sick a day in her life." Knowing of her connection with me, Beth said she'd tried to call me on Sunday, August 30, to tell me that Emily was in the hospital, and again on the night of September 2, after Emily's death. Beth's daughter, Stacey, was especially adamant that her mother contact me. Stacey had read some of Jane's books and had struck up an occasional correspondence with me.

Here I'll quote from my notes, made later that day: "I was stunned by Emily's death, to say the least. And I immediately connected the news with that gruesome dream of September 1. In that dream, I'd been led to the small building by a woman who combined my mother's attributes with someone else's—someone like Emily? That's a hindsight guess, but the Sept. 1 dream description of my grandmother's dream-death—the 'explosion' and resulting blood—connect, in my mind at least, with what happened to Emily's heart. Even Roy recalled a bloody dream that night . . .

"In my dream, my grandmother reappeared to me and then 're-died,' in typical dream fashion. Stacey has now lost a grandmother whose creative personality inspired her, as my grandmother Baker's inspired me as a child. On August 26—the date when Emily suffered the initial difficulty—my dream seemed to be gathering class-type folks together in preparation, and this felt especially connected with the September 3 dream of my grandmother's impending reappearance.

"The funny thing is, Emily and I discovered a few months ago that we were probably related, though very distantly, through my grandmother Baker's side of the family. But on August 29, my grandmother Mullin appeared in a dream that emphasized the genetic heritage of my *father's* side of the family (where, for example, lupus doesn't occur). Is this meant as a message of counter-balance, genetically speaking?

"The elements of this dream series—for it does feel like a definite series—have certainly served to make me think hard about beliefs concerning heredity, behavior patterns across generations, and certain personal connections with the past and present. Oddly, when I called Jane Roberts to chat with her about all of this, she said that in the past two or three days she's dreamed several times that both of her parents, as well as her grandfather, who are all deceased, had come back to life or had secretly been alive all along."

Here again, when you scrutinize this little batch of dreams for evidence, in usual terms, of "provable" precognition, nothing stands out either as foreknowledge or clairvoyance—in strict cause and effect, that is. Because what is *precognitive* about the dreams is in the nuance of *personal meaning for me.* The dream series seems to *include* Emily's death rather than predict it—although a precognitive air still whispers through it all. And I reacted powerfully to them, carrying the intangible weight of their meaning through my waking hours.

Days later, I was having what I call "repercussion" dreams, such as this one dated Sunday, September *13*: "A strange dream of dual realities. I 'recall' the 'forgotten' fact that I'd once been married to D., a friend from high school days . . . and as I wake up, this 'forgotten fact' becomes imprinted on reality in a confusing mix:

Did I marry him or didn't I? It seems logical and obvious that I did. Yet I also know that I didn't. It's at once an absolute memory and a part of my past; yet just as obviously *not* part of my past.

"Even after I woke up completely, I had to think hard about this to get the 'right' sequence in order. The feelings of past events—or more to the point, past *probable* events—rising up into my present is stronger than ever."

I wondered if this series were "finished"—or if there were more to come; if the symbols of days and dreams were pointing to other things that I couldn't yet see. But I decided to stop reading so much into it; I worried about getting carried away with my analytical imagination. How far can inner knowledge reach?

But then, just for the hell of it, I pulled out all of my ten-years' compilation of dream notebooks and began reading through all of the autumn-of-the-year dreams.

That's when I came across the dream that, I remembered, had unsettled me so much at the time: It was from September of 1973, and consisted only of an overvoice against a dark plain, saying, "Your father will recover from his present condition, but he will die of cardiac arrest in a parking lot." In 1973, my father was recovering from an emergency operation for a perforated diverticulum, but his general health, including his heart, was fine. That afternoon in 1981, I thought that it was an interesting coincidence to come across this old dream, given the circumstances of Emily's death by cardiac arrest. There hadn't been any reason in 1973 to think that anything of the sort would happen to my father. However, by 1981, physical complications from the stab wound he'd sustained years before were beginning to affect my father's health. And on December 13, 1983—ten years and two months after that odd voice-over dream—my father did indeed die of cardiac arrest . . . *while walking through his company's parking lot on the way to his car.*

And on September 5, 1984, my friend Jane Roberts died—at the age of 55, after suffering for several years from the effects of rheumatoid arthritis; her death resulted from infection and other complications of that condition. And . . . I remembered this autumn, 1981, dream series. Jane had told me then that she had dreamed of her dead parents "coming back" into her life in some strange way, just as I had dreamed of my grandmother's reappearance.

The connection that I make here is that Jane's symptoms at the end of her life were very much like those her mother suffered at the time of *her* death in 1972. My grandmother Baker died of a disease that in my mother's family is *familiar* in many senses of the word—symptoms that are known; a pattern that is familiar—even though certainly undesirable. A pattern that seems *shared*, even, by my mother, grandmother, and possibly my great-grandmother, who herself died in 1947 of an unknown ailment of the kidneys (organs often affected by lupus).[3] Each of these women was in her own way a gifted artist; each in one way or another *suppressed those artistic urges specifically because*—and these words are my mother's, mouthed many times over as I was growing up—*because they were women, and women have to wear blinders. They can't allow themselves to see. They can't look from side to side, or realize too much. They are not allowed. They have to hold themselves down.*

An autoimmune disease, attacking the body of the self. Three women; a painter (I still have several of Great-Grandma Templer's dark, brooding oils), a poet (my grandmother Baker's poems were published in literary magazines of the day; I even have some of the fan letters she received), a secret writer (especially gifted at humor, my mother had just begun a continuation of Great-Grandfather Asbury's family history when she died). Creative gifts, suppressed by beliefs that these impulses did not fit with what women were "supposed" to do; a chain of beliefs obviously universal—and deeply personal, as the universal always is. And so what is it that we really inherit—is genetic memory imbued with messages of disease, *or is it that we will follow our impulses whether "we" do or not, however long it takes us, even if it means following them down through the centuries, passing them on to our children like precious family artifacts growing older and more "valuable," psychologically speaking, the longer they remain intact . . .*

On Thursday, September 13, 1984, I recorded the following dream: "I am on the phone with my mother [who lived some 50 miles south of Dundee]. My father [at that date dead exactly nine months] is in the background, yelling things at my mother for her to relay to me. She has to keep interrupting what she is saying to me in order to repeat what Pa is saying . . . all very irritating [*and in fact a familiar telephone-scene*]. He is upset because I don't have any health insurance . . . he's shouting that I must get some, *now*, without delay. I wake up wondering if something awful is going to happen to me and I'll wish I had health insurance after all . . . But that isn't it; something else is going on here."

The next day, I called my mother and in the course of the conversation she admitted that she'd been having some bleeding ulcer symptoms and that she was going to call her doctor for a checkup. Then at noon the following day, I was suddenly struck with the strong impulse to call her again. Noontime was an unusual hour for us to call one another, as my mother often went out for lunch with girl friends—but the impulse was powerful and explicit: Call!

The phone rang five times, six times—seven times. I was about to hang up when I heard the receiver clatter off its hook and crash onto the floor. Finally, weakly, my mother came on the line. Apologetically, she confessed she'd had a little trouble getting to the phone—she'd apparently passed out and seemed to be bleeding from her mouth, in great gushes actually, and she didn't feel well at all . . .

Somehow, I got her to put the phone back on its receiver so I could call an ambulance. Even as I dialed the operator, I found myself congratulating this impulse-following act: my mother had been saved by the bell; by the bell of an impulse, how *neat*.

But later, I would find myself wondering just how *neat* it was after all. When icewater lavages didn't solve the bleeding problem, surgery revealed a malignant tumor in my mother's stomach—cancer that quickly spread to her liver (or possibly from it) and caused her death little more than a year after my "miraculous" impulse of a phone call had "saved" her. Had I—had *she* in fact—interfered with the process of her natural death, meant to be encountered in private on that autumn morning in the peace and quiet of her own kitchen? If so, what "truth" did my impulse contain? A last-minute change of heart on all our parts?

The means of her death seemed an end of a lifelong progression of more and more serious internalized ailments (and a dramatic reflection of my strange and bloody dream of August 26, 1981); and the last year of her life was for me a searingly powerful learning experience, as millions of human beings can attest, of course. My mother died at home on the morning of Saturday, October 19, 1985—peacefully, after slow weeks of struggle against the ongoing ravages of terminal illness. By far the greatest part of that struggle for my mother was her deeply-rooted belief that death meant personal extinction—that she was facing absolute annihilation of self. Nurses and others around her expressed great astonishment that she stayed alive, stubbornly, in spite of terrible physical deterioration (although she was never in great pain). More, she would not talk about her illness; it was not her way to burden others with her fears. Only her eyes, black sparking dots of fury, revealed any emotion whatsoever.

Finally, one afternoon a week or two before she died, my mother said to me, "You wouldn't believe the hallucinations that come with this," and went on to describe a series of visions involving geometric patterns, letters from the Greek alphabet, and mathematical symbols—along with gruesome nightmares of spilled intestines and bloody accidents (again reminiscent of my 1981 dream).

I could see that my mother viewed these experiences as frightening and somewhat demented; so I explained as best I could that these were a natural part of what was going on (really a difficult task, since the two of us never once discussed her obviously impending death) and that at least the hallucinations seemed a natural extension of her own interests (she had studied Greek classics in the original, for one thing). I suggested that the bloody nightmares might even be her dreams' interpretations of what was going on within her body. I don't know how much of this she accepted, as she listened without comment . . .

On the morning of Friday, October 18, 1985, I recorded the following dream for the night of Thursday/Friday the 17/18th: "I am standing in the driveway, in the dark, by my mother's house. Sharon S.—a former Dundee native who owned a beauty shop—appears as one of the nurses taking care of my mother. She is black—but black like the night, like black paint. She tells me that she is 'almost in life.' She says to me, 'I have come to take your mother away.' To escort her, she says—to show my mother how to leave physical reality.

"This woman then takes me on a 'trial run' or a demonstration of where she will take my mother. We fly up the backyard hill, over the family cemetery, and into the sky—which is filled with geometric shapes and odd objects; I feel that yes, this is the 'direction'—the doorway that Ma will go through to die. However, all of this feels somewhat alien to me and I tell the woman that while I can understand why this would make sense to my mother, this 'doorway' isn't one that I would take.

"'That is why I have come,' the woman says. 'I will come into your life for this reason and no other.'"

I told this dream to my friend Susan Benedict on Friday morning, after writing it down. I knew that my mother's death was close at hand; yet when my aunt called with the news the next morning (early Saturday), I still felt some quiet surprise. Sean and I drove to her house, where we were greeted by Shirley, the nurse who had been in charge of my mother's round-the-clock caretaking since mid-August. For some reason—impulsively, between making all the attendant phone calls and other arrangements—I told Shirley about my dream of the 18th—and she nearly fell off her chair!

It seemed that on Friday night, the nursing care organization had sent a new R.N., a woman none of us had ever met before, to substitute for a last-minute schedule change. The R.N.—a woman named Louise P.—was black. I later spoke with Louise about my mother's last hours. Among other details, Louise said that she and my mother spent most of that time in conversation; and that my mother expressed great interest in a blanket that Louise was crocheting (geometric patterns?) and in talking about the antiques, books, and other objects in the living room (where her bed was set up). At 6:00 a.m., my mother asked Louise for a talwin (a mild pain pill and relaxant) and basically did not respond to outside stimuli again. She died at about 8:45 a.m.

Many other details coincide here (including a strong correspondence between my mother, Jane Roberts, and me—details that I plan to expand upon in another book), but the main message of my October 18th dream—that my mother would be finally shown how to let go easily—was apparently borne out. Furthermore, my aunt Marie (my mother's sister) later filled me in on a detail of their childhood that I hadn't known: when she and my mother and their brother were all seriously ill with pneumonia, my grandfather had hired a neighborhood friend—a black man—to help nurse his children back to health. So a natural caretaking thread existed there to begin with.

A funny little side note here is that Louise's last name is the same as the woman who is in partnership with Sharon S. (of my dream) in her Dundee beauty shop, another detail I couldn't have known before I spoke with Louise on the phone that Saturday.

Thus, when I look across the spectrum of these dreams, I have to gaze and wonder: Did my psyche reach out across time and space and the probabilities of circumstance, unfettered by standard notions of possibility, and show me correlations that *could* exist—as well as those that *did* exist in this series of sad events? And in preparation—and perhaps with certain inner warnings—did my dreams give me, instead of a series of literal snapshots, the *meaning* in symbol and metaphor, of what was about to happen? Of things I was meant to realize?

Again, how far does the natural caretaker reach? On what infinite ground of knowledge do our lives, and world, reside?

DREAM, Monday/Tuesday, May 19/20, 1986: I meet my parents in a small white house near the ocean. They are both young and healthy, dark-haired, about 25 years old, and meticulously dressed (as was their habit in life) in wool tweed business suits. They are seated in white Adirondack chairs, my father nearest me; my mother sits with her calves crossed in a coy, rather old-fashioned feminine gesture; her skirt is just-below-the-knee, with stockings and heels—all very flattering and characteristic of her. Her hair is very full and pulled up in a dark chignon. They are both obviously very involved with one another, in a closely-tied association that seems, to my dreaming-eye, to be only marginally associated with their forty-year marriage: they seem to have a working comaraderie of purpose that simply escapes me—and in fact, they are nearly oblivious to me altogether. They exude a feeling of freedom, and of release from the material goods they accumulated and maintained while alive—these things are far behind, insignificant, lost in memory. They seem to be waiting to start out on a voyage, something like an ocean voyage of an older, more adventurous era.

I try to draw them into conversation. My dream-self is fully aware that they are both now dead and gone from my lifetime, though I'm only vaguely aware that this is a dream. However, I do sense that we're communicating on a level of consciousness other than the usual waking one. My father talks to me, but my mother only watches, peering around my father's shoulder in a manner suggesting youth, innocence, and a certain sweet girlishness. I ask Pa if they realize they're dead, in my terms. He glances at my mother and shrugs; it's unimportant—as I realize then that of course it would be to them. It's a question relevant only to *me*. The fullness of their life "here"—the reality they've created on this level—has a validity for them every bit as real as my own. That they found one another and can move on to new adventures comes as a profound relief to me—mixed with some envy.

Then I ask Pa, "When exactly did you realize you were dead? What was it that gave you the clue? I'm interested in how this happens." This seems to appeal to his natural interest in the mysterious, but as he responds, I'm struck by his recall of the realization of death—it's the same as recollecting a dream, or any other remarkable, funny little anecdote from his existence. The importance of his physical death is no more, no less, than other noteworthy events in his "life"—which I suddenly realize with a blow *includes* the physical life in which I knew him, plus the one this dream touches, and a life or thread of LIFE that I can sense, as they obviously can, stretching out in all directions from them in an infinity of possibilities. This is the voyage upon which they are embarking; this is the journey they've prepared themselves for, and which fills them with the passion, anticipation, and youthful *bloom* I see here . . .

I am again struck with the sense that they are done with the physical lifespan as I think of it, at least for a "while." I feel a pang of loneliness: Will they go beyond my ability to communicate with them? Yet, in certain respects they always were, at least as we knew ourselves in our family setup. How will they be changed, I wonder. Health issues were such overriding concerns to them, plus my father's shattering war experiences on Guadalcanal in World War II; his scientific and inventive talents presented difficulties for him too, as these were largely put aside after the war . . .

Anyway, he looks off to my right, and answers the question: "What clued me in was when I found myself sitting with my father [*who died in 1937, when my father was 17*]," he says. "I gave him some backtalk and nothing happened. Normally—"here, my mother rolls her eyes in agreement—"that would have resulted in his knocking me on my *can*. But he didn't move. And that caught my attention!"

He laughs, spreads his hands in a characteristic whaddya-gonna-do gesture. "Then I noticed I wasn't a kid, either," he says, "but there the Old Man was, and there we were, sitting in the old West Water Street house [*my father's childhood home in Elmira*]. So then I started talking it over with the Old Man, and realized that, Jeeze, we weren't like we used to be—stuck with time, you know." He smiles, shrugs in his old familiar way.

I think that the phrase "stuck with time" is a very neat description of their now-free perspective on physical life. Again, I feel an envy for their status, their freedom to experience the mysterious from that level. I am about to ask the same questions of my mother when I am *yanked* out of the dream. I wake with the lingering sensation that the "time" wasn't right for such questions to my mother.

I think, well we're all figuring stuff out, no matter where we are—but it seemed to fall on me to do such figuring in the *awake* world, maybe for them, too, who knows? All I know is that I've come to *like* my parents more and more as my "time" goes on without them and all the parent-child junk between us falls away . . . a perfectly normal living process, of that I'm sure . . .

(NOTE made in May, 1988:) Yet another fascinating dream-connection running beneath my family's shared associations came clear to me in the fall of 1987, two years after my mother's death.

Briefly (because once again, the details are myriad, complicated, and apparently literally endless), the scenario began just after my mother was admitted to the hospital in September, 1984, with bleeding ulcers. I dreamed the night after she was admitted that I was once again a teenager, ice skating with best friend Evelyn down the frozen stairway that the creek next to my parents' house made in winter. In the dream, I saw a jagged hole in the ice up ahead of me, but could do nothing to avoid it and plunged through, into very deep water (though the creek actually is shallow and no longer freezes in the same smooth, solid way). Falling down through the icy cold, my dream-self acquiesced to death with great ease and relief . . . but then at the dream's last minute, my friend Evelyn reached down through the hole, grabbed me, and saved my life.

It's plain enough to me now, years after my mother's illness and death, how this dream connected with my "saving" her from death by bleeding ulcer on her kitchen floor—"falling down through a hole" being an apt image, plus the connection with the emergency icewater lavages she received in the emergency room—but at the time, I thought this dream meant that I'd "saved" her from falling into a premature death from widow's despair.

I was to discover that hindsight contemplation of one's dreams can yield some shocks, however. Though my mother seemed to respond to the emergency treatment and returned home in a week's time, she was back in the hospital a month later with the same symptoms, and this time doctors recommended surgery for what they thought might be stomach cancer. As my accounts have said, this diagnosis was borne out; but on October 11/12, 1984, the night before my mother's surgery, I woke up from a vivid and powerfully *reassuring-feeling* dream that I thought at the time must be telling me otherwise. In the dream, I walked into my Dundee apartment's bathroom and found Claude, my Siamese cat, all curled up in the bathtub—which was full of water. My dream-me was horrified that the cat was not only drowned but *rotten* inside, and so would fall to pieces when I picked him out of the tub—but at that moment, Claude looked up at me and blinked a sweet, cross-eyed cat-kiss from beneath the water. He was perfectly all right!

Here, the dream went on to a scene involving an Elmira doctor and his wife who were long-time friends of my parents. Then I found myself walking back into my Dundee bathroom . . . and this time, Claude was curled up contentedly in a clear glass *bowl* of water underneath the sink. Again, though he was under water and therefore should have been dead, he was alive and well.

I recorded this dream in a euphoria of (actually somewhat smug) reassurance. The unmistakable symbolic and literal message of this dream—then as now—was the sense that no matter how it might appear, *everything was going to be all right*. I made extensive notes (many on coincidences and connections too lengthy or personal to go into here; they also included family mat-

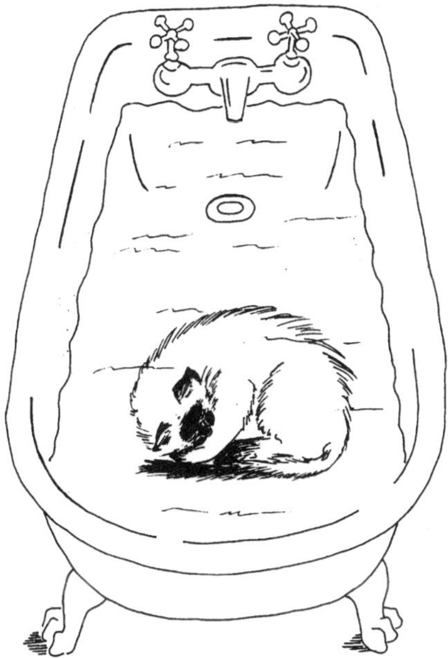

ters relating to the doctor and his wife) and dwelled at length on how Claude-in-the-tub must symbolize a benign-in-the-stomach condition that surgeons would find during that day's surgery—for that is how powerful the *feeling* of this dream was that everything was *all right*.

My interpretation of Claude-as-benign-mass was wrong, however. Months later, I came across those notes again and jammed them away in the bottom desk drawer, angry and humiliated with my apparently deluded optimism. But beneath it all, part of me remained convinced that this dream was not "false." No matter the outcome of my mother's travails, that part of me knew, the dream was simply *correct*. Yet if this were so, then either I wasn't making the right connections or I'd misinterpreted it from start to finish.

Two years later, my aunt Marie (my mother's sister) and her husband, my uncle Lou, and I met for lunch in Ithaca, N.Y., an occasional little get-together we all enjoy. I'd been aware that my uncle Bob (my mother and Marie's brother), who lives in New England, had been in and out of the hospital that summer with symptoms his doctor couldn't seem to diagnose; however, Uncle Bob wasn't consciously on my mind that pleasant fall day—until I walked up to Marie and Lou at our designated meeting-place. Immediately, my aunt said, "I have to tell you about this dream

I had last night, but it's really crazy and I wonder if I'm not really *sick*."

"Of course you're not sick," I joshed her in my old dream-shaman way. "Go on, tell it to me."

And as my aunt began to describe her dream, the hairs on the back of my neck stood right up in an electric recognition so startling that I felt a little dizzy (though we all walked casually enough along the Ithaca sidewalk). I had never described my "Claude in the Tub" dream to Marie and Lou, or to anyone else as far as I know—and in fact I'd consciously forgotten all about it by then—but there was Aunt Marie, telling me this dream:

"I was looking at a bunch of sheep grazing under the water at the bottom of a river," my aunt said. "Even though the water was flowing over them, they were perfectly content and were eating grass growing on the riverbottom. Then as I watched, it seemed that they turned from white to a murky brown, all at the same time, from top to bottom, so they were all mud-colored. But still, they went right on grazing. I thought they would be all . . . you know, *mushy* inside, from being under water. But they weren't."

She looked up at me. "Whatever do you think that means?" she asked. "I was thinking about Bob last night, so I thought maybe it had something to do with him—but what?"

I don't think I've ever experienced such a slam-wham gut-reaction instant *recognition* of dozens and dozens and *dozens* of connections and parallels and possibilities between dreams, waking reality, and *purposes* of same as I did in that moment. In fact, the sensations running through me (for I instantly saw how Marie's sheep-in-the-river fit with my Claude-in-the-tub) were so powerful and distracting that I hardly said anything to her for the rest of the afternoon, though I did reassure her that no, it wasn't a "sick" dream by any definition. Later, I wrote a letter to her explaining some of my thoughts.

For one thing, there is the obvious parallel of the animals existing peacefully beneath the water—alive when they should be dead. My mother and her brother were remarkably alike in many ways; close with a solid wordless understanding and sharing of many intangibles, including an odd feeling-tone of despair and nostalgia for things that never quite *were*. It seemed plain to me that my aunt and I had both perceived a common belief-bond that ran between my mother and Uncle Bob and which probably gave rise to their separate hassles with physical difficulties.

In my dream, the Siamese cat goes from a tub of water to a bowl of water—interesting that my mother's surgery removed about a third of her stomach (a bowl-like organ), thus making it smaller. In my aunt's dream, the sheep are in a flowing river. Several months *after* the dream, in March of 1988, my uncle Bob underwent major surgery on his *intestines*—the function of which could be likened to that of a "flowing river."

Also, our family has always had Siamese cats—sometimes four or five at the same time! *But the only female Siamese cat I ever owned, a fiesty-tempered curmudgeon named Piwacket, died of liver cancer in 1973* . . . another associative reason for my Siamese to appear in the dream-tub rather than, say, my American shorthair cat. Claude's presence was prescient, then, of other "inner" conditions to come.

And how odd that one of my most vivid childhood memories has always been of the days-long, rather vitriolic argument my father and Aunt Marie got into one Thanksgiving over whether or not people could catch anthrax (also known as "the wool-sorter's disease," since it's carried by sheep and indeed for centuries has been the cause of many human deaths; as Aunt Marie is a nurse and should know, I couldn't figure out why my father was being so stubborn in the opinion that people can't be infected with it—except that he relished the idea of goading people into preposterous arguments, which he was very talented at achieving)—yes, and odd, this memory's reference to sheep, my aunt Marie's connection with it, and my father's intestinal surgery in 1973 that involved the same techniques as in my uncle's case (no malignancy was found in either of the two men) . . . and then there is this *memory* I've had for years, and which I thought of as Marie told her dream, of my mother once telling me how her brother came down with anthrax while he was in the Army (though Aunt Marie says that this isn't true at all) . . .

I looked back upon that Claude dream, and my aunt's sheep dream, and the reassurance I felt so powerfully began to fall back into place. Though the passing of time could have much to do with my re-interpretation, it seems clear to me now that the Claude in my dream represented a combination of animal "level" contentment and understanding—and acceptance—and that in those terms, my mother knew exactly what she was doing—that "beneath the water," everything is always all right—which I do believe is true, even in the face of apparent disaster. In my dream of plunging through the ice, the feeling of acquiescence was pleasant and desirable—my rescue was not. Somehow, there is wisdom peeking through these dreams, and it is not meant to be ignored. Perhaps the caretaker self wills out no matter what.

NOTES

1 No longer uncommon, systemic lupus erythematosus is considered primarily a woman's disease, as 90% of all cases occur in females between 30 and 50. It is characterized by episodes of fever, fatigue, and an odd facial rash, plus numerous other loosely-aligned symptoms such as joint pain and swelling of the face, legs, and lymph glands, along with increased sun sensitivity and depression (even "mental disorders," according to some medical literature—making me think, cynically, that sticking *that* particular label on my grandmother—who indulged in rather uninhibited sexual experimentation long before such activity in women was considered permissible, or even "sane"—represents a certain Draconian approach to eccentricity, to say the least. My grandmother had been diagnosed earlier in her life as "schizophrenic"). Lupus as a defined disease has no medical cure at present. The body's connective tissues and organs—especially the kidneys, heart, and eyes—are affected; in my grandmother's case, her kidneys were destroyed, while my mother's heart, joints, and eyes were affected (and "complications of lupus" were officially part of the cause of her death). Doctors now prescribe combinations of immunosuppressive steroids and non-steroidal anti-inflammatory drugs to relieve lupus symptoms—drugs that obviously interfere with whatever natural immune system the lupus sufferer still has. The side effects of such drugs are numerous and under study; ironically, these can involve kidney and liver disorders—including cancer.

Another form of the disease, discoid lupus erythematosus, involves the skin only, the primary symptom being a rash or "butterfly" lesions on the cheeks, jawline, scalp, ears, neck or arms. Topical steroids are used these days to treat eruptions.

2 I note with interest here that my mother's first symptoms of lupus came upon her during my parents' annual trek to the Florida Keys in January of 1980. That year, their Marathon, Fla., apartment turned out to be right next door to one of the most fascinating places we ever discovered—a private orchid garden, with hundreds of blooms kept perfectly in a cool, inviting *slatted orchid house* by an older *white-haired woman*—who was working at a potting bench the first time we all peeked in on her, uninvited explorers of her miniature jungle.

3 And in that dream-series, seasonal dates connected too: Emily and Jane dying on September 2nd and 5th respectively, three years apart; my grandmother Baker dying in September of 1956; the dream about my father appearing in September of 1973. I also find it eerie and provocative that Jane's first "psychic" experience—the rush of information later entitled,

The Physical Universe as Idea Construction, essentially the birth of the Seth material—occurred on September 9, 1963.

Writing this, I looked it up—Great-Grandma Suzie Davis Templer died on November 11, 1947—no coincidence there. Everybody dies *some*time, after all.

A note: I believe that I also received dream information on my father's death just before it happened. Although my father had been dealing with severe breathing problems for about a year (serious enough so that by that fall he was on oxygen 24 hours a day, even carrying a portable oxygen tank between larger tanks at home and work), his death on December 13, 1983, was unexpected. Three days before, on December 10, I recorded the following dream: "A strange dream about President Ronald Reagan. I see him clearly. He reaches out to me beseechingly: he looks old and tired, and somehow threatened. I wonder [in the dream] if he's about to die."

The day before that, Dec. 9, I'd dreamed of a terrorist "attack" on my father's Elmira business, of which he was *president* and general manager at the time of his death. Once more, as my Dundee dreamers said to me many times—these dreams were not so much precognition of the event as they were preparations for it; when my mother finally reached me late that evening as I returned home from a village board meeting, her statement of his death—"He had a cardiac arrest and they couldn't save him," was all she said—was like a telegram from myself; an acknowledgment of something I'd realized, and only momentarily forgotten.

APPENDIX TWO

Probable Glitches, Possible Worlds

Another such experience of something . . . slipping . . . in Chapter 10's window-way is described in Chapter 14, page 393, of *Conversations with Seth.* There, my friend Ellen R. describes a mystery surrounding a Polaroid 320 camera that she'd assumed was stolen out of the van during her family's move to a New York City apartment in 1971.

". . . the losses were sad, but not the end of the world, and . . . we bought me a Square-Shooter Polaroid camera to replace [it]," Ellen said in a letter to me dated April 20, 1974. "Today, I was hanging up clothes in my closet, and there was my 320 Polaroid, hanging on a clothing rack right next to the door!

"Sure, you're thinking, Ellen is a slob, and she probably didn't notice it until today. BUT THAT IS NOT WHAT HAPPENED!! I always use that clothing hook and I have cleaned my closet lots of times, and even [her husband] has cleaned my closet, and when we first moved in we searched the entire apartment, including my closet for the missing [camera].

"So now I have two Polaroid cameras and I can't believe my eyes. The only believable explanation for me is that some otherworldly being borrowed the camera for a while, and now returned it! Can *you* think of another explanation . . . I am reeling from disbelief!"

A few years later, I experienced another of these jarring little "it happened-yet-it-didn't" co-events, this time involving Sean's report card. "A strange juxtaposition of events and non-events," I recorded in my notebook on April 23, 1982. "Sean brought home his report card yesterday. For this current marking period, he had an 88 in reading—but written in ink for the previous marking period was a 73. I stared at this grade in surprise, knowing that it was wrong (the 73) . . . the last time I'd seen this report card, the grade had been a *93.* But this grade of 73 hadn't been erased or changed—only my memory of it was different. Sean *also* remembered it as a 93—that high mark had been a pleasant highlight of the day for him.

"I decided to send a note to Sean's teacher about this—acknowledging that I could be mistaken, though it was all very mysterious. A few days later, the teacher called me up. She'd checked the report card against the central computer in the school office and discovered that the previous marking period's grade was actually a *96*! How the 73 got on the report card was beyond her, too—as she'd *also* been sure it was a 93!

"Where had we all "seen" that grade of 93 before? On what report card . . .??"

—And just recently, a friend related to me his unnerving experience of discovering his own initials carved into the porch railing of his house—initials which, he insists, were never there before . . . and yet, the initials were obviously of long-standing, since they were worn and covered over with several layers of paint . . .

* * * *

(Here's a tale of glitched directions, written to me by C., a fan from Florida.)

Feb. 2, 1982

Dear Sue,

I feel compelled to write to you: I am rereading *The Nature of Personal Reality* for the third time and I am shocked at missing entirely the basic premise of the whole thing! Never, I could swear, did I ever read this before—it seems I was in for an added treat: the book changed while it sat on the shelf!

But I wanted to tell you about this experience: Not very far from where we live, my aunt and uncle have a home, to which I've been a few times. Now, my husband calls me after that Indian guide in *The Last of the Mohicans* because my sense of direction and memory of how to get here or there is so good. However, it seems, my aunt & uncle's house moved—although all insist I am just recalling it all wrong. The house is a block away from where I insist it was!

I have driven there myself two or three times, as well as several times with others, and I will swear that we *never* made that turn into the block on which they live. Just as I will swear I *never* saw in *The Nature of Personal Reality* what I am now reading. I am still in a sort of semi-shock state over the house business. I can describe *exactly* where I *believed* it was! This is very confusing, to say the least . . .

Cheers . . .

* * * *

(Here's an amusing article clipped from the July 15, 1979, edition of the New York Times Book Review. *It caught my attention for several reasons, not the least of which is the intriguing glimpse into the mechanics of idea production . . .)*

"[*The author Robert Ludlum writes:*] A little over a year ago something happened that was at first amusing, then disturbing, ultimately not a little terrifying. I lost two and a half hours of my waking life. Whether due to advanced years—52, to be precise—or intellectual infirmity, or a poor tired mind, I cannot say. I would have rejoiced had I been able to blame it on the grape, but unfortunately it was one of those noxious infrequent times when I was temperate. Regardless, two and a half hours of my life had been removed from me, obliterated, a shadow of vapor without images.

"I had finished a novel, and my wife Mary and I were tending to several domestic concerns long overdue for attention. We were having morning coffee when she put down The Times crossword puzzle long enough to say:

"'Don't you think you ought to shave and get dressed?'

"'Why? I have labored long in the fields. I will grow a beard and walk naked among mine enemies and friends.'

"'Not with this mortgage you won't. Seriously, Ed's expecting you in his office in a half-hour.'

"'What for?'

"'You said you'd be there.'

"'When did I say that?'

"'Yesterday. When you signed the papers for him.'

"'What papers? Ed wasn't here yesterday.'

"'Who was it? Henry Kissinger?'

"I did not know what she was talking about. Cautiously, I telephoned my friend who keeps me out of jail and inquired softly as to whether he expected me. He did; he had everything in order pursuant to yesterday's meeting at the house. I had no memory of the meeting or of the documents he referred to.

"Amusement rapidly deteriorated into fear, fear into a sense of helplessness. It *was* terror. Brief but deeply felt.

"Now the what-if syndrome is the writer's springboard. It's been responsible for more story-telling than any other form of prodding, except possibly outrage. And I used it. I found myself fascinated by the occurrence, called knowledgeable people, and discovered a great deal about a thing called amnesia. I learned primarily that there are no rules; it can manifest itself in many ways, evolve through physical dislocation or emotional depression or hysteria. It can be whole or partial; brief, long-standing, or permanent.

"What if . . . a man trained for a maximum-stress situation lost his memory—only his memory. Not his skills or talents—they still exist intact but he can relate them to nothing. His reactions are the natural products of his whole life experience, but that life is nowhere to be found for him.

"I started an outline for a novel. Its title is 'The Borne Identity.'"

* * * *

(I wrote the following notes on the morning of Thursday, November 29, 1979, in my second-floor apartment in Dundee. Sean was nine years old.)

"A VERY STRANGE mental experience. As I was falling asleep last night, I thought about a friend of mine, a man, of about 35 or 40. His image, background, and personal characteristics came vividly into my mind. He seemed to know other people in Dundee, and I particularly remembered an incident involving this man's seven or eight-year-old son. In my recollections, this man was wearing a light brown corduroy jacket and jeans.

"Then, with the peculiar sensation of everything being sucked down a drain, this man disappeared from my field of awareness—and I realized with a jolt that I didn't know him at all; had never met anybody remotely resembling this person. Yet in this 'recollection,' I had known him very well . . . again, like waking up from dreams of a past that never was.

"AND THEN ON Thursday afternoon [*of the 29th*], the same sort of thing happened—only while I was wide awake. This time, I was washing dishes and my thoughts drifted to a woman friend and her job at Taylor Winery in nearby Hammondsport, cleaning out the antique wooden wine barrels for a grape-processing demonstration. I did know that Taylor was planning for its centennial celebration, so this probably had to do with it . . . but again, there was an absolute, though fleeting, knowledge of this woman and her background and characteristics. And then she swirled away, sucked right out of my brain, so the details vanished as though they'd never been. Which in ordinary terms they hadn't—the woman doesn't exist in my life at all. Both times, I knew that these people do not appear in the reality I know; both times, I felt that I'd somehow bridged probabilities—at least on a limited mental level.

"I seem to remember doing this all the time in childhood (could this be a source of 'invisible' playmates?). I wonder if Sean's peculiar difficulties in understanding chronological time, or in describing people he meets, has to do with this. And what about the Strange Case of the $5 Bill, as we call it? Sean found $5 on the street and then lost it in the house, practically in front of our eyes. I watched him put it down on his bookcase and two minutes later it was gone—and we never saw the $5 again, no matter how many times we searched, cleaned, tore things apart, etc. Two days later, Sean's cue ball, a rummage-sale treasure, followed the $5 into that mysterious void, disappearing from one minute to the next from the living-room rug. I told Sean that the færies took the stuff as payment for maintaining gravity—and sometimes I wonder!"

* * * *

(Here are some other twists on the "probability" feeling as written to me in a letter from Peter Danison, who was living in Anaheim, California.)

"In 1974 (while living in New York State), I had an application for a CAPS grant—an arts-grant program, if you didn't know. I had a rock opera co-written with a NYC poet. The title was *Sam.* It was five years old by the time I heard about CAPS, but I thought I'd send it in anyhow. I wasn't crazy about the opera, but what the hell.

"So I sent it in. Today, on the 4th of December, 1980, I was wondering whatever happened to the application, if they'd heard the opera recording.

"I never sent it in. I decided they wouldn't be interested in it, since it wasn't very artsy—it was more pop music.

"But I DID send it in, I remembered very clearly. It came as clear as a bell—I'd done both things. I filled out the form and sent the tape in. I filled out the form and DIDN'T send it in.

"What difference either memory made, I couldn't tell. Maybe the one said to my present, 'at least you were trying to do something about your [*poor financial*] situation.' But the other said 'you knew in any case it wouldn't have mattered, so you were smart not to waste the energy.'

"That's a brief one, anyhow. These experiences seemed obviously to be something about probabilities, and just as obviously an adventure in following personal beliefs to one extent or another. Any dream at all, or any fantasy or reality is a probability, right?—the delineation being defined by the consciousness that experiences it. These here seemed to serve as some kind of self-therapy affecting my unsatisfactory belief-arrangements in the present."

APPENDIX THREE

More Animal Tales

THE FISH THAT FLEW

On Sean's eighth birthday in 1977, I bought a 22-gallon aquarium with about a dozen kinds of tropical fish. We were both absolutely enchanted by this miniature universe, and instead of television (which I banished to the closet), we spent our evenings watching the fish wander inside their separate world.

One of the fish, a pearl gourami with long whisker-like tentacles, spent most of *his* time just behind the tank glass directly in front of our faces, apparently watching back. We peeked around behind the aquarium to see if the fish were merely looking at his own reflection, but the glass was transparent from the inside out, so the gourami could see out as well as we could see in. Whenever we walked through the living room, the gourami would follow us as we passed by, swimming in graceful languor from one side of the aquarium to the other, keeping his fishy eyes glued upon us. None of the many other fish that we had over the next five years ever did this—they just swam here and there in expected fish-form.

About a month after I purchased the tank, Sean and I left to spend the weekend at my parents' house, about fifty miles south of Dundee. That Friday night, I had a vivid dream of the gourami—except that in the dream, he was huge, the size of a house, his eyes big as picture windows. He floated in the air, turning his head from side to side, staring directly into my dream-face.

"Fish dreams!" I said to Sean later that day. "Next we'll be buying them Christmas presents." But I couldn't get the dream out of my mind. At about 4 o'clock in the afternoon, feeling very silly, I called my landlady, who lived downstairs in the big old house where my apartment was, and asked her to please go up and check my fish tank. Well, better to be safe than sorry, I rationalized. I didn't have to *tell* anybody why I thought the damn tank needed checking.

We came back home Sunday afternoon, and as we climbed out of the car, my landlady rushed out of the house to tell me that I'd better go right up and do something about my aquarium. She said that when she'd checked it out for me on Saturday, she didn't think at first there was anything wrong—until she leaned over to look in the top. "The water felt awfully hot," she said, "and then I noticed that the fish looked sick, so I unplugged the heater, and I hope that was the right thing to do."

Sure enough, the aquarium heater's thermostat had malfunctioned, driving the water temperature up way too far, which meant certain tank-fish death if the heater had been left on another day. As it was, several fish hadn't survived the ordeal—but there was the gourami, swimming placidly back and forth, light as milkweed, very much alive.

Two years later, I woke Sean up for school and he told me this little dream before he got out of bed: "I dreamed the gourami jumped out of the tank and flew all around the room," he said. "Then he came in my room and flew around my bed and out the window, where he flew away through the trees." Then we walked out into the living room and looked into the aquarium, as we did every morning. The gourami (by now very old for a gourami), was lying on the gravelly bottom, dead and half-eaten by his ungrateful tank-mates.

"Maybe he was practicing all this time to be a bird," Sean said as we gave the gourami a ritual flushing-down. And maybe if we do go somewhere after physical death, the idea that a fish might go flying away through the trees helps me think that I might go that way myself. Or that if we send calls for help out into the universe, we'll get the help we need on some level or another. He was a *smart* old fish, he was.

THE DAY OF THE DOGS

(At the time of the incident that I think of even now, years later, as "The Day of the Dogs," my journal recounts that I was having many "double" dreams[1] and some other odd waking experiences—as usual, I suppose—including a funny little run-in with an Elmira College professor I interviewed for the *Observer*. I drove out to his place in the woods above Dundee, having heard from local coffee shop gossip that this fellow had built a solar-heated, energy-efficient log cabin. Though I didn't know the man, he seemed like a good subject for a story. I maneuvered down the narrow, winding forest driveway and stepped out of my car just as the professor walked out the front door of his cabin.

We took one look at each other and without saying a word bounded across the few yards between us and embraced, both of us nearly in tears. Seconds later, the shock of what we were doing zapped us apart. We'd never met before in our lives—what the hell was this all about? He was about forty, good-looking in a rugged way and certainly huggable—but this had definitely been the embrace of two people separated by time and space beyond comprehension. That feeling was still there, hanging in the air as clearly as the wind brushing through the trees all around us, even though by then we were both speechless with embarrassment. I couldn't think of a thing to say—so I finally went on with introductions and the interview and pretended that nothing out of the ordinary had happened at all. I never saw the man again; later, I would recall the "Dr. Wilt" encounter Jane Roberts describes in several of her books.[2]

(Anyway, the next day, my son Sean and I drove to my parents' house for a weekend visit . . . and an encounter that the four of us, my parents and Sean and I, would never forget.)

(*excerpted from my journal, September 25, 1978*)

That Saturday, Sept. 23, was a lovely, sunny autumn day. I remember I woke up thinking that I wanted to tell my father how mad I was about some things he'd said the night before during a heated discussion about dog leash laws—and then decided that it was too nice a day to get into that sort of thing—typically, nobody in my family ever sat down with anyone else to have a "serious talk." At the time, my father kept an old BB gun in the kitchen which he used on dogs that came into the yard. My parents' house is located next to a small farm in a sparsely-populated suburban/rural neighborhood, so wandering dogs were something of a problem; and in the past, they'd killed newborn kittens, torn into the garbage, etc. But beyond this, my father seemed to feel mortally threatened by the *idea* of strange dogs trespassing on his property and would get so furious about it that he often talked about getting out the .22 and blasting the dogs to bits.

The thing was, the stray dog situation infuriated me also, but the specter of my father blasting animals into bloody corpses was terrifying, mostly because he was not like this in any other situation—he had extraordinary diplomatic skills, in fact. I don't know why he never confronted the dog owners, for instance; yet I had to admit that underneath my anger about the situation, I often felt like shooting the damn dogs myself, especially after they'd killed the kittens. I think that part of my dilemma was that I wasn't "supposed" to feel the desire to shoot anything, and so I was irritated with myself, too.

On this Saturday, my mother and I sat at breakfast talking about the house and the family collection of antiques. It was about 10 a.m.; my father was out in the garage sharpening lawn mower blades. My mother had been speaking of her parents, my grandmother and grandfather Baker, who lived in that house before my parents did and are now buried in the family cemetery on the hill up behind the backyard. "Sometimes I think these antiques are definitely under guard [*meaning supernaturally*]," she said—and then she glanced out the window and cried, "Look!"

Coming out of the trees surrounding the cemetery and moving across the lawn toward the house were two large dogs, one of them limping. Without pausing to sniff around or survey the territory, they walked around the back of the house and right up next to the French doors that open out into the side yard from the kitchen, where they stood still—looking in at us.

They were absolutely the most magnificent dogs I've ever seen anywhere, before or since. They seemed to be one of those Husky-wolf breeds; their fur a rich copper color, their chests cream. Their ears were wide and packed with cream-colored hairs; their tails curled up over their backs like an elkhound's. Both had extraordinarily deep blue eyes. The male was larger, powerfully built, about the size of a German shepherd. His fur was extremely thick and curly and shining clean—not a speck of mud or a burr on him. He could have stepped right out of a dog show magazine. The female had longer, shaggier fur and although smaller, was as powerfully built. But she was a mass of those ugly round, tough burrs and sticktights. She was also holding one forepaw up off the ground.

They continued to stand there, staring in at us—but the male was staring right into our faces in a way that took my breath away. I recalled the day I'd walked into the Bronx Zoo monkey house and looked up into the most intelligent, compassionate eyes I'd ever seen—the gorilla's. These dogs were not cringing, begging creatures—they were intelligent and proud. That fact leaped out at us. I was awed.

At that moment, my father stepped out of the garage and spotted the dogs. "Hey! You! Get outta here!" he yelled. He ran down the driveway, into the house, grabbed the BB gun, and rushed for the door. But the minute he'd laid his hands on the gun, the male dog had nudged the female and they'd walked around the house away from the back door. My father ran in the other direction and met them in the driveway with the BB gun. There they were, facing one another. Nobody moved.

My father took a breath and drew a bead on the dogs. The dogs continued to stare at him steadily, unmoving. I honestly don't think that my father would have shot at them, since the end of the gun was only a few inches from their noses—but the question is moot, because all at once the male dog *stepped forward and licked the gun muzzle.* Then the dog very carefully put his mouth over the end of the barrel, pressing gently on it with his huge teeth.

My father was flabbergasted. He turned around and walked into the house, his face a map of astonishment. "How the hell can you shoot something that licks the god-damned gun?" he moaned.

He seemed ashamed and amused at the same time—but also drained of the mighty belligerence he'd been wrapped up in seconds before.

In other words, the dog had made the one psychologically correct move. Running or growling, or even cringing at that point, would probably have gotten them a stinging BB shot on their butts. Now they were safe, and they seemed to know it. They turned and walked to the open porch on the other side of the house, the female limping now in obvious pain.

I went outside and watched them as they lay down on the porch's cool cement floor. The female stretched out on her side, apparently exhausted. The male sat right beside her, looking at me, his eyes alert—and bottomlessly blue, like the sea, or an October sky. I couldn't resist. I walked up to them. Would they think I was going to hurt them and growl or bite? (There hadn't been a dog in the family since my early teens, and I am not comfortable around strange dogs.) But these dogs made no moves at all, not even friendly-doggie stuff. I held out my hand for the male to sniff, but he didn't—he just kept his eyes on my face. There was no tension in his demeanor at all.

Finally, I rubbed the male's head and spoke to him. His fur was thick as sheep's wool. I remember wondering how he could possibly have fur as heavy as this, coming out of a hot and muggy summer.

And then this all becomes hard to describe. The male, who tolerated my touch with detached dignity, turned his head and looked down at the female's feet. Then he looked up at me. Then he looked down at her feet again—then back up to me. Of course I'd observed her limping, but I suddenly realized that a sort of tacit *permission* was being given to me. And then I also knew that these dogs had *known* us—had known that someone in the house would help them. They'd known something else, too. I groped for it, but it was elusive. The male was watching me, again, staring into my eyes. I'd never experienced anything like this. I began to understand that this was a plea, a request, and a statement of absolutes all at once. I could no more refuse this dog's message than volunteer to stop living.

"So you want me to help her, is that it?" I said aloud. I took the female's paw in my hand and turned it over. Instantly, the male put his nose down next to my hand, where I could feel his warm, soft breath on my skin. Hairs tingled on the back of my neck, but I kept on. Jammed up in between the pads of her paw were five or six of those wood-hard prickly stick-burrs. They must have hurt like hell. I started pulling at them as gently as I could.

Each time I removed one, the male would lick the female's paw—and my fingers too, of course—and then stop and wait for me to get the next one, his nose resting—*resting*—next to my hand.

The female never once moved or whimpered, and the male never made a sound. Then I checked her other feet. There were stick-burrs jammed up in the pads on every one. I don't know how she walked at all. Each time I pulled one out, the male would carefully lick her paw. There was some blood; not much.

It was without question a profound act of love between those two dogs.

I then picked all the burrs and sticktights out of the female's fur, the male watching my every move. The phrase, "a profound act of love," kept going through my mind. "There you are," I said when I was finished. "Rest a while." I got them a pan of water, which they drank. Then they curled up around each other and slept for an hour or so in the cool shade of the porch. I watched them the whole time—they were so beautiful. Finally, they woke up and trotted in concert back across the yard and up the hill and into the cemetery trees as though they'd remembered an appointment. We never saw them again.

We called every kid in the neighborhood, trying to find out who owned those dogs. My father had decided by then that he wanted to keep them—after all, they hadn't been wearing any collars or tags, so maybe they were . . . strays? I doubted that, somehow. We called the paperboy, the town sheriff, the dog warden, the fire chief, some area farmers—everybody we could think of—and nobody had ever seen a pair of dogs of that description. And nobody ever did see them, as far as we know, and we never figured out where they came from.

Of course, they could have belonged to someone visiting the neighborhood; or they could have escaped from a car and been rounded up after they left our house. But I wondered: Sticktights and burrs of all kinds grow in thick profusion throughout the woods around there. How come only the female got any in her fur and paws? And where did they come from, appearing out of the cemetery like that? (I ran up to look for them after they'd disappeared into the trees—but they were gone. The cemetery is an oasis of trees in the midst of wide, open fields, so *where* they'd gone was a mystery in itself; but gone they were.) And if they were strays, how come they were in such magnificent condition, aside from the female's burr infestation? And most important—how could the female have walked very far with all those nasty, unyielding burrs in her paws? *Where did they come from???*

"Those were *not* just dogs," my mother stated—her only

comment on the subject. And after that, my father stopped shooting at dogs—and dogs stayed out of the yard (by then they were all BB-trained anyway). That is, they stayed away until the day after my father died in December, 1983. That morning, the neighbor's dog trotted right up to the evergreen shrub by the back door and pissed all over it in what you might call a definitive substitute for the last laugh.

BONNIE'S LAST GIFT

In the summer of 1984, I received a sad and frightening letter from my friend Ellen, who lives with her husband and children in another state. It seemed that her husband had been bothered by some peculiar aches and pains, and an ordinarily routine visit to the doctor ended up in a horrifying diagnosis: M. had testicular cancer. His health and his life were in painful balance.

In the next few weeks, Ellen related a long and terrible sojourn in a series of letters. Eventually, her husband refused extensive surgery and chemotherapy and opted for a program involving positive imagery and special diet—and miraculously, against all medical odds given them, he recovered. Much later, in September of that year, Ellen sent me a postcard with the query: "Did I tell you about Bonnie?"

I wrote back that no, she didn't tell me about Bonnie. Was Bonnie a relative of hers I'd never met? What about her?

Ellen's next letter related the following story. I must emphasize that ordinarily, Ellen and her family don't consciously incorporate the ideas implied here in the context of their daily lives; although Ellen has read my books, her perspective on life is much more traditional than mine and I was surprised (though relieved) when she and her husband chose to take their chances with nonmedical cancer treatments—which worked, though perhaps with help from a most unexpected source.

(Letter dated Sept. 11, 1984)

"Dear Sue: Okay, here's something for you on 'coincidences.' Bonnie was the abused, battered dog I adopted a day before the shelter was going to put her to sleep, right after we moved [*to their present address*]. She was psychotic but very cute, good with children, and desperately in need of a family to take care of her. She was *extraordinarily* healthy and well behaved.

"Then in May of this year she started having urinary problems. This dog never had an 'accident' in all the five years we had her, but in May she lost control. We first thought the problem might be psychological—we'd just given away our cat and gotten another dog—but then we took her to the vet and got her on sulfa medication.

"This all started at the same time M. started having his (similar) troubles, before they diagnosed it for what it was. He too was on sulfa. The medication didn't work for either of them. Then M.'s real health crisis developed and the terrible weeks began.

"For a while, it looked as though Bonnie was getting better, but M. then was at the height of his problem and his 'infection' developed and spread. Then pathology gave an answer: M.'s disease was congenital, probably originating from the DES his mother took forty-plus years ago.

"At the same time, we took Bonnie for tests and they discovered she had tumors, too. *She was put on a DES medication.* And she deteriorated and died. And my husband recovered.

"It was as though their illnesses and their lives kept intersecting daily with their ups and downs, and medical diagnoses, prognoses, and plans of treatment. So it was very sad when Bonnie died. It was our decision to put her away rather than subject her to more tests and operations, which would provide more information but which would not cure her inoperable tumor. But in a way it was a relief because from that moment I felt that as Bonnie's life failed, my husband would be okay. It was odd because you could see her getting worse every day while my husband was making his slow recovery back—and without operations . . .

"My husband and Bonnie were about the same 'age.' At the end, I really wanted her to be out of her misery but could not make the decision—so it was my husband who took charge and took her to the vet's to be put to sleep . . .

"And that's the story. What do you think?"

What I *think*, of course, is that there was indeed an exchange here—a thank-you and a good-bye. A gift returned for a rescue; a gift in kind. A psychic balance achieved for reasons understood between the species.

Others have told me similar "exchange" stories since Bonnie's; and again, like the "confessions" of my unofficial Dundee dreamers, these were shared in an atmosphere of great secrecy. One example is the story related to me by T., who told me that years before, as a young man, he contracted a rare and usually fatal disease for which there was no known cure. Involved in the diagnosis of that disease was the appearance on x-rays of distinctive star-shaped lesions attached to his inner organs. T. said that doctors were baffled by the symptoms and recommended chemotherapy as a last-ditch hope.

But then, T. said, the strangest thing happened—his normally healthy dog suddenly took sick, curling up in a corner of the house and refusing to eat. T. finally took it to the veterinarian for tests—and to everyone's astonishment, the same star-shaped lesions showed up on the dog's x-rays. Eventually, the dog wasted away and died—and T. recovered.

Doctors told T. that the diseases were not related or contagious in any way, and wouldn't comment to T. further about it. T. added, however, that throughout those ghastly months before he was declared "cured," his youngest daughter woke up almost nightly with the same terrifying dream: that a skeleton was running all around the house, trying to eat everyone up. But one night, the girl dreamed that the family dog leaped out and ate the skeleton, thereby saving them all. The nightmares—and T.'s disease—went into permanent remission.

* * * *

"If whales and dolphins are supposed to be so smart," I overheard one of my son's friends say to him one afternoon, "then how come they beach themselves and die?"

"Maybe it's a religious ritual of some kind," Sean replied.

"All right, then, how come they never developed technology?" my son's friend demanded.

"I don't know, maybe they developed something else," Sean said. "Maybe instead of a technological reasoning, they developed philosophy to such a level that we just can't begin to comprehend it. Maybe all animals have done that—how do we know? Maybe they're trying to help us develop it ourselves, who knows?"

NOTES

1 There is excellent material on double dreams in both volumes of *The "Unknown" Reality* (Jane Roberts, 1977 & 1979, Prentice-Hall, Inc., Englewood Cliffs, NJ 07632). On page 155 of Volume 1 of that book, double dreams are described as "simultaneous material handled by the brain on unconscious levels of activity."

2 As in Chapter 6 of her *Adventures in Consciousness* (1975, Prentice-Hall, Inc.). There, she recounts the experience of walking into the office of a doctor she'd never met before—and walking straight into the man's arms in answer to his odd beckoning gesture. ". . . I felt as if the doctor and I were beloved colleagues at another level of experience—or in another life," Jane recalls. ". . . In a few months when the Sumari development began, I understood at least one reason for the instant recognition we'd felt. And now I wonder if that meeting was a trigger, one among others, that would initiate future events."

APPENDIX FOUR

Dreams from All Over

(Grassroots Enow)

What I've put together here is a collection of impulses, coincidental dreams and events; precognitive connections; some fascinating dream-correlations (including one in which a person I've never met apparently tapped right into a dream of mine); and some other "unofficial" desserts arranged to tempt your psychological palate as much as they do my own.

(I'll start with some interesting examples of precognition from others' dream records or experiences:)

(Letter from Carmen R., longtime friend, dated July 3, 1979:)

"Precognitive dreams:

"1. May 24, 1979. Dream: I am driving with [friends] in New York City. The traffic is crazy. I see a big bus nearly run over a little car that pulls up in front of it with no warning. All around are people driving too fast and taking too many chances. This is a terrifying nightmare, one that I wake up from with my heart pounding.

"Subsequent events:

"A. May 27—I accepted a ride with a couple I have never met to go to the wedding of a mutual acquaintance—a one-hour drive from here in Shirley, Mass. The couple arrived to pick me up one hour late and the man . . . drove very recklessly to get to the wedding on time. He passed to the right and left of cars in tight city traffic, ran a red light, drove consistently 20 mph over the speed limit. On the highway he wove in and out of traffic, hitting 85 mph. I complained three times for him to slow down—whereupon he pulled to the side of the highway and told me to get out. When I refused, he shouted, 'Shut up!' and went on. I arrived at the wedding thoroughly terrified and murderously angry—honest to god, Sue, I thought I was going to be killed. Needless to say, I got a ride home with someone else.

"B. June 4. I was driving with a friend in downtown Boston in his Porsche. We pulled up to a light to the left of a large city bus that had its left turn signal on. I saw it but my friend didn't. I vividly remembered this [May 24] dream and this prompted my speaking: I told my friend that the bus was going to turn and he pulled up in front so the driver could see him. When the light changed we went on straight and the bus did turn left.

"2. June 2, 1979, dream: I receive a letter from my friend O. telling me that her boyfriend has killed himself. She is very upset, of course. I travel to New York to be with her. She is extremely distraught and grief-stricken.

"Subsequent event: On June 3, O. called me from New York. She said she had tried to get in touch with me on May 31 because she was very upset—a guy she used to go with had just sent her 24 red roses and she didn't know how to react; wanted my advice. She also told me that she missed her boyfriend, who had left for Israel. She said, 'It's like he's dead; I can't get in touch with him at all because he's so far away.'

"3. I dream about someone I haven't seen in five years and then I run into him on the following Saturday."

[Note: Three years later, Carmen's fiance was killed in a vehicular accident just days before they planned to marry. A few days after the funeral, Carmen came to stay with me while she recovered as best she could—much like the scenario in her dream about O. Though her fiance's death was not self-inflicted, it's worth noting here that Carmen's other vivid precognitive dream in this group involved life-threatening traffic situations.]

* * * *

(From a letter about precognition written from Oakland, Ca., by Peter Danison:)

"Here's one for the books. DREAM, March '79: I dream that a friend has taken me to a hilly place somewhere in northern California. This friend says that these hills have abandoned mines in them. The mines are sealed now and filled with stuff—old bikes, cars, a helicopter—lots of stuff owned by a certain very rich family. My friend takes off and I ask—what am I supposed to be doing here?

"An old woman, about 70, thin, thin-faced and worn-looking, appears in front of me and explains that her daughter has been very ill.

"REALITY—January '81: I've been living in southern California for 1 year (the dream took place while I was living in Houston, Texas). I meet a loony, pumpkin-faced woman who says to me right off, 'I'm magic. I can make all your dreams come true.' Later we become friends. I find out she is the daughter of some Italian royalty that moved to San Francisco in the 1840s. She tells me that doctors have told her she has cancer of the uterus and may not live another 2 years. *Then* one day she tells me that her family owns mill property in northern California and that they used the abandoned mines to store family hard-goods. Old Rolls-Royces & stuff. At this point I remembered my Houston dream and dropped my jaw.

"I met her mom—same face & personality as in the dream . . ."

* * * *

(Here are some selected records of little precognitive dreams and funny psychic one-liners—from my dream notebooks and from records sent to me by fans and friends:)

April 1/2, 1979

DREAM: I go into the penny candy store I frequented as a child. The place is dirty and the cabinets are filled with rusty knives. A weird-looking young man hands me a package with an elaborately-written note attached to it. I read the note and discover, to my embarrassment, that it's an invitation to dress up in leather and beat one another with whips and chains! I run out of the place in terror.

[NOTE: I received a package of books from a friend in that afternoon's mail [April 2nd]. Included was a paperback entitled, *Nine and A Half Weeks,* a supposedly true story of a woman who spends that time with a man who chains her to the wall and whips her. Also included in the package was a copy of *Fat Is a Feminist Issue,* a humorous enough juxtaposition of reading material—note that my dream took place in a *dirty* candy store.]

April 24/25, 1979

DREAM: I meet my maternal grandmother, Lois Templer Baker, in the kitchen of my parents' house. She 'pops' into the room, wearing the nightgown and quilted housecoat that clothe my most vivid memories of her. Her gray hair is wild and curly, as it always was; she is holding a cigarette in a fancy holder.

[NOTE: In the 25th's mail, I received a letter from my cousin Joanne. She lives in another state and we rarely communicate. The letter, dated April 20, included this little aside, remembering our grandmother Lois: "My one memory of her is in the old kitchen (*meaning in my parents' house*) in short pants, an overblouse of some sort, rather wild hair, holding a cigarette."]

Wednesday, August 14/15, 1979

DREAM: The electricity in Dundee has gone haywire. Fires from surges of electricity have started in houses all over Harpending Avenue. I am watching these from Vera B.'s beauty shop. Rob Butts is standing next to me. One house bursts into flame from the second-floor windows, where the electric lines come into the house . . . then the house next to this one catches fire.

[NOTE: Wind had blown electric lines down along a village street on the Tuesday before this dream; the hot wires had burned bushes, trees, and asphalt and caused much concern among nearby residents before the NYSEG workmen could get to the scene.

[On Thursday, August 16, I went to Vera B. for a haircut and discovered during casual conversation that Vera spent her childhood in Sayre, Pa., and remembered Rob Butts and his father's machine shop (which Rob has mentioned in his notes in the Seth books) from those days. I've never met any other Sayre contemporary of Rob's, and even though I'd known Vera for a couple of years by this time, we'd never discussed her background before.

[Then in the next few days, two major fires destroyed structures in the area. One of these, on August 19, was a barn owned by a man whose mother's maiden name was "Harpending." The other fire, which gutted a house, was caused by faulty wiring, according to fire officials.]

Saturday, September 21/22, 1979

DREAM: I am trying to escape from a fire that is licking all around the edges of my place—only it doesn't seem to be my place.

[NOTE: This morning, Sean asked me what the name was "of that restaurant that burned down." I couldn't think of any area restaurants that had burned in recent years, so I just named off some of those around Dundee. None of these satisfied Sean—nope, he wanted to know which one had burned down, and that was that. Then sometime in the wee hours of Sunday night/Monday morning, a restaurant near Dundee burned to the ground in a spectacular blaze. Sean had never been to the place and as far as I know, never consciously knew it existed. For several hours on that Monday, rumors cuirculated that the owners might have been trapped in the blaze, as firemen found the couple's car parked in the restaurant lot. However, the people were later located in another town. A lengthy insurance debate ensued over the incident, and even though the restaurant had been a popular place, it was never rebuilt.]

August 30/31, 1979

DREAM: An image of the first Dundee *Observer* that Susan B. and I published together: A line drawing of an old brick gristmill in a nearby township dominated the front page.

[NOTE: The following week, the September 6th edition of the *Observer* carried a front-page story on 'The Old Stone Mill,' the same building I'd seen in my dream and from that old 1974 front page. By August of 1979 I wasn't working regularly on the paper and I had no idea what was going to appear that week.]

Sunday, November 24/25, 1979
Webbs Mills, N.Y.

DREAM: I am sitting in Roy's car, which is careening down a backwoods road somewhere in the Finger Lakes area. The car goes more and more out of control, finally hurtling around a corner, going into a spin, and skidding backwards off the road, where it rams into a concrete post, smashing the back end. I wake up abruptly.

[NOTE: I dreamed this while visiting my parents for Thanksgiving. When I returned to Dundee Sunday afternoon, I went out to the farm to visit Roy. His first words to me were, "Go up and take a look at my car." I went out of the barn and walked up to the storage shed. His small sports car was parked at one end of the shed, its back end smashed in. Roy then explained that he'd been driving through a nearby Finger Lakes village that afternoon—on Sunday, the day following my dream—when he lost control of the car on a curve, spun around several times on the frosty highway, and slammed tail-first into a bridge abutment. Roy wasn't hurt, but his car was certainly banged up—not to mention his feelings when my reaction to it all was to dance around gleefully and shout, "Oh, boy! Hot dog! Wait until you hear about my dream!!!"

[Roy was not, understandably, impressed.]

May 22/23, 1980

DREAM: I see a hummingbird in a square bird feeder, which is boxed in on all sides but one. I look into the dark interior of the feeder and the hummingbird is there, bright against the darkness.

[NOTE: Later that afternoon, I dropped by Al and Adrienne's house. We sat at the dining room table to have coffee. There on the table was a black box. I turned it around and discovered that it was a sonar unit from a fishing boat. One side of the box was recessed, and inside this recessed area was a picture of a hummingbird in flight! The brand name of the unit, printed on the box, was 'Humminbird' (*sic*). I don't know anything about fishing gear and had never seen such a gadget before this.]

Thursday, October 15/16, 1980

DREAM: Hazy, murky war dream. Atom bombs fall. The explosions resound over the top of the house, and my dream-self waits for the blast. I wake up from this dream thinking that this is inevitable—that the world can't possibly avoid it. Depressing.

[NOTE: Later this afternoon, Nora M. (*see Chapter 11*) told me that she'd had "a murky war dream" (her words) last night. The next day, I read in the October 17th edition of the Rochester newspaper that the Chinese government had detonated a nuclear bomb in the atmosphere early Thursday morning (our time). The article noted that the previous detonation by the Chinese a year before had "circulated radiation around the globe for months."

[Also, early Friday morning, October 17, a natural gas well located up the valley from us exploded, blowing an eight-foot hole in the ground and spewing rocks some thirty feet in the air, according to reports. No one was injured. There are many natural gas wells around this area, and they do explode upon occasion . . .]

October 30/31, 1980

DREAM: I'm helping Jane and Rob Butts write a series of indexed acknowledgments that will appear at the front of a new Seth book. Some of these entries are people's names; one specific name is "Sarah Genesis," who in this dream is an ancestor of mine. I write her history up for Rob. The Seth book seems to be about genetics—about the psychic heritage of genetics and the "genetics" of this country as a whole. Another name I see clearly in this index is "West," meaning the author Jessamyn West.

[NOTE: Today I received the week's *New Yorker* magazine in the mail. I opened it right up to an ad for Jessamyn West's new book (which I hadn't known about—I don't follow West's work). According to the ad, this book is about researching her ancestral heritage and looking back on a trip she took through Europe in 1929. In addition, Jane's book, *Dreams, "Evolution," And Value Fulfillment*, which Seth began dictating in September of 1979, not only includes information on genetics, as in the Vol. 1 chapter, "Genetic Heritage and Reincarnational Predilections," but in its published form contains a series of introductory essays by Robert Butts involving Jane's background and the circumstances of her life and work.]

June 29/30, 1981

DREAM: Our oldest brood mare aborts her foal. We are in someone else's farmyard when we see this. To find out what happened, we open up the mare's stomach. She is awake and standing up, unconcerned, as we do this. We find a huge red blanket inside her, intact; it looks like Roy's old quilted red work jacket. We wonder why on earth she would eat this.

[NOTE: This mare was supposed to foal in January of 1982. As her time approached, we sent her to our trainer's, whose farm provided indoor heated stalls. However, a veterinarian discovered that in spite of all appearances and positive blood tests, she was not pregnant after all. In many ways, this was a humiliating discovery, since we'd paid a large sum of money to send the mare to a nationally-known Appaloosa stallion—a fact we'd advertised exuberantly, even though Roy had doubted that the mare was in foal; but after all that time and expense, he didn't want to believe it either. Our veterinarian later speculated that the mare had probably re-absorbed the foal fetus, as mares will sometimes do, or aborted it unnoticed in a springtime pasture.

[The odd thing is that when we sent the mare out to the stallion in February of 1981, we'd purchased a new red blanket for her to wear in the trailer . . . And in February of 1982, another brood mare of Roy's *did* eat this red blanket—although apparently without doing herself harm, so this dream isn't quite as outlandish as it sounds. (The trainer discovered a small pile of red fuzz and a very thirsty horse in the stall one morning.) A funny combination of future events, certainly . . .]

July 18/19, 1981

DREAM: Roy's hired man has gone blind from some infectious disease. He is standing out by the barn, his eyes all gloppy and stuck shut.

[NOTE: This afternoon, I noticed that one of the barn kittens was blind in one eye, apparently the result of injury. A day later, I found another one of the kittens with an eye suddenly gone so messy with distemper that it had literally popped out—glaack. Later, the hired man of this dream offered to put the kitten out of its misery, which he did with merciful swiftness.]

August 13/14, 1981

DREAM: I dream about policemen. They come to tell me something important. There are at least two of them, but I only speak with one. They come to the house, an unusual situation that makes me feel angry and uncomfortable.

[NOTE: That afternoon, a salesman came to the door and tried to sell me a set of teaching manuals by using the Dundee elementary principal's name as reference. I turned him away and then checked with the school and found that they knew nothing about any salesmen. For some reason I was indignant enough about this to call the Yates County Sheriff's Department and report it. Later, deputies called me back for details. Turns out there were actually two salesmen, although I only spoke with one. I'd never called a police agency to complain about anything before this.]

August 14/15, 1981

DREAM: I see a book review of *Conversations with Seth* in thc *New Yorker* magazine. Wow!

[NOTE: My weekly copy of the *New Yorker* arrived in the mail that afternoon. I opened it to the book review section and saw this:

CONVERSATIONS with
Katherine Ann Porter

[I was a bit miffed by the similarity! However, the fact is that I dream frequently about subjects that later appear in some form in the *New Yorker*, a magazine that since my childhood has symbolized literary aspiration and achievement.]

October 12/13, 1981

DREAM: Dr. X., an area veterinarian, dies suddenly. For some reason, his wife and I travel to Fulton, New York (an upstate village near Syracuse). This community seems related to Doc's untimely demise. We pass television crews photographing something on the highway.

[NOTE: Even though I'm a Syracuse University graduate, I've never been to Fulton, N.Y., and have no connections there. A couple of days after this dream, I happened to watch the Syracuse television news at 6 p.m. Events included a report on two women who were fatally injured in an auto accident on Rt. 38, near Syracuse. One of the women was from Fulton. I rarely watch this news program and didn't know either of the women.]

Tuesday, December 14/15, 1981

DREAM: I am on journey by horseback to a small New England town. I get off my horse and inspect an old library, where I notice a small, delicate leather-bound book entitled *The Sketches of E.B. White.* I leaf through this treasure (does anyone else know about this, I wonder) when E.B. White himself walks up to me. I tell him that when I was a young child, his stories were sad, but as I got older, they became funnier. He laughs. As I wake up, I wonder if White has died.

[NOTE: In that afternoon's edition of the Elmira newspaper was an article on the death of author Nathaniel Benchley, who had passed away on Monday, December 14, 1981. He was the son of humorist Robert Benchley. While growing up, I spent most of my reading hours with the works of Benchley, White, Thurber, Perelman, and others of that era; that Monday night, I'd read some of

Benchley's essays to Sean at bedtime and he'd asked me if Benchley and E.B. White (author of *Charlotte's Web,* a favorite of ours) wrote in the same time period. "They sound like the same person," he said. And incidently, one of my favorite movies is "The Russians are Coming! The Russians are Coming!" which is based on a story by Nathaniel Benchley and humorously evokes my memories of Martha's Vineyard.

[But again—why not just dream of Benchley's death? Very peculiar.]

[NOTE: But when E.B. White did pass away on October 1, 1985, I did not dream of that event—rather, my dream records show that on the night of September 30/October 1, 1985, I dreamed only of an empty double bed in a large, dark room; and of teaching my mother, who was in the last stages of terminal cancer, how to fly. In that dream, we were both in our pajamas, soaring like airplanes over the grass and fields behind my childhood home; and I watched her glide silent as an owl up toward the little family cemetery where my father's ashes (and now her own) are buried. Later, I thought this dream was a perfect, subtle connection with White's death—both my mother and I admired White's writings and always took along our well-worn copies of his essays wherever we traveled.

[I read of White's death in the Rochester newspaper while eating breakfast in a Dundee restaurant the morning of October 2nd—as I'd read of S.J. Perelman's death a few years before while in the same restaurant. Precognitive elements surrounded both events and touched my private life; Perelman was another childhood favorite my mother and I shared. My immediate reaction was that the news of E.B. White's death would help ease my mother through the same doorway; by then she'd been under twenty-four-hour nursing care at home for nearly six weeks and was plainly near death. It struck me that the connective threads among these dreams, my mother's rapidly approaching demise, and White's death were not accidents; for the love of literature was the one common bond between my mother and me, and the only language we could ever speak to one another.

[And if there is "elegant timing" in one's birth and death, my mother named another factor herself: "I always thought I would die when Halley's Comet came back," she said on October 3, as that object was indeed becoming visible in the sky on its 75-year return cycle. Sixteen days later, my mother was dead.]

December 14/15, 1981

SEAN'S DREAM: I saw a big train rushing through the landscape. It was like a large model train. I could also see a gasoline storage tank near the train. The tank had letters on it—I remember the "R."

[NOTE: Unknown to Sean at this time, I had purchased a Western Auto electric train set for a Christmas present. I stored the train set at the Dundee Western Auto and didn't tell anyone else about it, although Sean could very well have seen the set on the store's shelf at some time. The set included an ARCO gasoline storage tank as part of the set-up. Who says kids don't have access to Santa Claus?]

February 24/25, 1982
Webbs Mills, N.Y.

DREAM: A strange, murky dream. I see, from above, a naked fetus-figure of Sean [*who at that time was twelve*] lying on a sheet-swathed table. This is a late fetus, with umbilical cord attached; the face is barely distinguishable but resembles Sean's early baby photos. It has been born too early, though it's still alive, moving in spasms. I wonder if it will live; it reminds my dream-self of that scene last May when the tortoiseshell cat aborted her kittens and left hairless fetuses moving in slow, doomed spasms lying all around the driveway (*see Chapter 11*). All vaguely sickening.

[NOTE: On February 26, I came across an article in the Elmira daily newspaper entitled QUADS DIE. According to the story, the first set of quadruplets born in the Elmira area had arrived about five months premature at 7 a.m. Thursday morning, February 25, in an Elmira hospital; and all four babies had died within a minute of birth. As I read this, I remembered that I'd dreamed precognitively the year before of our cat's premature kittens, and that there were four kitten fetuses involved. But why would I pick up on an event concerning a family I'd never met and knew nothing about? Was it the coincidence of timing; a connection in my memory of the underlying symbolism within? To my knowledge, I'd never dreamed before of human infant death. (I attached this newspaper article to my dream records, as I have many others that correlate.)]

August 14/15, 1982

DREAM: Lou Grant (the television series character portrayed by actor Ed Asner) has been killed—shot through the left eye. I see this wound clearly. The character was apparently walking out of an executive office when it happened. I recall Bobby Kennedy's assassination—there's a vague connection with liberal politics.

[NOTE: A day or two after this dream, I received the August issue of *Mother Jones* magazine in the mail. The cover story was entitled "Who Killed Lou Grant?" and displayed a full-color cover photo of actor Ed Asner—holding to his left eye a black button reading, "Politically Correct." The inside article examined the reasons behind the cancellation of the series, which *Mother Jones* claimed was ordered by CBS executives for political reasons—mainly Ed Asner's liberal stand on controversial issues of the day.

[I find this precognitive "hit" very interesting indeed. Many of my precognitions involve newspaper articles, which isn't surprising given my newspaper background. The TV series "Lou Grant" concerned the workaday world of a big-city newspaper editor. This program first aired in September of 1977 and was cancelled in May of 1982 amidst controversy not only over Asner's politics, but high-level accusations that ideas expressed in the show were "too liberal."]

Thurs., September 21/22, 1983

DREAM: A dream about artist friend George Rhoads (whose illustrations appear in *Conversations with Seth* as well as this book). He seems to be on a tropical island; maybe a tropical version of Martha's Vineyard (where we met in 1968). Brilliant color. George is wearing his usual tie-dyed cut-off sweat pants and a multi-colored tie-dyed T-shirt.

[NOTE: That day in the mail, I received the following three letters:

1. A letter from a friend who lives in a small town near George's upstate home. Enclosed was a newspaper article about George from that town's daily newspaper. The accompanying photo showed George dressed in a pair of cut-off sweat pants and a plaid shirt. The article featured George's audio-kinetic sculptures, particularly the one installed in the new Port Authority Building in New York City. When I met George on Martha's Vineyard, he was working on his first pieces of audio-kinetic sculpture. (An article on George and these sculptures appeared in The New York Times Sunday Magazine on May 31, 1987.)

2. A note from my friend Ellen, who asked, among other things, "Whatever happened to George? Is he still making sculptures and paintings? I am buying a Haitian painting of people going to a pink church." And further on in the letter, Ellen wrote, "I like Hawaii a lot . . . in Hawaii, everyone is enjoying Utopia."

3. A letter from Nancy Ashley, author of *Create Your Own Reality,*[1] asking for releases to quote from my own book, *Conversations.* Her return address, handwritten on her self-addressed return envelope, was Waialeena, Hawaii. Up to this point, I had no idea where Nancy lived.]

January 14/15, 1983

DREAM: I am performing on stage somewhere, singing effortlessly (a talent I don't actually have!). I play a Dorothy Lamour type, singing the old number, "Personality."

[NOTE: Today, I was rummaging through a box of my newspaper clippings and came upon a copy of the words to "Personality," which was sung by Dorothy Lamour in one of the old Bob Hope-Bing Crosby "Road" pictures. Consciously, I'd forgotten this was in my clipping box; I was sorting through them trying to find something I'd written long ago for the Elmira newspaper.]

Wednesday, May 25, 1983

SEAN'S DREAM: Sean told me this morning that he'd had a dream about a major earthquake and he "knew" that one would take place within a week.

[NOTE: On Thursday, May 26, newspapers reported an earthquake of 7.7 Richter Scale magnitude in Japan.]

Monday, July 24/25, 1983

DREAM: Susan Benedict's grandmother, who died July 7, 1983, tells me that I must give the following message to Susan: that a missing family ring (which the grandmother had promised to Susan) is under the foot of the bed mattress in a small box inside a larger white cardboard box, along with cash and other jewelry.

[NOTE: Several weeks after this dream (which I told to Susan), the missing ring was found in a bunch of *kleenex* (white stuff from a box?) in a pocketbook (used to carry cash) under the foot of her grandmother's bed mattress. This is the only time I recall actually locating a physical object through dream imagery; but in this case, my friendship with Susan and her late grandmother (whom everybody, including me, affectionately called, "Ma"), plus my own family's strong tradition involving the preservation of heirlooms, probably fueled my incentive to find the ring, which Susan had feared was lost for good.]

* * * *

(From a letter written November 25, 1981, by Michigan fan S., with whom I have an occasional correspondence:)

"Last night, November 24, I dreamt I got a card from you with a very few lines on it. Odd thing was that the card was as tall as a movie screen! And then later today I received your unexpected post card. Not only that, but I also received today a brochure from a company called WATKINS, which among other things sells soap and stuff . . ."

November 14/15, 1982

A dream of Roy's, described to me on the afternoon of November 15: "I dreamed I saw my house on fire, only it wasn't exactly my house. I wasn't home, but I could see the fire. The fire department was there, but I worried about people running into the house and stealing my horse trophies. The front of the house was chopped off."

[NOTE: On the front page of the November 17, 1982, Elmira newspaper was a large photo of the aftermath of a local house fire. This home was owned by folks Roy and I had met a year or two before through a horse-coincidence: they owned a gelding out of an old mare of Roy's. We'd visited the couple's home once. Their bookshelves, like Roy's, were lined with silver horse show trophies.

[I think Roy was quite shocked by the dream connection. "Now, that's downright mysterious," he said, pointing at the newspaper story. "I even saw the front of the house missing." In the photo, firemen were clearing away charred debris from a large gap in the front wall. There were no reports of missing trophies, however.]

Letter from a fan, dated July 30, 1982:

". . . You mentioned in your book [*Conversations*] that you would be interested in hearing about others who had precognitive dreams about that great flood of 1972 [along the Tioga-Chemung-Susquehanna River on June 23rd of that year]. I had just graduated from college and was staying for a week or so with my parents in their house on River Street in Forty Fort, Pennsylvania, just across the Susquehanna River from Wilkes-Barre and so I was evacuated along with the rest of the area when the flood hit . . .

"It wasn't until I was reading through my dream journal that I discovered a dream I'd had while in Boston in February of 1972. In the dream I saw people from Wilkes-Barre being evacuated from the city. I saw thousands of people walking over the city's *bridges.*"

(Here's a funny little precognitive dream experience written down at my request by a friend who protested exquisite embarrassment about the whole thing:)

"Dream June, 1984 (can't recall exact date).

"It was [in the dream] about 11:20 p.m. when a person knocks at my door. To my surprise it was Z., an area police officer and friend.

"Z. and I have coffee. We sit down on my couch—which wasn't my real couch, it was much nicer—and we have a great conversation about a lot of things, nothing special.

"The next thing I know, Officers W. and S. have busted my door down! I remember waking up (in the dream), watching this parade in my living room—Deputy Z. and I had both fallen asleep, each on different ends of the couch.

"Officers W. and S. were accompanied by other patrol cars. They told Deputy Z. that they had been searching for hours to find him. His car wasn't visible because in the dream my house was hidden behind several trees and shrubs.

"At any rate I was suffering embarrassment and woke up!

"REALITY—July 2, 1984.

"At about 10:15 p.m., Deputy Z. stopped for a visit at my office where I was working late. We chatted for more than an hour. His portable radio sat on my desk, not more than a foot away from either of us. We were engrossed in conversation and didn't realize the radio hadn't made so much as a static noise . . .

"Approximately 11:20 p.m., Officer S. went whizzing by the office, down Main Street in his patrol car—and came to a quick halt when he spotted Z.'s patrol car parked by the office door. Officer S. backed into the parking lot and Z. went out. We both realized at that point that his portable hadn't been working.

"Z. immediately got into his patrol car. I went out and confirmed the fact that the radio hadn't been working. They both left on an emergency call. The next day, the police department dispatcher told me that he'd sent *two* patrol cars out in search of Z. and was just starting to call in off-duty officers to help in the search when Z. was found at my office!

"YIKES!!! I was mortified!!!"

* * * *

(Probably the most commonly-recalled precognitive dreams are those that accurately predict disasters. My own specialty in that department seems to be airplane crashes—not surprising, given my absolute terror of flying and my reporter's interest in "newsworthy" events.[2] *My dream notebooks are filled with specific "hits" involving airplane disasters, such as the following:)*

Monday, Jan. 26/27,1981

DREAM: Something about an airplane that is getting ready to leave from the Rochester (or other large city) airport. Another woman and I refuse to get on the plane because we know it's going to crash. We stand in a small nearby village and watch while the plane takes off, barely getting off the runway, stutters, and slips sideways out of the air and slams into a suburban area. This is repeated three times. No explosion, however—but flames and leaking fuel. A body of water is nearby (is it Lake Ontario?).

[NOTE: Over that January 31st weekend, there were three airplane mishaps reported in the national news. No one was killed in any of these. Another engine fell from a DC-10, which landed safely (this in reference to the May 25, 1980, disaster at Chicago's O'Hare airport caused by an engine breaking loose form a DC-10). In New York City, an incoming Eastern airliner's landing gear collapsed, breaking a wing and spilling fuel on the runway; but no fire erupted. The third incident occurred in California when a large commercial jet's landing gear stuck down and the pilot returned to the airport. According to reports, the pilot was worried that the landing gear would malfunction upon landing, but this didn't happen.]

Wednesday, January 12/13, 1982

DREAM: Remember only a crowd of people involved. Of these, I see only my cousin, Joanne B., in some kind of terrible danger. I jolt awake, sick with fear—I seem to be experiencing some kind of claustrophobic fear on her (or someone's) behalf.

[NOTE: Joanne and her husband live in Washington, D.C. That (Wednesday) night, television news carried the story of the Air Florida 737 crashing into the Potomac River after hitting the 14th street bridge, killing all but five passengers and also several commuters on the traffic-packed bridge.

[I immediately called a friend living in nearby McLean, Va., who commutes daily across the Potomac. She told me that she and her husband had driven over the 14th street bridge a half hour before the Air Florida crash; that in fact she'd demanded "for some reason" that the two of them leave work early that night and get home—she'd been adamant, "almost hysterical," about getting out of the city early, she said. My friend then reassured me that my cousin would have taken a different bridge to get home and would be safe (which was the case).

[I knew intuitively that this dream was connected with that disaster—but once again, why such a murky message? Why not the whole picture??]

Wednesday, July 7/8, 1982

DREAM: Roy and I are driving to Florida to see his mother. I wake up from a nap in the front seat and discover that we are in

Louisiana. I look at a map and point out that we are far away from Central Florida, where Roy's mother lives. Mysteriously, on my map the finger-like land configurations that jut out around New Orleans loom large before me, filling the dream sky. I can't figure out why we're going to Florida this way. The map is huge, significant. I wonder if we'll ever *get* to Florida.

[NOTE: This is the first and only time that I can recall, at least in recent years, of dreaming about Louisiana, a state holding no personal connections for me whatsoever. On Saturday, July 10, 1982, newspapers again carried front-page disaster news of a major airplane crash. Pan American World Airways flight 759, originating in Miami and heading for Las Vegas, crashed two minutes after takeoff from a stopover in New Orleans International Airport, killing all 145 aboard and at least ten in the suburban neighborhood where the plane came down.

[Weirdly, the Geneva, New York, daily carrying this story displayed two maps of Louisiana on the front page—one of these showing in enlarged detail the geographic location of the crash: a finger-like peninsula of land jutting out between Lake Pontchartrain and Lake Borgne, by New Orleans. I didn't know anyone involved, but reading the newspaper articles (now attached to my dream records) made my heart pound in a sickening vicarious fear reaction. I had no doubt that this was a precognitive dream—visually vague, perhaps, but emotionally powerful.

[I've also observed in the last couple of years that my dreams are often filled with images and sequences involving tornados right before commercial plane crashes, although why this should operate is a mystery. Personal symbolism probably, combined with the magnet of my flying phobia (which has impelled me to cancel trips and spend unavoidable flight time in a state of sweaty, weeping despair). However, it's interesting that I've never dreamed of actually being *in* an airplane crash—just these sickening, half-formed images of other people's ghastly endings. My dreams know my psychological limits, I suppose—although I'd like to think I can count on them to give me a straight warning if I ever need one . . . *if* I ever fly again, that is.]

* * * *

Another fascinating quirk of dreams is the enigma of correlations among dreamers who may or may not know one another, or even live in the same geographic area. As I've demonstrated in *Conversations,* Jane Roberts' ESP class kept a lookout for these kinds of dream-connections and automatically granted meaning beyond "mere" coincidence to their existence. Of course I think dream correlations are normal and commonplace; and if more people had the habit of keeping good dream records, this facet of the dreaming focus would become obvious, particularly among family or group members.

But for some real surprises, you might try setting up a dream-correlation experiment with distant friends, as several fans and I did quite spontaneously through regular correspondence. We soon discovered that the contents of our letters contained dozens of correlations with each others' dreams. For instance, I'd write to California friend Peter Danison on a Thursday and later find out that he'd dreamed on the previous Wednesday of subjects I covered in my letter—often things I hadn't written about to him before—which then connected with events in the lives of the other correspondents. Or for the fun of it we'd send the same week's worth of dreams to one another and find all sorts of strange similarities between them.

Details of such correlations wove endlessly, on and on, through the fabric of our private lives, making me wonder again (as I have many times throughout this book's dream experiments) if indeed *all* thoughts and events, no matter how fleeting, are acknowledged and stored somewhere in a collective, interconnected consciousness.

Anyway, here are a few simple examples of dream correlation, starting with a funny little dream-waking life synchronism . . .

Wednesday, February 12/13, 1980

MY DREAM: Several of us are in my apartment when I make the room "take off" from the rest of the house and fly out over the sea, toward Europe. Halfway across the ocean, we see a pod of humpback whales and land on the water near them. They come over and sing to us. I show them how to play a violin, which is also a bicycle(??). The whales grasp the bow in their fins and play the instrument with ease and joy. It's a trade of abilities between two species. The feeling is of great warmth and excitement as we communicate.

[NOTE: That morning, I went in to work at the Dundee radio station and talked with "Morning Man" Jim W., who told me that he'd had several dreams lately—one the night before—in which he was talking to a group of monkeys, one of which was playing the piano.]

GEORGE RHOADS' DREAM of Wednesday, February 12/13, 1980 [received in the mail a few days later]: I was on a farm, apparently in Africa. There were lions rolling in the dust in the barnyard. You came to visit. We were both landlords and had contracts or deeds on perforated tapes. Then I went to a place where the earth flowed like magma, but cool. I strayed into underground caverns and emerged by the sea. People came in with unicorns and other animals. At first they considered me dangerous. Later I was given a strangely shaped document and became one of the animals. We merged.

[NOTE: Jim W., like George, is an artist who has published cartoons and comic strips. They've never met, however, and live in different towns.]

(Here is a coincidence of nightmares experienced by my son and me after watching an episode of the "Buck Rogers" television series [the updated version] in which Buck came up against a mysterious box holding within it doorways to the 4th dimension . . .)

Friday, January 29/30, 1981

MY DREAM: A nightmare, from which I was awakened at 4:30 a.m. because Sean was yelling for me from his room, in the throes of a nightmare of his own.

In mine, two small creatures of some alien origin appear on the earth—specifically, in downtown Elmira, N.Y. I catch each of these creatures one at a time, wrap them up in a certain way, and place them in a microwave oven, where they heat up and boil. The second creature rolls through the room while I do this to the first one—and with good reason, because the microwave treatment is horrible. All of this is revolting and frightening.

SEAN'S DREAM OF THE SAME NIGHT: The girl from Buck Rogers had that box. She looked inside it and saw a woman in there who was rotting. The girl threw the box into a fire. As it was burning, a man and a woman crawled out, and the man said, "So close to freezing." That meant that they would have been frozen together forever, but now they were burning. This was terrible. And then my kitty stepped on my head and woke me up, but I heard steel clanging after I woke up and that scared me, too.

[NOTE: Oddly enough, the Buck Rogers episode, which Sean and I agreed was the source of these dreams, didn't have anything in it about anyone being burned or physically hurt in any way. But something about the idea of a box holding the 4th dimension called up some fearful—and similar—associations for both of us. Incidentally, as I awakened from this dream, hearing Sean's cries, I thought that I'd heard the barn door banging outside. But I checked it, and the door was locked tight and there was no wind.]

Monday, February 9/10, 1981

MY DREAM: Two sets of events going on at the same time with one set of characters, like a double dream. In one set, Sean and his cat, Chief Investigator, and I move to an apartment in the building on Elmira's West Water Street where I lived ten years ago. The other part of this dream involved Roy and me and an all-*black* cat (not the Chief, who is white with black spots, tail, and ear muffs) moving into a tiny apartment. I ask Roy to try a "quantum leap" in his thinking. This I demonstrate by making a peculiar physical leap, twisting my body around in the air and landing on my feet, facing him.

SEAN'S DREAM OF THE SAME NIGHT: I dreamed that Chief Investigator had a white tail and he kept sticking his whiskers in a light socket, making his tail lash back and forth real fast, like it does when he's mad!! Then he stuck his *tail* in the socket and it turned all black like it is! Then he jumped up in the air and twisted around like he does when he jumps up after bugs.

[NOTE: The next day, a cat with coat colors similar to Chief Investigator's showed up at the back door. This was an unfixed, aggressive tom who spent the day challenging all the barn cats—except for the Chief, who studiously ignored him. We named this cat "Mr. Hyde." Turns out he belonged to a family in Dundee who dumped him by Roy's barn ("moved" him, in effect) to fend for himself.]

Friday, January 22/23, 1982

MY DREAM: Sean and I are living in an area of the country where tornados are an expected feature of the weather. Our house is small, built on two levels of a hill, with a cellar built back into the ground for tornado protection. And a storm does come up, and tornados do strike—dozens of them. I am myself here and also the weather reporter—I see the black funnels forming up in the dark sky, hooking down to the ground. Two of these rush toward the house. Sean and I run for the cellar. I see more tornados forming all the while from the dark, swirling clouds overhead. I try to rescue Sean's stuffed animals.

SEAN'S DREAM OF THE SAME NIGHT: You and I were someplace where there were lots of dark hills. Then we saw about a hundred tornados come out of the black clouds and come toward us. They were coming all around us from the sky. I grabbed my toys and we ran for it!

[NOTE: While tornados do occasionally occur in the Finger Lakes area, January isn't tornado "season" anywhere in the northeast, as far as I know.

[A few days after I recorded these dreams, I received a letter from Peter Danison, who was living at the time in Anaheim, California. He described a series of "tornado dreams" he'd recorded from Friday, January 22, through Sunday, January 24; and also the following, recorded January 21:]

"Well, back to Gansevoort (a town near Saratoga Springs, N.Y., where Peter had previously lived). In between other things, I woke during the dream (*meaning within it*) and decided to do something, so long as I was awake—what the hell, I'll fly over and see Sue Watkins, I decided.

"With a little effort, I managed to get up in the air, and went across a field of high-power electric wires. Then I went over a field of brightly-colored toys of all kinds—toy trucks and cars and other things. Most interesting. I was thinking, though, that I'd have to be careful, and not lose my concentration or I wouldn't have enough to get me to Sue's, and I started imagining how I'd get there. Imagine a map? Which direction to go?

"Decided I didn't know how to get to Sue's, so I went on to something else. Next time I WILL have the presence of mind to pay her a visit, though."

[Peter also mentioned in his letter that he'd heard from a friend living in the midwest who's said he'd been having dreams lately about dozens of tornados roaring down out of a dark sky . . .]

* * * *

DREAMS AND THE MAIL: On August 17, 1984, I received two letters in the mail—one from Peter Danison, the other from a fan, Lenny S. (Both letters are attached to my dream records.)

In Peter's letter, mailed August 13 from Oakland, California, he asks if I ever receive fan letters from people who dream about me; and also mentions a friend of his from Ballston Spa, N.Y., a town near Albany.

Lenny's letter, mailed August 15 from Ballston *Lake*, N.Y.(basically the same as Ballston Spa) was made up of a dream about Seth, Jane's class, and me.

MOST CURIOUS OF ALL was the dream correlation between me and Marcia F., a fan writing to me from Stanton, California. We'd never met in person and were not regular correspondents; in fact I hadn't heard from her in at least six months at the time of this incident.

On the night of January 17/18, 1984—a month after my father's death—I awoke from a dream so brilliantly detailed and full that it seemed an absolute natural for a novel. Set in a straightforward story line, the dream began with me and some friends living in a mountain cabin in Jackson Hole, Wyoming (which I've never visited, although in the dream I clearly saw the rugged, bare rock formations and the stark beauty of the Rockies).

Briefly—because the dream was pages long— the main character (me and yet not me) finds a crack, or doorway, into a parallel universe. She walks down from the mountains into this parallel world, discovering that it is almost the same as her own—except that nuclear weapons don't exist and a semblance of world peace has been achieved. Once she figures out what she's discovered, however, a bundle of dilemmas present themselves, starting out with the possibility that a parallel version of herself—and her deceased parents—might be alive there. Should she go find them? Should she go back through the doorway to her own world and live her life there as was intended? Or should she return to the relatively safe parallel world, taking friends along with her?

The ideas in this lengthy dream turned all of my creative buttons to "ON"—but other chores were weighing heavily upon me then; and so I denied the impulse to work day and night on the story within and filed it in my "future stories" drawer.

Then on January 24, I received this letter from Marcia :

"Dear Sue: I haven't had a dream about you in a long time, but this one cropped up on 1-18-84 and I thought I'd drop it off to you:

"I am visiting Sue Watkins. She lives in the mountains. Carla V. [*a woman Marcia and I both met on separate occasions*] is there, and also a man . . . The mountains are very rocky and especially difficult to climb because the rocks are all smooth-sided pyramids jutting out in all directions from the side. But I have faith in my surefootedness and am soon on a grassy clearing. I try to pick up impressions. Suddenly I know that just before I reached the area, Sue was up here . . . and received an important insight into a long-standing challenge. I run off to catch up with her hoping she'll tell me what it was all about.

". . . I come to a house set back off the path. It belongs to Sue's mother who lives there by herself. I am just in time to see Sue run up and greet her mother on the side porch. I gather from the excited conversation that Sue has just received the greatest inspiration for a NOVEL she will write. All barriers have been lifted—green lights all the way on this project!"

* * * *

(*Lastly, here are some fan letters that I received while I was writing this book—interesting that each in its way is "about" portions of* Dreaming Myself *and each coincidently showed up in my mailbox at the "right" time . . .*)

"Dear Sue. Here's something about coincidences. For the record, 'Irv' is my husband; 'Carob' is our springer spaniel. Also, when I was 20 years old, I legally changed my name from Linda to Roxanne. My brother Mike never got used to the name and still called me 'Linda.'

"Copy from my journal dated June, 1976.

"This morning, Irv took Carob to the 'Poodle Parlor' on his way to work for the dog to be groomed. We discovered this tiny dog-grooming shop on one of our afternoon walks a few days ago. It's about a half-mile from home in the old part of town.

"Irv jotted the 'Parlor' phone number down on a pad after calling for Carob's appointment. I was to call later in the day to find out when she would be ready to come home.

"At about 12:30 I was vacuuming the carpet near the telephone and I noticed the number of the Poodle Parlor and decided I'd better call and check on Carob. As I turned off the vacuum and reached for the phone, I was startled by its sudden and timely ringing. I answered the phone and a very pleasant male voice said, 'Hello, may I speak with Linda?' Positive it was my brother, I jokingly said, 'Linda doesn't live here any longer, but Roxanne is here—can she help?'

"There was silence for a moment. The voice finally said, 'Well, I was told to ask for Linda—has she moved to another business?' Now I realized that the voice wasn't Mike's and it was my turn for a bit of silence. Flustered, I said, 'Oh, gosh, I thought you were someone else . . . you see, my name used to be Linda and then I . . . (good grief! I thought to myself, this poor guy doesn't care about all of that!) . . . anyway, you must have the wrong number!'

"He laughed politely and then he said he was sorry—he was trying to reach the Poodle Parlor at this number!

"Now I was *really* confused and thought for an instant I misunderstood him. Did he say he was calling for the Poodle Parlor? So I blurted out, 'Oh, is Carob ready to be picked up?'

"More silence from that end, then, finally, he said, 'Who is Carob?' I sighed and said, 'Did you say you were calling from the Poodle Parlor?' 'No,' he answered cautiously, 'I am trying to *reach* the Poodle Parlor.'

"I told him that my own dog was at the Poodle Parlor and hung up after giving him the number of the place . . . which incidentally was *nothing* like my own phone number . . ."

* * * *

"Dear Susan. First I would like to thank your very thoughtful reply to my previous letter. It was much more than I expected, especially since I really wasn't expecting a reply . . . Actually, it seemed to set off, or be part of, a very interesting set of events.

"I had been reading and studying Seth and Jane [Roberts'] books constantly for over five months. Reading them gives me a sense of nostalgia; a feeling of remembering something long forgotten. I also got a touch of what I call the 'too-good-to-be-true' syndrome. It all seems real yet somehow unreal. So I decided to write to Jane Roberts, hoping for a reply which would help me feel that she was a real person out there. I wrote and she replied.

"Around this time, though, I came across your books [*Conversations with Seth*], which I read . . . It seems to happen that when I begin to wonder about one thing or another the right books seem to get to me, usually by an impulse to buy a book, which I may have already known to be there all along . . . But what I see now that I really needed, most of all, was a subjective experience.

"On the morning of October 5th I had a dream. In this dream I found myself sitting at work (I am a computer operator in the print distribution division of a securities firm) at a desk reading a letter from you. Also on this desk were my Seth books and notebook, which I almost always have with me, and a bundle of Halloween 'drag.' Then suddenly there were these billowing black smoke clouds, which oddly reminded me of steam clouds. So I got up from where I was sitting, and thinking there was a fire, I turned on the fire-alarm. I went back and got my books, your letter, and the costumes, and left. The dream faded.

"Later on that morning, I called a friend and while talking, he mentioned that he was going to try to get off early that day to shop for Halloween drag. Just getting out of work early is unusual for him. I told him that I'd dreamed about Halloween drag. I didn't think much about this, though—I've had 'small' precognitive dreams before.

"That afternoon, though, when I checked the mail—there was your letter!! This made me think a little more since I wasn't even expecting it. Also was the surprise that your letter was so extensive and written with thought. It wasn't until later, when I was thinking all these events over, and reread your letter, that I realized your advice was in perfect answer to questions I'd been asking (quote, 'There's a line somewhere between not knowing where your reality springs from and in being too analytical. Finding that alone can help. Also try remembering that action around you is as symbolic—and as literal—as any dream; that your body never lies to you; and that un-followed impulses *will show up* in the "exterior" world.')—all of this without my having mentioned any personal data or related questions in my letter to you.

"But the coincidences continued . . . Your letter really cheered me up and made me realize that I had been over-analyzing somewhat. And, in my impatience with myself, forgetting what I had been learning in my studies.

"I decided to relax a little and be more open to my impulses. My first was to go work out. On the way to the gym, though, the sky suddenly turned black and the rain poured down. It was pretty bad so I detoured to a friend's place of work. While there, I told him about my dream and your letter (we don't usually talk about dreams). So this reinforced the impact of it all, while giving me a witness! Then I joked about how all I needed now was for my office to burn up and I would be a bonafide psychic.

"Well . . .

"After I'd gotten to work on my shift that night, I mentioned to my co-workers that I had dreamed the place caught fire. Later, while we were all busy, my supervisor came back from the restroom to tell us we'd better get out because the fire alarms were going off!! (Of course I hadn't mentioned my dream to him.) We couldn't hear the alarms [because of] the [computer] printers, so we stepped out into the hall. Sure enough, they were blasting away. I almost fainted! Everyone headed for the elevators. I went back and got my book and *your letter*, which I had taken with me, and got out of the place. Thankfully, there wasn't a fire. Somehow, one of the smoke alarms in the basement just malfunctioned and went off.

"Dreaming the highlights of the whole day, the fact that all this *happened*, when you 'happened' to mention a planned book about coincidences and dreams. Coincidence?? I think not . . ."

* * * *

(*The following fan and I discovered that we'd been pen pals more than thirty years ago, when we were both in the third grade and I lived in Elmira, she in Wisconsin.*)

". . . well, since you are the tribal shaman now, I'm sending you some pages from a journal recorded many months ago . . .

"I can remember only one dream where I actually woke up yelling and very distressed. While carrying my second child [in 1980], which [as in the first pregnancy] I also knew was going to be a boy, I dreamt one night that the child, then about one and a half or two, was playing on the edge of a beach. Suddenly, he began slowly going out in the water. There was no visible sign of malice, just the child pulling away and going into the water further out of reach. I awoke on the edge of the bed with my hand out trying to reach him, and screaming. I was in a cold sweat and so perplexed and upset with this dream that I couldn't sleep for an hour. It was 2:00 a.m.

"That pregnancy had been a very strange one with a small weight gain, very little movement of the fetus and a different body chemistry . . . The boy was stillborn after nine months but the doctor estimated that it had died at the end of the seventh month. This was about the same time that I had the dream. The dream ended up being a comfort to me rather than a bad experience. It perplexed me that I did not know exactly when the baby ceased to exist on its own within me & I strongly felt that the baby's soul left my body that night . . .

"I have had only two significant dreams since then. The first was about 5:00 a.m. I dreamt that I opened my eyes and saw a white bird fly into the bedroom and land behind the bed. My eyes were open during this time & I began looking for the bird and I awoke my husband, who checked the bedroom and the rest of the house and could find no bird. I could see no significance in this dream at the time—but felt since the bird was white that perhaps it was a good omen.

"But two days later, our parakeet died, a bird we had lived with for eight or nine years, took camping, taught to talk—and dearly loved.

"My second dream was an out-of-body experience significant only to me as an experience, I guess . . ."

* * * *

"Dear Ms. Watkins.

"There is a question that I'd like to ask you if I might. It deals with the 'past.' You said [in *Conversations*] that you read in an article where scientists had changed their conceptions about a certain dinosaur after examining new skeletal finds.

"You then hypothesized that what actually may have happened was that the past was changed.

"I hope I can explain what I want to know.

"If the past can change what happens to memory? For example, I remember a certain set of events. I know what happened. Here's an example.

"I know from memory that, say, the Beatles recorded these certain songs. Could the past, say, change and 'new' Beatles songs arise? How would my memory be altered to include these new set of facts? And what about my old memory that knew certain facts to be true? Does it just go out the window? Am I hypnotized out of the old memory?

"I do know this. Reality is not at all what it seems. Even in the physical world the past and the future don't occur as they seem to. They actually emanate from the present and this, I believe, can be clearly perceived . . .

"What has happened, if you ask me, is that we have for the most part accepted our parental concepts on reality in scores of areas like time, emotions, expression of feelings, etc. . . . If you can shed a little light on my question concerning the past I'd appreciate it. I am still a little confused about the mechanics (or dynamics) of the past changing.

"Thank you."

* * * *

"Dear Susan Watkins. Within the last week I had been wondering what it would be like to live as 'intuitively' as possible; I think intuition and impulse may be similar . . .

"I am a scientist and in my career followed my 'gut' feeling on many occasions. I think there is a definite scientific basis for precognition—the physicists are on to it—most of the great physicists were all mystics. My own interpretation is based upon the complementary theory: light has both wave and particle properties. We perceive the physical/material world by translating the light waves we see into definite objects with discernible properties. Much of the Eastern philosophical teachings as well as those given by Seth tell us that the past, present, and future are all occurring simultaneously—so for precognition—I believe that some individuals' senses are so developed that they are actually picking up the waves of events that are happening before the rest of us can. I think it is very similar to the practice of using barnyard animals as predictors of earthquakes: their sense of hearing is developed so they can pick up the sounds of the sliding of the earth plates—most cannot.

"If you have not read it already, I highly recommend the book, *The Dancing Wu Li Masters*. It looks at the physical/scientific basis for a variety of events . . ."

* * * *

"Dear Sue. A question: By not following my impulses, am I acting on impulse not to follow them?

"I am an enthusiastic reader of yours and Jane [Roberts']. However, I have been troubled by Seth's repeated statements that we should follow our impulses, almost without reservation. After some thought, it seems to me that we can only do so if we have been telling our inner selves good, positive things about ourselves.

"Let me elaborate. I have a serious behavioral problem. It is not alcoholism, but for current purposes, let us say that it is alcoholism. To deal with my problem, I make up a conscious list of do's and don't's. As long as I am able to consciously force myself to follow this list, things go well.

"But, meanwhile, I keep feeding my inner self negative information about myself, and my situation. I review all the circumstances in the past . . . which seem to have resulted in my present circumstance, always with a great deal of bitterness.

"I have timed myself, and at the longest, I may manage to go three weeks following my proscribed schedule. At that point, following what seems to me like an irresistible impulse, the whole system collapses and I go on an unrestrained binge, indulging in the most self-destructive behavior, which I have been trying to avoid . . .

"It seems that as long as I use my conscious mind to generate a negative self-image, my impulses will be self-destructive, and I cannot really 'trust' them. I can trust my impulses to be in accord with my *conscious* image.

"What is your opinion in all of this? Just now, playing a game I like to indulge in—imaginary conversations with 'Seth'—I believe I can hear 'Seth' saying, 'If you listened closely to your impulses, even in the circumstances you are describing, they would lead you away from your negative self-image.'

"I am considering using self-hypnosis to be able to concentrate on a more positive self-image . . ."

* * * *

"Dear Susan—I am quite interested in studying, examining, and experiencing the conscious and 'unconscious' . . . I'm consistently on a relaxed alert, searching for new materials that echo my thoughts and needs. On occasion when I do find something unexpectedly, I almost literally jump for joy. This search of mine has been a very rewarding experience by itself—many, many avenues have opened up to me—avenues I didn't even realize existed. The only 'rub' is that the more I search and ask, the more and more I find that sharpens and enlarges my conscious perceptions, which in turn increases the mental pain . . . The only way to lessen this pain, I figure, is to increase my understanding of myself and my reality to the point where this pain would diminish . . . I believe (but not 100% positive!!) that I have passed the point where my gained understanding allows me to handle my situation. Therefore, a tremendous driving force helps me to lock into everything, leaving no stone unturned.

"Out of the corner of my eyes I continually scan events that are happening 'outside' of me—recently I've noticed a strong grassroots movement that operates as a network, or web of actions that are non-traditional, radiating outward. People *are* questioning what authorities tell them and questioning their own beliefs.

"It seems contradictory, but in spite of the pain, there is hope for individual betterment and indeed the only thing that I have is hope . . ."

* * * *

"Dear Sue: I guess my favorite dream happened in June of 1957. I dreamt that I and a girl I didn't know were in a field of white, dancing around and around, and wearing war paint and laughing like loons! The feeling of joy and exuberance was *so* intense as to be almost painful.

"A few weeks later, I started on my vacation. On the bus chartered by the small resort I was going to, I met my future wife. We spent 3 days together, and then she left to keep a vacation date with a girlfriend at a dude ranch. I returned to N.Y.C. and received a post card saying she was returning to the resort for a second week. I, of course, returned as quickly as possible, and the dream came true!

"We were reunited in a field of Queen Anne's Lace, dancing around like a pair of loons, with her lipstick smeared all over our faces, like so much war paint. At that point, I recalled the dream and recognized her as The Girl of My Dreams. This part is crystal-clear.

"What happened when I read her postcard is the experience I find difficult to recall. Call it for want of a better description a moment of illumination. I was a nexus of past, present, and future. I stood in a whirlwind, and my consciousness exploded outwards and inward. I was not frightened, just amazed.

"I always believed, and still do, that the Best is yet to come. Life has never disappointed me."

* * * *

"Day after day," Jung says in *Memories, Dreams, Reflections,* "we live far beyond the bounds of our consciousness; without our knowledge, the life of the unconscious is going on within us." And yet, I think that the map to that so-called unconscious world exists openly in the Atlas of our conscious musings—in the eccentricities of our subjective experience.

NOTES

1 *Create Your Own Reality*, by Nancy Ashley, 1984, Prentice-Hall, Inc., Englewood Cliffs, NJ 07632.

2 The nationally-reported dreams of Cincinnati car salesman David Booth—who in May of 1979 dreamed for ten consecutive nights of a plane crash that accurately described the demise of the American Airlines DC-10 at O'Hare Airport—has apparently inspired (if that is the word) several dream collection centers whose goal is to keep records of such precognitive warnings—and perhaps use these to prevent disasters.

INDEX

Available from Kendall Enterprises Inc.

The Seth Video

This 60-minute videotape contains the only visual record we have of Seth speaking through Jane Roberts, as well as the only filmed interview of Jane and Robert Butts. (Transcript and corresponding audiotape also available.)

Jane Roberts: The San Francisco Interview

An extraordinary 90-minute interview with Jane Roberts recorded December 4, 1975. Jane also answers questions from callers. Includes 2 cassette tapes, an 80-page paperback containing the text of the interview, plus a custom-designed case to house the tapes and text for future use.

Seth, Dreams and Projection of Consciousness

A limited number of copies [hardcover edition] autographed by Robert F. Butts.

Conversations with Seth

A limited number of copies [Vol. 1, hardcover edition] autographed by Susan M. Watkins.